Abraham Lincoln and Making a Case
The Story of a Master

Joseph F. Roda

authorHOUSE®

AuthorHouse™
1663 Liberty Drive
Bloomington, IN 47403
www.authorhouse.com
Phone: 1 (800) 839-8640

© 2018 Joseph F. Roda. All rights reserved.

No part of this book may be reproduced, stored in a retrieval system, or transmitted by any means without the written permission of the author.

Published by AuthorHouse 11/15/2018

ISBN: 978-1-5462-6394-4 (sc)
ISBN: 978-1-5462-6393-7 (hc)
ISBN: 978-1-5462-6392-0 (e)

Library of Congress Control Number: 2018912272

Print information available on the last page.

This book is printed on acid-free paper.

Because of the dynamic nature of the Internet, any web addresses or links contained in this book may have changed since publication and may no longer be valid. The views expressed in this work are solely those of the author and do not necessarily reflect the views of the publisher, and the publisher hereby disclaims any responsibility for them.

I dedicate this book to my wife, Elizabeth; to my four living children, Daniel, Joseph, Joshua, and Anastasia; and to my deceased son, Michael, a history student and kindred spirit, whose thoughts and suggestions for this book would have been so welcome.

Contents

Preface ix
Prologue xiii

Part I

Chapter 1: Born to Speak 3
Chapter 2: Best in the State 9
Chapter 3: The Road to the White House 15
Chapter 4: Mr. President 37

Part II

Chapter 5: Personality and Intellect 87
Chapter 6: Knowledge of People 94
Chapter 7: Preparation and Timing 101
Chapter 8: Credibility 110
Chapter 9: Clarity 121
Chapter 10: Facts 135
Chapter 11: Logic 140
Chapter 12: Emotion 147
Chapter 13: Conclusion 161

Index 203

Preface

ABRAHAM LINCOLN BEGAN his famous speech at the Cooper Union Institute with the statement:

> The facts with which I shall deal this evening are mainly old and familiar; nor is there anything new in the general use I shall make of them. If there shall be any novelty, it will be in the mode of presenting the facts, and the inferences and observations following that presentation.[1]

The same might be said of this book. Its facts are not new. They can be found in any number of books and articles about Lincoln. If the book offers anything new, it is the presentation of those facts and the observations about them.

This book looks at one thing about Abraham Lincoln, and only one: his ability to make a case, to persuade, on his feet in speeches, and on paper in written messages. It looks at how good he was at this—as lawyer, politician, and president—and what made him so good.

The book's genesis was Doris Kearns Goodwin's *Team of Rivals*.[2] Full disclosure: Ms. Goodwin (then Kearns) was my senior thesis advisor at Harvard, and I have been a fan of hers for many years.

I have also been a trial and appellate lawyer for forty-two years, and reading *Team of Rivals* prompted an interest on my part on the influence that Lincoln's career inside the courtroom had on his approach to persuasion outside it.

That in turn led to a continuing legal education presentation to my local bar association entitled "Abraham Lincoln: Trial Lawyer in Chief," the thesis of which was that Lincoln's almost twenty-five years in the courtroom—in hundreds of trials and appeals—so shaped his approach to persuasion that he never stopped being the courtroom lawyer even outside the courtroom, in politics and the presidency.

That presentation led to others, to both lawyers and laypersons, and their scope grew to encompass two things: the success that Lincoln had in making a case in all three of his adult "careers"—lawyer, politician, and president—and what led to that success.

Each new presentation prompted more reading and notes, the notes grew into "sections" and a manuscript, and this book is the result. It collects information from many sources, and puts it together in a way that might hopefully be a handy, one-stop reference, for others with a kindred interest in what makes a successful case, and Lincoln's singular ability at doing so.

His ability at making a case caught the attention of observers early on, when he was but a young man fresh off a life of manual labor. It distinguished him in politics and the courtroom from his earliest days in both arenas. It distinguished him still more in the turbulent politics of the later 1850s, when the threatened expansion of slavery beyond the Deep South became the hot-button issue of the day. And it then distinguished him equally, if not more, in his four years as president.

Time and again over Lincoln's adult life, one reads of contemporaries—even those ideologically disposed against him—praising a speech or writing of his in terms reserved for very few, calling it a "masterpiece" or "the best" they had ever heard or read.

Admission: this book looks at Lincoln's *success* at making a case, with the emphasis thus on the positive. It does not do this blindly: it does not contend that Lincoln batted a thousand, or even close. It notes shortcomings that he had, especially in his younger efforts, and that even his best speeches and writings, especially as president, had critics, lots of them. But the book does not dwell on the critics or their criticisms. Even giving the critics and criticisms their due, the fact is that Abraham Lincoln enjoyed undeniable and remarkable success at persuasion, and that is the story this book seeks to tell.

I am indebted to the many authors whose works have provided the information on which this book relies. Without their marvelous efforts, this book would not be.

I am also especially indebted to one of them, Professor Matthew Pinsker of Dickinson College, a nationally recognized scholar on Lincoln and the Civil War, and the author of the acclaimed *Lincoln's Sanctuary*.[3] To my very good fortune, Matt is also a friend, who graciously helped me prepare that first presentation on Lincoln for the bar association, and then enhanced that program immensely, not only by attending, but also by participating in a dialogue with the audience that followed. Then, as if that were not enough, he graciously reviewed the manuscript that became this book, and again offered valuable suggestions. Matt has also put together a wonderful research guide on Abraham Lincoln, which was most helpful, and can be found at: http://housedivided.dickinson.edu/sites/lincoln/research-guide/.

A special thanks is also due to another good friend, Philadelphia attorney Dennis R. Suplee, a nationally recognized litigator who was the prime mover in arranging three of my presentations on Lincoln—to the International Academy of Trial Lawyers, the University of Pennsylvania Law School's Inns of Court, and the Union League in Philadelphia—as well as a steady proponent of enlarging those presentations into this book, and a thoughtful reviewer of its draft.

I am likewise indebted to Professor G. Terry Madonna of Franklin and Marshall College, the Honorable Louis J. Farina (retired) of the Lancaster County Court of Common Pleas, the Honorable Lawrence F. Stengel (retired from the federal bench), and David McCormick, my literary agent, for their review of the manuscript that became this book and for the very helpful suggestions that they offered. David also guided me through the process from completion of the manuscript to publication, for which I will always be in his debt.

A deep gratitude also goes to two longtime members of my law office, attorney Jennifer Snyder and Jill-of-all-trades Diane Brown. Both have been invaluable colleagues for decades, and have distinguished themselves with their help on this book as they have with their help on so many other efforts. Jennifer's research, fact-checking, attention to detail, and substantive suggestions were excellent, as always, right up to publication, and Diane likewise provided hours upon hours of dedicated and excellent work, in research and organization.

Special thanks also go to my talented artist cousin, John ("Bot") Roda, for his work on the book's cover, and to my son Joshua Roda and his staff for their contributions to the same.

And finally, thanks go to my wonderful wife, Elizabeth, for her unfailing patience and encouragement throughout this effort. She could not have been more understanding and supportive, notwithstanding the countless hours that passed with her husband squirreled away in the home office. She is indeed a blessing, without whom this book might never have been more than a dream.

My hope is that this book may enhance for others, as it has for me, the appreciation of the person and talent who was our sixteenth president. He was fond of giving advice on persuasion, and perhaps through this book, in at least a small way, that advice might continue. He is, and always will be, a model for those who would persuade, at any level, and in any forum.

Joseph F. Roda, October 2018

Prologue

HE WAS CONSIDERED the best courtroom lawyer in his state.

He was a political marvel, rising rapidly from a local, out-of-office politician to a national political figure, presidential contender, presidential nominee, and finally the presidency itself, despite having none of the traditional credentials of a presidential hopeful.

He was the nation's greatest president, holding his country together in its greatest challenge, and leading it to emerge better, truer to its professed bedrock principles.

He was Abraham Lincoln, and he was all of these things because of his ability to make a case, his ability to persuade, on his feet and on paper.

We remember him for many things, but without this one ability, we would remember him for nothing. We would never have heard of him, much less had him as president.

He did not come to national attention and popularity as other American presidential candidates have. He was not a founding father, military hero, or national government figure—a vice president, senator, governor, cabinet member, or ambassador. He was not a member of a prominent family, or a noted author.

His family was poor, illiterate farmers.

His military "career" was but a few months in the Black Hawk War, with no distinction other than being elected captain of his unit.

His political resume was limited, primarily local, and without national distinction. He represented his district in four, two-year terms in the Illinois legislature and one in the United States Congress, for which he did not seek reelection, and which he left on an unpopular note because of his opposition to the Mexican-American War.

He had not written anything of public prominence. That would come only later, in his presidency.

No, Abraham Lincoln came to national attention and popularity only because of his ability to make a case, specifically the case he made, beginning in the fall of 1854, against efforts to expand slavery beyond the Deep South, and into the federal territories and free states. He made that case in speech after speech for the next six years, from the Midwest to New England, with each speech increasing his recognition and standing, and each whittling away at what would have been thought to be significant obstacles for any hope on his part of becoming president: his lack of "national" political credentials, his lack of formal education, and his physical appearance.

His formal education "did not amount to one year," he would later sadly note, and was gathered only in short snatches ("by littles," he called it),[1] when work on the farm allowed, in backwoods, one-room schoolhouses, with curricula limited to reading, writing, and arithmetic to the Rule of Three.[2] When asked at age forty-nine to describe his formal education for a Dictionary of Congress, he did so in one word: "defective."[3] It created the image of a hayseed in the eyes of the better-educated, an image that would plague him his entire adult life, even into his presidency.

His physical appearance was an equal problem: it was anything but "presidential." He was six feet four inches tall, and only about a hundred-eighty pounds, with arms and legs so out of proportion to the rest of his body that his critics called him the "gorilla,"[4] "ape,"[5] or "baboon."[6] His face could at best be called "homely," and his movements and gestures were often awkward. He lifted and planted his whole foot when he walked, rather than moving heel to toe,[7] and he used "singularly awkward, almost absurd, up-and-down and sidewise movements of his body" when he sought to lend emphasis in his speeches.[8]

Even those who supported him could not avoid negative comments about his appearance. His cousin Dennis Hanks, nine years older, said later in life that while the newborn Lincoln "looked jist like any other baby, . . . he didn't improve none as he growed older. Abe never was much fur looks."[9] And when Lincoln's hometown newspaper sought to compliment him and wish him well as he left for Congress in 1847, it could not avoid a negative comment on his appearance, saying that he would "find many men" who did not have "half . . . [his] good sense"—even if they had "twice the good looks."[10]

One political writer described Lincoln as a "lean, lank, indescribably gawky figure, [with] an odd-featured, wrinkled, inexpressive, and altogether uncomely face."[11] And that writer was a *Republican* who *supported* him.

The *Houston Telegraph*, which opposed him, was much less kind, saying in 1860 that "Lincoln is the leanest, lankest, most ungainly mass of legs, arms and hatchet-face ever strung upon a single frame. He has most unwarrantably abused the privilege which all politicians have of being ugly."[12]

Lincoln himself had no illusions about his looks. He liked to tell, true or not, of a homely stranger who gave him a jackknife, saying that another stranger had given it to him to keep until he found someone uglier, and that, in Lincoln, he had finally found his man.[13]

But his ability to make a case overcame his negatives—his lack of impressive political credentials, formal education, and looks. It vaulted him from the local stage to the regional and the national. It made him a candidate for the United States Senate, then a contender for the Republican presidential nomination, then at least everyone's second choice for that nomination, and ultimately the party's nominee and first president.

The same ability—to make a persuasive case to the public—was then critical to him as president. He faced the most difficult period in the country's history, and the most difficult currents of public opinion that any president has ever encountered. These easily could have swamped a presidential administration, but they did not swamp his, because time and again, he was able to meet those currents with carefully crafted public messages that made his case.

He did not persuade everyone, of course: no one could have. He did not come close. The passions of the day were far too high. He had critics with every message, lots of them. But he did persuade *enough* people, enough to keep the power he needed to pursue his goals—victory in the war, preservation of the Union, and (later) emancipation. Under the circumstances he faced, that was an undeniable success, one that was anything but inevitable.

His is a remarkable story: in an age of oratory, when orators were celebrities, every good school taught oratory and rhetoric, and highly educated and trained orators abounded, a poor son of illiterate farmers, with no such education or training in oratory or rhetoric, and next-to-no formal education of any kind, rose above all others, to the highest office in the land, and the enduring respect of his nation and the world.

He would be called, after his death, "the foremost *convincer* of his day—the one who could do his cause more good and less harm by a speech than any other living man."[14]

The pages that follow explore why.

PART I

Chapter 1: Born to Speak

ABRAHAM LINCOLN WAS drawn to public speaking from his earliest days. His stepmother, Sarah Bush Johnston Lincoln, said that, even as a boy, Lincoln "would hear sermons preached—come home—take the children out—get on a stump or log and almost repeat it word for word."[1] His older cousin Dennis Hanks likewise said that the young Lincoln, even at work, "sometimes would mount a stump—chair or box and make speeches—Speech with stories—anecdotes & such like thing[s]."[2]

Thus would begin one of the great legacies of public persuasion, through both speech and pen.

Perhaps his first "debate" for which there is a "record" came in 1830, when the twenty-one-year-old Lincoln, while "driving a team of oxen, breaking prairie," encountered Peter Cartwright, a well-known "circuit-riding preacher and politician."[3] William Butler witnessed the encounter and later recalled it:

> Cartwright laid down his doctrines in a way which undoubtedly seemed to Lincoln a little too dogmatical. A discussion soon arose between him [Lincoln] and Cartwright, and my first special attention was attracted to Lincoln by the way in which he met the great preacher in his arguments, and the extensive acquaintance he showed with the politics of the State—in fact he quite beat him in the argument.[4]

In the summer of the same year, the young Lincoln similarly impressed observers with a speech at a political gathering, which another of Lincoln's older cousins, John Hanks, later recalled:

> A man by the name of Posey Came into our neighborhood and made a Speech: it was a bad one and I Said Abe could beat it.... Abe made his Speech [and] ... beat him to death—his subject being the navigation of the Sangamon River. The man after the Speech was through took Abe aside and asked him where he had learned So much and what he did so well. Abe Explained, Stating his manner & method of reading and what he had read: the man Encouraged Lincoln to persevere.[5]

Not long after this, the twenty-two year old Lincoln struck out on his own, leaving home and moving to New Salem, Illinois, where he soon began attending meetings of the town's Literary and Debating Society. He stood to speak for the first time after just a few months,[6] and impressed the group's leader, James Rutledge, who reportedly told his wife that Lincoln "was already a fine speaker; that all he lacked was culture to enable him to reach the high destiny which he Knew was in store for him."[7] Rutledge's son, who was also present when Lincoln first spoke, echoed that sentiment, saying that Lincoln "pursued the question [to which he spoke] with reason and argument so pithy and forcible that all were amazed."[8]

The next year (1832), at the age of just twenty-three, Lincoln made his first try at elective office, running as a Whig against twelve other candidates for four available seats in the Illinois House. He finished eighth,[9] but even in losing "acquired a reputation for ... speech-making," according to John Todd Stuart, a prominent Springfield politician and lawyer who would later become Lincoln's first law partner.[10]

Lincoln then made a second run for the Illinois House two years later, in 1834, and this time was successful. He was quiet as a freshman legislator, making "no formal speeches and only two brief sets of remarks,"[11] but then "emerged as a prominent and effective Whig spokesman" when he ran for re-election in 1836.[12] He campaigned not only in rural areas, as he had in his first two runs, but also in towns and villages,[13] and according to a Whig colleague, Robert L. Wilson, took "a leading part" in presenting "the Whig side" of questions, showing "skill and tact" in debates, and presenting his arguments "with great force and ability."[14] According to Wilson, the young Lincoln, at just twenty-seven and off the farm only five years, "was by common consent looked up to and relied on as the leading Whig exponent . . . the best versed and most captivating and trenchant speaker on their side."[15]

On one occasion in that 1836 campaign, Lincoln's skill at making a case reportedly stopped a Whig and a Democrat from trying to kill each other, when a confrontation between them became so heated that a duel looked imminent. Lincoln saved the day with what an observer called "one of the most eloquent and convincing speeches he ever made, carrying the crowd with him almost to a man."[16]

On another occasion in the same campaign, Lincoln further enhanced his reputation by "skinning" a leading Democrat—a Methodist minister and physician known as "The Fighting Parson"—with a rebuttal that "became a legend" in Lincoln's county.[17] The parson had disparaged a leading Whig, and Lincoln rose to the Whig's defense, with a response so good that by the time he was finished, "his reputation was made . . . [and] he had placed himself, by a single effort, in the very front rank of able and eloquent debaters."[18]

Lincoln showed the same skill, again in that campaign, in defending himself from an attack by one of the most experienced and highly regarded political speakers of the time, George Forquer. As Lincoln's friend Joshua Speed recalled the event, Lincoln spoke first, with a "very able" speech that used Whig principles "with great power and originality," and "produced a profound impression—The Crowd was with him."[19]

Forquer then arose, condescendingly announced "that this young man [Lincoln] would have to be taken down,"[20] and delivered a speech against Lincoln in that same, arrogant tone. But when Forquer finished, Lincoln rose again, and "with great dignity and force"[21] hoisted Forquer on his own petard. In a series of "fortunate" events, Forquer had recently switched from Whig to Democrat, been appointed Register of the land office, and built the best home in town, complete with a lightning rod—a novelty of that time.[22] In his rebuttal, Lincoln cleverly used the latter to his advantage, saying that while he, Lincoln, desired "place and distinction as a politician . . . I would rather die now than like the gentleman live to see the day that I would have to erect a lightning rod to protect a guilty Conscience from an offended God."[23]

Speed, who heard Lincoln speak many times, in court and out, said that he never saw Lincoln in better form than on that occasion.[24]

Lincoln won a second term in that 1836 election, and carried his speaking prowess into the Illinois House, where he became a Whig leader and colleagues regarded him as "a natural debater."[25] When a group of legislators pushed to move the state capital from Vandalia to Springfield, for example, they looked to Lincoln as one of their two spokesmen, and their effort succeeded.[26] Lincoln's success in distinguishing himself in that session of the Illinois legislature was all the more remarkable, as Ronald White, Jr. has noted, considering the talent in that session: "three future governors, six future U.S. senators, eight congressmen, a cabinet member, a number of generals, two presidential candidates, and one future president."[27]

Lincoln then won a third term in the Illinois House two years later, in 1838, this time beating fifteen other candidates, and was by now so well regarded for his speaking ability that his party made him their choice for Speaker of the House.[28] While he lost to the Democrats' nominee, and instead became "in effect minority leader,"[29] his party's regard for his ability to make a case was clear.

The next year (1839) featured a preview of an encounter that would repeat itself many times in the years to come, with ever increasing importance on a national level: Lincoln twice debated a Democrat named Stephen Douglas. The issue then was the differing economic policies of their respective parties, and the Bank of the United States, a point of especially heated contention. Lincoln did badly in the first debate, but redeemed himself in the second with a speech that a Whig colleague said "transcended our highest expectations," calling it "a triumphant vindication" of a magnitude that the colleague had never before heard or expected to hear.[30]

Eight days later, Lincoln gave another speech that was reportedly so "powerful . . . it became the Illinois Whig Party's textbook for 1840,"[31] and drew compliments even from Democrats.[32]

The thirty-one-year-old Lincoln then continued to distinguish himself in campaigning the next year (1840) for the Whig presidential candidate, William Henry Harrison. John M. Scott, an attorney who later became Chief Justice of the Illinois Supreme Court, said that Lincoln was by that time considered "one of the ablest of the whig speakers,"[33] and the *Quincy Whig* wrote that, in political debate, no Democrat could "hold a candle to him."[34]

Lincoln then campaigned again for the Whig presidential candidate, his hero, Henry Clay, four years later, in 1844. Lincoln made stump speeches for him throughout Illinois, again debating Democrat counterparts, impressing his audiences,[35] and adding "much to his already well-established reputation as a stump speaker."[36]

James C. Veatch, who heard Lincoln speak on tariffs in that campaign, said it was "the most remarkable speech that . . . [he] had ever heard,"[37] on any topic. Joseph J. Lewis similarly wrote that another Lincoln speech in that campaign "presented arguments . . . with a power and conclusiveness rarely equalled."[38] D. W. Bartlett, the Washington, D.C. correspondent to the *New York Independent* and *Evening Post*, similarly praised Lincoln for the same speech, writing that it established Lincoln's reputation as the "ablest leader" of the Whigs "in the great West."[39] Yet another observer, David Davis, a politically connected lawyer and judge who reportedly presided over more of Lincoln's trials than any other, said that by the 1844 campaign, Lincoln had become "the best Stump Speaker in the State."[40]

After that 1844 campaign, Lincoln successfully positioned himself to win his district's congressional seat in 1847, in which he served one term, with two high points, both challenging President Polk on the Mexican-American War. The first came on December 22, just two weeks after Lincoln took his seat, when he introduced resolutions against that war,[41] and the second was a floor speech that he made three weeks later, on January 12, 1848, which Michael Burlingame writes "was among the bitterest antiwar speeches delivered in the House up to that time."[42]

Lincoln then headed north with his family during the congressional summer recess in 1848, to give campaign speeches in seven Massachusetts cities, again for the Whig presidential candidate, this time General Zachary Taylor. He did not disappoint. With past as prologue, he again distinguished himself.

The *Boston Courier* wrote that Lincoln gave "a most forcible and convincing speech" that "drew down thunders of applause."[43] The *Boston Daily Advertiser* wrote that Lincoln gave a "truly masterly and convincing" speech in Worcester, "carrying the audience with him in his able arguments and brilliant illustrations."[44] Henry J. Gardner, later a Governor of Massachusetts who heard the same speech, later recalled that Lincoln utterly captivated his audience:

> He repeated anecdotes, told stories admirable in humor and in point, interspersed with bursts of true eloquence, which constantly brought down the house. . . . [W]henever he attempted to stop, the shouts of "Go on! go on!" were deafening. He probably spoke over an hour, but so great was the enthusiasm time could not be measured. It was doubtless one of the best efforts of his life.[45]

The *Lowell Daily Journal* reported that a Lincoln speech in Lowell, Massachusetts "was replete with good sense, sound reasoning, and irresistible argument, and spoken with that perfect command of manner and matter which so eminently distinguishes the Western orators."[46] And the *Old Colony Republican,* in Taunton, Massachusetts, enthusiastically and colorfully praised a Lincoln speech there, writing:

> Argument and anecdote, wit and wisdom, hymns and prophecies, platforms and syllogisms, came flying before the audience like wild game before the fierce hunter of the prairie.
>
> There has been no gathering of any party . . . where the responses of the audience were so frequent and so vigorous."[47]

But his success in New England notwithstanding, when his term in Congress ended in March the next year (1849), Lincoln returned to Springfield with no plans for further elective office. He would focus for the next five years on his law practice, and it would be solely in the courtroom, during this period, that he would show his ability to make a case.

Chapter 2: Best in the State

LINCOLN BEGAN THE study of law in the early 1830s while working in a general store in New Salem and serving in the Illinois House. As with his non-legal education, he studied on his own,[1] unlike "most law students of his day," who served "an apprenticeship with an established lawyer."[2] He was found qualified to practice in Illinois on March 24, 1836[3] at age twenty-seven, and then moved to Springfield the next year, where he practiced for the next twenty-four, until February 1861, when he left for Washington as president-elect. He practiced during those years in three successive firms, each with one other law partner, the first being John Todd Stuart, the second Stephen T. Logan, and the third William H. Herndon.[4] His practice largely was a general one, like that of most lawyers then, but it was in trials and appeals that he set himself apart.

He handled cases in the Illinois trial courts, both state and federal (in Springfield and Chicago),[5] as well as in the Illinois Supreme Court, and even the U.S. Supreme Court,[6] where he argued one case and was counsel in four others.[7] He was involved in more than 5,100 cases,[8] a number that, as historian Douglas Brinkley has written, is "truly staggering."[9]

He tried cases year round, six months in Springfield (his county's seat) and six months outside it, riding from one county seat to another, along the Eighth Judicial Circuit of Illinois.[10] The Circuit was in the middle third of the state, encompassing more than ten thousand square miles and a ride of four to five hundred miles through fifteen (later fourteen) counties.[11] Lincoln rode that circuit with a judge and other lawyers, and was one of but a few who rode the full circuit all six months, and perhaps the only one who did so consistently.[12] Frederick Trevor Hill, who studied Lincoln's career, said that Lincoln probably

> tried more cases between 1849 and 1860 than any other man on the Eighth Circuit. He was the acknowledged leader of the local bar, whose services were constantly in demand, and the one man who could be relied upon to take a case in any of the counties comprising the circuit, for he alone covered the entire route.[13]

He tried the cases that most lawyers handled in his day—debts, divorces, slander, the replevin of horses and mules[14]—as well as two medical malpractice cases in which he represented the defendant doctors,[15] and cases that many lawyers did *not* handle, among them patent infringement and admiralty cases (the latter involving ships on the Mississippi).[16] He also had a significant number of cases involving railroads, as they expanded throughout the country. He represented them in seventy-one cases and opposed them in sixty-two.[17]

He also tried murder cases, twenty-seven in all,[18] the first in October 1838, just a year into his legal career, when he and his first senior partner, John Todd Stuart, were hired with three other lawyers for the defense.[19] Stephen Logan, one of Springfield's most senior attorneys (and later Lincoln's second law partner), served as lead defense counsel, but the team chose Lincoln for the all-important closing argument,[20] even though he was the youngest and least experienced member of the team. Logan later complimented Lincoln's speech as "short but strong and sensible,"[21] and their client was acquitted.

Lincoln tried at least one murder case as late as 1859,[22] just a year before his election as president, and his best known murder case the year before that, in May 1858, several months before his famous debates with Stephen Douglas. The latter case was *People v. Armstrong*, in which the state accused William "Duff" Armstrong and another man of killing a third man in a late-night fight, on the outskirts of an evangelical camp meeting, where whiskey sellers had set up wagons.[23] The prosecution alleged that the other defendant had hit the victim with a three-foot board,[24] and that

Armstrong had hit him with a "Slung Shot,"[25] a lead weight wrapped in a leather pouch that could be swung.[26] The prosecution tried the other defendant first, won a conviction,[27] and then turned to Armstrong.

Armstrong's parents had befriended the young Lincoln when he came to New Salem many years earlier, and when Armstrong was charged, his widowed mother asked Lincoln to help with the defense, which he agreed to do.[28]

The key witness claimed that he saw what happened, even though it was late at night and he was some distance away, because of bright light from the moon high overhead.[29] On cross-examination, Lincoln patiently asked him to repeat his story a number of times (the exact number varies according to different accounts), always emphasizing the importance of the moon high above.[30] Then, after thus establishing the importance of the supposed moonlight, Lincoln produced an almanac showing that the moon had not been high overhead at the time of the incident, and had instead been within an hour of dropping below the horizon.[31]

Lincoln then gave a closing that not only urged Armstrong's innocence, but also emotionally told of how good Armstrong's parents had been to Lincoln years earlier in New Salem, how Armstrong's mother was now a widow, and how her son Duff should be returned to her.[32] According to some reports, when the jury left to deliberate, Lincoln told Mrs. Armstrong that the jury would acquit before sundown,[33] and they did.

Attorney and judge David Davis believed Lincoln had few equals in the courtroom,[34] and others thought the same—or *more*. Lawrence Weldon, a fellow lawyer who would become a judge, said that of those who rode the circuit, "Mr. Lincoln was the star; he stood above and beyond them all."[35] Hugh McCulloch, who would become U.S. Secretary of the Treasury, went even further, praising Lincoln as not just the best lawyer on the circuit, but also in the state and beyond: "as a lawyer and advocate," he said, "Mr. Lincoln had no superior in Illinois and few superiors in the older States."[36]

Contemporaries especially and repeatedly noted Lincoln's ability with juries. Chief Justice John M. Scott of the Illinois Supreme Court said: "Few lawyers ever had the influence with a jury, Mr. Lincoln had,"[37] and attorney Leonard Swett reportedly went beyond that, saying that if Lincoln ever had a superior before a jury— . . . he, Swett, never knew him . . . and that what Lincoln could not accomplish with a jury no man need try.[38]

Another fellow attorney, Isaac N. Arnold agreed, saying that Lincoln was "the strongest jury-lawyer we ever had in Illinois,"[39] and Frederick Trevor Hill, in researching Lincoln's legal career, found that all Lincoln contemporaries shared that opinion: they all considered Lincoln "the best all-around jury lawyer of his day in Illinois."[40]

Given this, Lincoln not surprisingly loved trying cases before juries. "If I can free this case from technicalities and get it properly swung to the jury," he would say, "I'll win it."[41]

Among his courtroom skills that contemporaries admired was his ability with witnesses, especially on cross-examination. According to Hill, it was "conceded by all his contemporaries that as a cross-examiner . . . [Lincoln] had no equal at the bar."[42] Chief Justice Scott agreed, writing that Lincoln

> had a most remarkable talent for examining witnesses—with him it was a rare gift . . . a power to compel a witness to disclose the whole truth. Even a witness at first unfriendly under his kindly treatment would finally become friendly and would wish to tell nothing he could honestly avoid against him, if he could state nothing for him.[43]

Indeed, attorney Arnold said, Lincoln could "compel a witness to tell the truth [even] when he [the witness] meant to lie."[44]

By 1850, a year after Lincoln left his term in Congress, the *Illinois Citizen* would write that he stood "at the head of his profession in this State,"[45] which was a significant compliment given the high quality of the Illinois bar. His ability in the courtroom drew clients from beyond Springfield, the Eighth Circuit, and even Illinois itself, especially later in his practice, because of both "his ability and learning as a lawyer and his clear and forcible mode of presenting a case either to a jury or to a court."[46] As Frederick Trevor Hill noted, Lincoln was attorney for the Illinois Central Railroad, the greatest corporation in the State, and one which doubtless had its choice of legal talent; he was also counsel for the Rock Island Railroad, and other corporations and individuals with important legal interests at stake; he was sought as legal arbitrator in the great corporation litigations of Illinois and he tried some of the most notable cases recorded in the courts of that state.[47]

In 1853, when an Illinois county taxed a railroad that ran through it, and the railroad sued to nullify the tax, the case had huge implications for *all* railroads and counties, not just in Illinois but beyond, and the lawyer whom *both* sides wanted was Abraham Lincoln. He gave the county first rights to his services, but when the county delayed in retaining him, he signed on for the railroad, won the case, at trial and in the Illinois Supreme Court, and then—ironically—had to sue the railroad to get his fee.[48]

When Cyrus McCormick, inventor of the famous reaper, sued another Illinois company in Chicago in 1855 for patent infringement, the Illinois defendant hired the best patent lawyers in the country, and when that team wanted to add an Illinois lawyer with stature and the trust of the judge, Lincoln was the lawyer they approached.[49]

In 1856, when a steamship hit the first railroad bridge built over the Mississippi, and the country's shipping and railroad interests went head to head in a case of epic proportions, the defendant bridge company hired Lincoln to lead the defense, at the recommendation of Norman Judd, himself a leading railroad attorney whom the bridge company had already retained.[50] Lincoln, Judd said, was "one of the best men" that Judd had ever heard at stating a case "forcibly and convincingly," his (Lincoln's) "personality will appeal to any judge or jury hearabouts," and he (Lincoln) was the only man "who can without doubt win that case."[51]

Scholars tell us that Lincoln's three partnerships took more than a thousand jury trials to verdict.[52] If Lincoln tried even half of these, that would be remarkable, and he likely tried many more than half, since he was the trial lawyer in his third partnership,[53] which accounted for two-thirds of his years in practice.

Scholars also tell us that Lincoln was equally the "go-to" lawyer in

Illinois for appeals. He and his partners appeared in more than four hundred cases before the Illinois Supreme Court, and in roughly half of these were hired just for the appeal.[54] Appeals allowed him to use his ability to make a case in both speaking (oral argument) and writing (briefs).[55] He wrote his own briefs for appeals,[56] just as he wrote his own pleadings in the trial courts.[57] Stephen B. Oates has written that Lincoln did "his most influential legal work" in the Supreme Court of Illinois, where he "won most of his appeals" and "earned his reputation as a lawyer's lawyer, adept at meticulous preparation and cogent argument."[58] John Duff has likewise written that it was in the Illinois Supreme Court on appeals, and not on the circuit in trials, that Lincoln "had his greatest impact as a lawyer."[59]

A decision that Lincoln won before the Illinois Supreme Court, on the right of corporations to amend charters in the public interest, was thereafter cited in twenty-five other cases throughout the country.[60] Lincoln won the case for the Alton & Sangamon Railroad against a stockholder who had refused to pay the balance on his pledge, after the railroad changed its route away from the stockholder's land, thereby rendering his land less valuable. The decision "helped establish the principle that corporation charters could be amended in the public interest."[61]

Similar recognition would come in another case, in which Lincoln sued Springfield for a man who had broken his leg on an unrepaired city street. The common law gave the man no claim, so Lincoln sued under the city charter, arguing that it required the city to keep its streets in safe condition. He won at trial and in the Illinois Supreme Court, the opinion of which would be widely cited in municipal law.[62]

Had he so chosen, Lincoln could have remained an increasingly successful lawyer for the rest of his life, or as long as he wanted to continue in practice. But fate had other designs on his ability to make a case, and would call on him to use it outside the courtroom and in politics once again, this time in a "case" of infinitely larger proportions than he or his country had ever faced.

Chapter 3: The Road to the White House

FOR FIVE YEARS after leaving Congress, Abraham Lincoln showed no sign of heading to further elective office. His family and his work were his focus.

And then, in the spring of 1854, everything changed. Under the leadership of Democrat Stephen Douglas, now a United States senator from Illinois and a nationally prominent politician, Congress passed the Kansas-Nebraska Act, which President Franklin Pierce signed into law on May 30. It removed the northern boundary[1] on slavery that the Missouri Compromise had set in 1820 for territories gained in the Louisiana Purchase, and made slavery a matter for settlers in each territory to decide, under the label of "popular sovereignty." It created a firestorm in the North, outraged Lincoln, and started him on the path that would lead to the presidency.

He first spoke against the Act on August 26, 1854, in Winchester, Illinois, at the request of a political ally running for reelection to Congress.[2] He gave a speech that the local newspaper called a "masterly effort . . . equal to any upon the same subject in Congress,"[3] and then made a second speech against the Act to a German-American group on September 12, in Bloomington, Illinois.[4] Two weeks later, in the same city, he tried to debate Stephen Douglas, who was on a statewide tour defending the Act,[5] but Douglas refused, so Lincoln invited the crowd, after Douglas gave his speech in the afternoon, to come hear him respond to Douglas that evening.[6]

A week later, on October 3, with Lincoln and Douglas both at the Illinois State Fair in Springfield, Douglas again refused to share the stage with Lincoln, so Lincoln again invited the crowd to come hear him, saying that he would "answer" Douglas the next day.[7] He then did,[8] in what Horace White, a reporter who heard the Springfield speech, later called "one of the world's masterpieces of argumentative power and moral grandeur,"[9] and Doris Kearns Goodwin has called Lincoln's "first great antislavery speech."[10]

Lincoln then repeated the speech two weeks later, on October 16, in Peoria, two hours after another Douglas speech,[11] and gave copies of the speech to the press, which published it in its entirety and magnified its reach.[12] In the speech, Lincoln made a passionate case for reinstating the Missouri Compromise, tracing first the steps of the founding fathers—who, he noted, included slaveholders—to keep slavery out of both the Northwest Territory[13] and the territory gained in the Louisiana Purchase.[14] He then traced the Missouri Compromise itself, its importance in resolving tensions between North and South, and the thirty-four years of respect it had enjoyed from all quarters, *including* Stephen Douglas, who had praised it, and not touched it in his initial drafts of the Kansas-Nebraska Act.

Lincoln argued that repealing the Missouri Compromise was wrong, in both "its direct effect" and "its prospective principle."[15] He also professed his "hate" for the "*declared* indifference" of Douglas to the spread of slavery because of its "monstrous injustice," and "because it deprives our republican example of its just influence in the world," making the United States instead look like "hypocrites."[16] While he recognized the shared blame of both North and South for the existence of slavery, and the difficultly of removing it, he denied that either of these justified allowing slavery to spread.

He then addressed each of the arguments that Douglas and others offered in defense of the Act.

He denied that the need for a territorial government in "the Nebraska country" justified the Act: the Nebraska country could get that government without repealing the Missouri Compromise.[17] He denied, with detailed facts, that the public had "ever repudiated the Missouri Compromise" or called for its repeal.[18] He denied that the repeal was "intrinsically right."[19]

He further decried the South's attempt to undo the Missouri *Compromise* without giving anything in return, when the Missouri Compromise itself had come about only through concessions from each side. It was as though, he said,

> two starving men had divided their only loaf; the one had hastily swallowed his half, and then grabbed the other half just as he was putting it to his mouth![20]

He denied, as a "*lullaby*," the argument that "climate" would keep slavery out of the Kansas and Nebraska territories, pointing out that five slave states lay *above* the northern latitude set by the Compromise.[21]

He rejected the argument that "as you do not object to my taking my hog to Nebraska, therefore I must not object to you taking your slave," because he rejected the premise that "there is no difference between hogs and negroes."[22] And on this point—the *humanity* of the "negro"—he gave example after example showing that "the great majority, south as well as north," recognized this.[23] He cited:

- the Constitution's failure even to mention the words "slave" or "slavery," and its provision setting a twenty-year deadline for ending the African slave trade;
- the series of laws that Congress had enacted, beginning in 1794, cutting away at the slave trade; and
- the South's almost unanimous support in 1820 "in declaring the African slave trade piracy, and in annexing to it the punishment of death," a punishment that he noted was *not* levied upon traders of hogs or other animals.[24]

He cited further the loathing that southerners themselves showed to the "SLAVE-DEALER" and even his children.[25]

> If you cannot help it, you sell to him; but if you can help it, you drive him from your door. You despise him utterly. You do not recognize him as a friend, or even as

an honest man. Your children must not play with his; they may rollick freely with the little negroes, but not with the "slave-dealers" children. If you are obliged to deal with him, you try to get through the job without so much as touching him. It is common with you to join hands with the men you meet; but with the slave dealer you avoid the ceremony—instinctively shrinking from the snaky contact. If he grows rich and retires from business, you still remember him, and still keep up the ban of non-intercourse upon him and his family.[26]

By distinct contrast, he pointed out, southerners showed no such disdain for "the man who deals in corn, cattle or tobacco."[27]

And, he continued, the liberation of so many slaves, at great financial cost to their masters, was further evidence of the tension between slavery and conscience:

There are in the United States and territories, including the District of Columbia, 433,643 free blacks. At $500 per head they are worth over two hundred millions of dollars. . . . All these free blacks are the descendants of slaves, or have been slaves themselves, and they would be slaves now, but for SOMETHING which has operated on their white owners, inducing them, at vast pecuniary sacrifices, to liberate them.[28]

All of this, he argued, showed that the vast majority, North and South, recognized the slave as a human being, not an animal, and the intrinsic wrong of ignoring this.[29]

In an impassioned plea, he warned that the "spirit" of the Revolution of 1776 and the "spirit" behind the Kansas-Nebraska Act "are utter antagonisms; and the former is being rapidly displaced by the latter."[30] He called for all "fellow countrymen—Americans south, as well as north . . . to arrest this" displacement, and to "repurify" "our republican robe," which was now "soiled, and trailed in the dust."[31]

> Let us turn slavery from its claims of "moral right." . . . Let us return it to the position our fathers gave it. . . . Let us re-adopt the Declaration of Independence, and with it, the practices, and policy, which harmonize with it. Let north and south—let all Americans—let all lovers of liberty everywhere—join in the great and good work. If we do this, we shall not only have saved the Union; but we shall have so saved it, as to make, and to keep it, forever worthy of the saving. We shall have so saved it, that the succeeding millions of free happy people, the world over, shall rise up, and call us blessed, to the latest generations.[32]

Frederick Trevor Hill later wrote that Lincoln's speech "fairly astonished" not only the general populace, but also Douglas himself, who Hill wrote was "the most amazed man in the community" at the speech.[33]

> He [Douglas] had known him [Lincoln] as a local practitioner and effective stump-speaker and country attorney, but he was not prepared for the logical, lawyer-like arraignment to which he found himself subjected, and after two more encounters with this new antagonist, he called a truce, proposing that neither he nor Lincoln should make any more speeches during the rest of the fall campaign.[34]

The "truce" notwithstanding, Lincoln's speeches in Springfield and Peoria had made their mark. Within weeks, he was elected to his fifth term in the Illinois House—his name having been put on the ballot by friends, against his wishes.[35] He never served that term, however, because the surge in his popularity led him to make a run at Illinois' other United States Senate seat (the one not held by Douglas) four months after his election to the Illinois House, in February 1855, and Lincoln believed he could not run for the Senate seat as a member of the Illinois House, which, like all state legislatures in those days, selected the state's United States senators.[36] He just narrowly missed winning that Senate seat, but one thing was now clear: in just four months, because of his speeches in

Springfield and Peoria, he had gone from an apparent political "has been" to a statewide political force.

In the months that followed, he left the Whig party and became a leader of the new Republican party in Illinois, in the process giving what may have been the greatest speech of his life, at the party's organizational meeting in Bloomington on May 29, 1856. It was the closing speech of the meeting, lasted ninety minutes, and was reportedly given without notes—and without any record of what he said: it is called his "Lost Speech." One explanation—the "legend"—is that what he said in his opening moments so captured reporters that they stopped writing.[37] Another is that the speech may have been considered *too* impassioned, too radical, and was "lost" on purpose or by agreement.[38]

Whatever the explanation, the speech appears to have been one of Lincoln's best. William Herndon, his last law partner, later called it "the grand effort of his [Lincoln's] life,"[39] and Chief Justice Scott, who also witnessed it, offered a similar opinion and this description of the event:

> After others had spoken Mr. Lincoln came forward and stood upon the platform. . . . A sudden stillness settled over that body of thoughtful men as Mr. Lincoln commenced to speak. Every one wanted to hear what he had to say. When he commenced, he spoke slowly as if selecting words that would best express his views and until he could get his subject well in hand. Gradually he increased in power and strength of utterance until every word that fell from his lips had a fullness of meaning not before so fully appreciated. The scene in that old hall was one of impressive grandeur. Every man, the venerable as well as the young and the strong, stood upon his feet. In a brief moment every one in that before incongruous assembly came to feel as one man, to think as one man and to purpose and resolve as one man. Rarely if ever was so wonderful an effect produced by an oration. It was the speech of his life in the estimation of many who heard it. . . . It was an extraordinary oration . . . a triumph that

comes to but few speakers. It was an effect that could only be produced by the truest eloquence.[40]

Jesse Dubois, who would soon become State Auditor, praised the speech as "the greatest . . . ever made in Illinois," and—in a prediction way ahead of its time—said it "puts Lincoln on the track for the presidency."[41] Several weeks later, Lincoln was among fifteen persons nominated, in Philadelphia, at the first Republican presidential convention, for the vice presidential spot on the first Republican presidential ticket. While Lincoln ultimately finished a distant second in the voting,[42] he also finished well ahead of the remaining thirteen nominees. The Springfield lawyer was no longer just a political force in his state: he had also reached prominence at the national level.

In the presidential campaign that followed, Lincoln was invited to speak in Indiana, Michigan, Wisconsin, and Iowa, all in "recognition of his growing national stature within the Republican Party."[43] He accepted only one out-of-state invitation, however, to speak in Kalamazoo, Michigan.[44] He otherwise confined his speeches to Illinois, with approximately fifty such efforts in support of the Republican ticket, headed by John Fremont.[45]

But while his speeches were nominally for Fremont and the ticket, they focused more on the case Lincoln had been making for the past two years. In his speech of August 27, 1856 in Kalamazoo,[46] for example, Lincoln referred to Fremont, by last name only, just a handful of times, and indirectly (by "him" or "his" or "the man") only a few times more, instead focusing on what he said at the outset of the speech was "not only the greatest question, but very nearly the sole question. . . . Shall slavery be spread into the new Territories, or not?"[47]

By the next year (1857), Lincoln had set his sights on another run for the United States Senate, this time for Douglas's seat, which would be on the ballot the year after that (1858), and fired his first shot in that campaign after the United States Supreme Court announced its decision in the *Dred Scott* case on March 6.[48] While all nine justices wrote opinions, Chief Justice Taney's opinion commanded the concurrence of the 7-2 majority,[49] and declared (among other things) that slave owners had a constitutionally protected right to their slaves as "property" under the Fifth Amendment, with which neither the federal government nor the territories could interfere. This decision trumped the "popular sovereignty" principle of the Kansas-Nebraska Act, since the "popular" vote in a territory would not matter against a constitutionally protected right, and raised the firestorm over slavery in the territories to a new level.

Three months after the Court announced its decision, Stephen Douglas defended it in a speech, which Lincoln attended,[50] and Lincoln responded two weeks later, on June 26, in the Illinois statehouse in Springfield.[51] Marching into the room with a collection of law books under his arm,[52] he gave a scholarly speech assailing Chief Justice Taney's majority opinion on both its facts and logic, with the aim of undercutting the opinion as incorrectly decided and worthy of reversal.

He attacked, as incorrect in fact, Justice Taney's statement that "negroes were no part of the people who made, or for whom was made, the Declaration of Independence, or the Constitution."[53] The truth, Lincoln noted, as Justice Curtis had in his dissenting opinion, was that in five of the thirteen states there were not only "free negroes" when the Constitution was adopted, but they were also entitled to vote, and were thus not only "included in the body of 'the people of the Unites States,' by whom the Constitution was ordained and established," but also "had the power to act, and, doubtless, did act, by their suffrages, upon the question of its adoption."[54]

Lincoln similarly challenged, as errant fact, Taney's implication "that the public estimate of the black man is more favorable *now* than it was in the days of the Revolution."[55] The truth, Lincoln noted, was "decidedly the other way."[56] Two states that had originally allowed free blacks to vote—New Jersey and North Carolina—had since revoked that right, and New York had severely abridged it. "Legal restraints" that amounted "almost to prohibition" had now been placed upon the right of masters to emancipate their slaves.[57] The Kansas-Nebraska Act had removed the restriction on expanding slavery into the territories, and the Supreme Court had declared that any such restriction would be unconstitutional. Far from being better off, Lincoln said, "the black man" now faced ever-increasing barriers to freedom.

Lincoln equally took the majority opinion to task for its logic, first addressing Chief Justice Taney's statement that in declaring all men to be created equal, the Declaration of Independence was only "speaking of

British subjects on this continent being equal to British subjects born and residing in Great Britain."[58] Lincoln's response:

> Why, according to this, not only negroes but white people outside of Great Britain and America are not spoken of in that instrument. . . . [T]he French, Germans and other white people of the world are all gone to pot along with the Judge's inferior races.
>
> I had thought the Declaration promised something better than the condition of British subjects; but no, it only meant that we should be *equal* to them in their own oppressed and *unequal* condition. . . . [I]t gave no promise that having kicked off the King and Lords of Great Britain, we should not at once be saddled with a King and Lords of our own.[59]

Lincoln further attacked Taney's conclusion (which Douglas also advocated) that the founders could not have intended the Declaration of Independence to include "negroes" since the founders "did not at once, actually place them on an equality with the whites."[60] Lincoln pointed out the logical error of concluding that because the founders did not "declare all men equal *in all respects*," the founders did not intend "negroes" to be equal in *any*, and specifically those in which the founders *did* say all men are equal: life, liberty, and the pursuit of happiness.[61]

Furthermore, Lincoln argued, the Declaration was not meant to assert that all men were *at that point* "actually enjoying that equality," or that the Declaration was about "to confer it immediately upon them."[62] The Declaration was instead meant to "declare the *right*," to be enforced "as fast as circumstances should permit," and to set the goal for the country, the "standard" principle of "free society, which should be familiar to all, and revered by all; constantly looked to, constantly labored for, . . . even though never perfectly attained."[63]

And finally, Lincoln took aim, both logically and factually, at a favorite theme of Douglas and the pro-slavery camp—their "horrified" contention that what Republicans really wanted was "amalgamation," the "mixing [of] blood by the white and black races."[64] "I protest against that counterfeit logic," Lincoln said, "which concludes that, because I do not want a black woman for a *slave* I must necessarily want her for a *wife*. I need not have her for either, I can just leave her alone."[65]

As a matter of fact, Lincoln pointed out, the most recent census (of 1850) showed that there were 405,751 "mulattoes" in all the states, with only 56,649 of these in the free states, and most of them born not in those states, but in the *slave* states. "In New Hampshire," Lincoln continued, "which goes farthest towards equality between the races," there were just 184 "mulattoes," while there were in Virginia alone 79,775, which was 23,126 more "than in all the free States together."[66] "These statistics," Lincoln said, "show that slavery"—not freedom—"is the greatest source of amalgamation; and next to it, not the elevation, but the degeneration of the free blacks."[67]

The *Illinois State Journal* published Lincoln's entire speech and offered copies for sale, and Republican newspapers in Illinois also published the whole speech or portions of it.[68] A letter to the *New-York Daily Tribune* praised Lincoln's "masterly effort," and its "complete refutation of the sophistries of Douglas," and sent a message to those outside Illinois about the stature that Lincoln now had in his home state:

> Mr. Lincoln is too well known in Illinois to need a word of commendation; but it may be interesting to Republicans at a distance to be informed that there is not a man in this State whose opinions on political subjects command more universal respect by all classes of men, than his.[69]

Lincoln's race against Douglas for the Senate seat then began in earnest in May of the next year (1858), when Illinois Republicans unanimously nominated him to run against Douglas, and Lincoln hit yet another home run with his acceptance speech.[70] The latter cast the country as a house divided over slavery, predicted that it could not remain that way, and warned of a pro-slavery plan to end the division in slavery's favor, by making it legal not just in the territories, but in the free states as well.

In support of his case, he cited a series of events that conveniently fit together: the Kansas-Nebraska Act; the *Dred Scott* decision; the support for that decision that each of the last two Democrat presidents, Franklin Pierce and James Buchanan, had urged even before the decision was handed down, suggesting that they knew what it would say; and the attitude that Stephen Douglas was now urging upon the country—as the Democratic leader in Congress and presumed front-runner for the Democratic presidential nomination two years hence—not to "*care* whether slavery is voted *down* or voted *up*."[71]

All that remained for the pro-slavery effort to succeed, Lincoln said, was "another Supreme Court decision, declaring that the Constitution of the United States does not permit a *state* to exclude slavery within its limits."[72] "Welcome or unwelcome," he said, "such decision *is* probably coming, and will soon be upon us, unless the power of the present political dynasty shall be met and overthrown."[73]

And to this latter cause—meeting and overthrowing "the present political dynasty" and its plan—he then summoned Republicans—the "undoubted friends [of the cause]—those whose hands are free, whose hearts are in the work—who *do care* for the result."[74] His reference to "*do care*" was aimed at Douglas and those in Republican circles, including Horace Greeley, the influential editor of the *New-York Tribune*, who advocated that Republicans back Douglas, because he had split with pro-slavery forces over whether a pro-slavery convention at Lecompton, Kansas qualified as the "popular sovereignty" vote that the Kansas-Nebraska Act envisioned. Could Republicans, Lincoln asked, who passionately *did care* whether slavery went into the territories, align themselves with someone—Douglas—who had repeatedly said, "I *don't* care?" No, Lincoln said, the responsibility for stopping the spread of slavery could be trusted only to Republicans, to whom he then directed this stirring peroration:

> Two years ago the Republicans of the nation mustered over thirteen hundred thousand strong.
>
> We did this under the single impulse of resistance to a common danger, with every external circumstance against us.

Joseph F. Roda

> Of *strange, discordant*, and even *hostile* elements, we gathered from the four winds, and *formed* and fought the battle through, under the constant hot fire of a disciplined, proud, and pampered enemy.
>
> Did we brave all *then* to *falter* now?—*now*—when that same enemy is *wavering*, dissevered, and belligerent?
>
> The result is not doubtful. We shall not fail—if we stand firm, we shall not fail.
>
> *Wise counsels* may *accelerate* or *mistakes delay* it, but, sooner or later, the victory is *sure* to come.[75]

Republican newspapers throughout Illinois ran the speech on their front pages, and some editors published a pocket edition.[76] Greeley himself, though not happy about Lincoln's nomination, also published the speech.[77]

When Douglas learned of Lincoln's nomination, his response spoke volumes. "I shall have my hands full," he said.[78] "He [Lincoln] is the strong man of his party—full of wit, facts, dates—and *the best stump speaker . . . in the West*."[79] That was high praise indeed from a man himself considered one of the country's best stump speakers—the so-called "Little Giant"—and also from "the West." "If I beat him," Douglas said, it would be only through a hard battle indeed.[80]

Lincoln reportedly gave sixty-three speeches in his campaign against Douglas,[81] but it was their seven debates, between August 21 and October 15, for which Lincoln and the campaign are remembered. While Lincoln started his campaign by again following Douglas (and his national press corps) around, and giving speeches after Douglas spoke, he then upped the ante and challenged Douglas to formal debate.

Douglas was a highly skilled debater, the "Master of the Senate"—the nation's paramount debate forum—but wanted no part of debate with Lincoln. He had privately called Lincoln "the most difficult and dangerous opponent" he had ever met,[82] and had declined (as noted above) to debate him four years earlier (in 1854), when Lincoln had first spoken against the

Kansas-Nebraska Act. Douglas again dodged Lincoln's challenge in 1858 as long as he could, but finally had to give in or lose face.

Lincoln—the confident jury lawyer—wanted as many as *fifty* debates with Douglas,[83] but Douglas would agree to only seven, one in each of the seven congressional districts where he and Lincoln had not already recently spoken.[84] Scholars differ on who "won" the debates, but Lincoln at least held his own, which was itself a victory, given his opponent. The debates received national press because of Douglas, and that moved Lincoln now solidly onto the national stage. As one writer put it, "he had become the voice of the aroused conscience of a nation."[85] The *Chicago Press & Tribune* wrote of the "memorable and brilliant canvas" that Lincoln had made, and the "national reputation" he had "created for himself," which was "both envied and deserved."[86]

Douglas retained his Senate seat because Democrats won a 54-46 majority in the Illinois legislature (which as noted above chose the state's United States senators), but Republicans pulled more votes for legislative candidates statewide, and Lincoln began to be mentioned as a possible presidential candidate himself, primarily in "the West." He held off declaring himself a candidate, given the much better credentials of the Republicans already in the ring, but put his debates with Douglas to continued work by publishing them with his biography in a two-hundred-page scrapbook, which became a best seller and led to more invitations to speak.

Lincoln had to decline invitations until August of the next year (1859) because of financial considerations and the demands of his law practice (which had taken a back seat in his senatorial campaign). But when he did resume speaking in August, he then gave nearly two dozen speeches between that month and December, in five midwestern states (Iowa, Ohio, Wisconsin, Indiana, and Kansas) other than Illinois.[87]

Lincoln went to Ohio because Stephen Douglas—who else?—was campaigning for Democratic candidates there, and Lincoln agreed to do the same for Republicans.[88] Douglas had recently published an article in *Harper's Magazine* arguing that the founders had essentially taken a "hands off" policy to the people of the territories and colonies in "all things affecting their internal polity," including slavery,[89] and Douglas had then repeated that argument in a speech on September 7 in Ohio, adding that "our fathers, when they framed this Government under which we live, understood this question just as well, and even better, than we do now."[90]

Nine days later, Lincoln responded[91] with a two-hour speech that went at Douglas on all fronts.[92] He attacked Douglas's "insidious" version of popular sovereignty, that "if one man chooses to make a slave of another man, neither that other man nor anybody else has a right to object."[93] He attacked Douglas's idea that slavery was "one of those little, unimportant, trivial matters which are just about as much consequence as . . . whether my neighbor should raise horned cattle or plant tobacco."[94] "I suppose the institution of slavery really looks small to him," Lincoln said: while "a lash upon his back would hurt him, . . . [a] lash upon anybody else's back does not."[95]

He attacked even harder Douglas's suggestion that the founding fathers had thought as Douglas and his supporters did, when the unassailable evidence was that they thought *exactly the opposite.*

> And now he asks the community to believe that the men of the revolution were in favor of his great principle, when we have the naked history that they themselves dealt with this very subject matter of his principle, and utterly repudiated his principle, acting upon a precisely contrary ground. It is as impudent and absurd as if a prosecuting attorney should stand up before a jury, and ask them to convict A as the murderer of B, while B was walking alive before them.[96]

The "naked history" to which he referred was the Ordinances of 1784 and 1787—which, Lincoln noted, Douglas had conveniently omitted from the "history" of slavery in his recent article and speech. Lincoln especially emphasized the Ordinance of 1787, which Lincoln pointed out was drafted at the same time, and by the same men, as the Constitution; had passed *unanimously*, even among those who were slaveholders; and had specifically *forbidden* slavery in the Northwest Territory (which became the states of Ohio, Indiana, Illinois, Michigan, and Wisconsin, and part of Minnesota).

Francis P. Blair, Jr., a Missouri lawyer, soldier, and politician (who would later serve in the Union Army), called Lincoln's speech in Columbus "the most complete overthrow Mr Douglass ever received."[97]

Throughout his midwest swing in the late summer and fall of 1859, Lincoln impressed even those who disagreed with him. A Democratic newspaper in Indianapolis said that "for deep thought, historical research and biting criticism, [Lincoln's speech had] not been equaled by any Republican orator in the West, or the East either."[98] A pro-slavery leader from Virginia reportedly called a Lincoln speech in Atchison, Kansas "the greatest antislavery speech he ever heard."[99] An Indiana newspaper said that Lincoln's speech in Cincinnati "ought to be read by every body interested in American politics,"[100] and the *Cincinnati Gazette* said it had "such dignity and power as to have impressed some of our ablest lawyers with the conclusion that it was superior to any political effort they had ever heard."[101]

And in November, in the midst of this swing, Lincoln received what would become his most important invitation of all: to speak in Brooklyn, New York, as part of a lecture series at the church of the Reverend Henry Ward Beecher, the brother of Harriet Beecher Stowe.[102] It would be his first exposure in the all-important, delegate-rich East, and a make-or-break moment for him, as he knew.

The date was pushed back to February 27, to give him time to prepare, but even then, Lincoln and his friends "had many misgivings" about the invitation, right up to his departure for New York.[103] Lincoln reportedly told Lawrence Weldon, a fellow lawyer, "I don't know whether I shall be adequate to the situation; I have never appeared before such an audience as may possibly assemble to hear me."[104] But notwithstanding these apprehensions, he honored his commitment and went.

The change in the date put the speech beyond the lecture series, and a new sponsor stepped in—the Young Men's Republican Union of New York—which then moved the speech to the Cooper Institute in New York City[105] when the anticipated audience grew too large for Beecher's church. The audience included all of New York's finest, "all the noted men—all the learned and cultured"—of the Republican party in New York, "editors, clergymen, statesmen, lawyers, merchants, critics."[106] Indeed, the crowd went beyond just Republicans: the *New-York Daily Tribune* wrote that there had not been "a larger assemblage of the intellect and mental culture of our City" to hear a political speaker since the days of Clay and Webster.[107]

This audience knew Lincoln only from newspaper accounts, as the prairie lawyer and the uneducated "rail splitter," and came to see if he was for real, or just had good press. When they first saw him, his physical appearance took many aback, as it had the sponsors themselves. The committee member who had greeted Lincoln on his arrival in the city reportedly had a "My God, what have I done?" moment at that first sight, which he later recalled:

> I faced a very tall man wearing a high hat and carrying an old-fashioned, comical-looking carpet-bag. My heart went into my boots. . . . His clothes were travel-stained and he looked tired and woe-begone, and there was nothing in my first hasty view of the man that was at all prepossessing. On the contrary, . . . there came to me the disheartening and appalling thought of the great throng which I had been so instrumental in inducing to come. . . . For the instant I felt sick at heart.[108]

Other committee members had the same reaction when they visited Lincoln on the day of the speech, calling him "the most unprepossessing public man . . . [they] had ever met."[109]

At the event itself, an observer reported that one leg of Lincoln's new suit (purchased just for the occasion) was about two inches above his shoe, the back of his coat was too large, his sleeves were too short, and "his hair was disheveled and stuck out like rooster's feathers."[110] Another said that Lincoln was "tall, tall—oh, how tall! and so angular and awkward that I had, for an instant, a feeling of pity for so ungainly a man."[111]

Lincoln then did nothing to help his cause when he began his speech with "Mr. *Cheerman*,"[112] in his Kentucky / Indiana / Illinois twang,[113] and momentarily lost his place.[114] But he then *did* change impressions, and rapidly, when he got beyond that moment and into his speech.[115] Picking up where he had left off in Columbus, he announced as his theme the statement of Douglas that "*Our fathers, when they framed the Government under which we live, understood this question just as well, and even better, than we do now.*"[116] He said that he "fully indorse[d] this" statement, and that it simply left the question of what the fathers' "understanding" was.[117]

He then proceeded to answer that question with the fruit of three months' research. He identified the "fathers" as the thirty-nine signers of the Constitution, and then presented—in meticulous detail—how each had voted (if each had) on six pieces of legislation between 1787 and 1820 that involved whether to allow slavery in the territories. Specifically, he showed that, of the thirty-nine "fathers:"

- twenty-three had taken a position on the issue, and of those, twenty-one—a clear majority—had consistently voted to prohibit slavery in the territories, which clearly implied that those twenty-one believed, as Republicans now did, that the federal government could and should bar slavery from the territories; and
- only two had voted against a federal prohibition of slavery in the territories, and it was impossible to tell why those two had voted that way: was it because they believed the federal government could not or should not bar slavery from the territories, or because of some other, unrelated objection to the bill on which they were voting?

The "fathers'" votes thus showed without question that Douglas was wrong: the fathers' "understanding" of the issue—which Douglas had said should now guide the country—was *not* that of Douglas and the pro-slavery forces. It was that of *Republicans*, and having established this, Lincoln then repeatedly used all or portions of Douglas's anchor words—"our fathers," who "understood this question just as well, and even better, than we"— against Douglas, to the delight of the audience.

In the second part of his speech, Lincoln then addressed southern accusations and misimpressions about the Republican party, one by one, arguing that they were baseless. He spoke to the "unconditional condemnation" that southerners had for anything Republicans had to say, a condemnation that he said appeared to be "an indispensable prerequisite" for any southerner even to be allowed to speak.[118] He asked southerners "to pause and to consider whether this is quite just to us [Republicans], or even to yourselves," and to listen with an open mind to Republican answers to southern "charges and specifications."[119]

He addressed—and denied—the southern charge that Republicans were "sectional," that Republicans were "revolutionary," and that pro-slavery forces were "conservative."[120] He pointed out that it was Republicans who wanted to keep things as they had been—keep the Missouri Compromise intact—and Douglas and the pro-slavery forces who wanted so drastically to change things, by overthrowing that long-respected compromise.

He denied the accusation that Republicans "stir up insurrections among your slaves," or had anything to do with John Brown's failed raid at Harper's Ferry, Virginia, attempting to instigate a slave rebellion.[121] John Brown was not a Republican, Lincoln said, and southerners had produced no proof of any connection between Republicans and Brown's raid. He also denied that Republicans were seeking to disallow any "plainly written" constitutional right of slave holders.[122]

Then, having "spoken" to the South, Lincoln returned to his fellow Republicans in the third and final part of his speech. After emphasizing that Republicans wanted that *"this great Confederacy shall be at peace,"* he identified the only thing that would satisfy the South: for Republicans and the North to "cease to call slavery *wrong,* and join them in calling it *right.*"[123] This, he said, Republicans could never do, and given that, he summoned them, in another stirring peroration, to do what they must:

> If our sense of duty forbids this [allowing slavery to spread in the territories and free states], then let us stand by our duty, fearlessly and effectively. Let us be diverted by none of those sophistical contrivances wherewith we are so industriously plied and belabored—contrivances such as groping for some middle ground between the right and the wrong, vain as the search for a man who should be neither a living man nor a dead man—such as a policy of "don't care" on a question about which all true men do care—such as Union appeals beseeching true Union men to yield to Disunionists, reversing the divine rule, and calling, not the sinners, but the righteous to repentance—such as

invocations to Washington, imploring men to unsay what Washington said, and undo what Washington did.

Neither let us be slandered from our duty by false accusations against us, nor frightened from it by menaces of destruction to the Government nor of dungeons to ourselves. LET US HAVE FAITH THAT RIGHT MAKES MIGHT, AND IN THAT FAITH, LET US, TO THE END, DARE TO DO OUR DUTY AS WE UNDERSTAND IT.[124]

The speech lasted an hour and a half,[125] and was a stunning success. It made not only the case that Lincoln expressly sought to make—that Republicans must stop the expansion of slavery—but also his all-important "secondary" case: that he, Abraham Lincoln of Illinois, the prairie lawyer and "rail splitter" about whom the audience may have had their apprehensions, was indeed a viable candidate for the nation's highest office.

One person who had initially pitied Lincoln for his looks later said that, after Lincoln began speaking, "I forgot his clothes, his personal appearance, and his individual peculiarities. . . . I was on my feet with the rest, yelling like a wild Indian, cheering this wonderful man."[126] And when a friend asked him after the speech what he now thought of Abe Lincoln, "the rail-splitter," he said, "'He's the greatest man since St. Paul.'"[127]

Richard McCormick, a member of the sponsoring committee, said that Lincoln was "captivating," that he "held the vast meeting spell-bound," and that McCormick had never seen "an audience more thoroughly carried away by an orator."[128] William Cullen Bryant, the poet and longtime editor of the *New York Evening Post,* called Lincoln's Cooper Union presentation "the best political speech he had ever heard,"[129] and Horace Greeley concurred,[130] with his paper going even further, praising Lincoln's ability as a persuasive speaker without limitation to the speech he had just made. "Mr. Lincoln," the paper said,

> is one of Nature's orators, using his rare powers solely and effectively to elucidate and to convince, though their inevitable effect is to delight and electrify as well. . . . The

vast assemblage frequently rang with cheers and shouts of applause, which were prolonged and intensified at the close. No man ever before made such an impression on his first appeal to a New-York audience.[131]

In his book, *Lend Me Your Ears*, William Safire wrote that in ancient Greece, when Pericles spoke, the people said, "How *well* he speaks," but when Demosthenes spoke, the people said, *"Let us march!"*[132] Abraham Lincoln, at the Cooper Institute on February 27, 1860, made the people want to march.

Lincoln would later say that his Cooper Union speech, and the photograph Mathew Brady took of him before it, made him president.[133] Newspaper accounts of the speech brought still more invitations to speak, and Lincoln essentially repeated the speech nine more times, in a tour of the Northeast over the next nine weeks. Four of those speeches were in New Hampshire, the last being in Exeter, where Lincoln's son Robert was in school. Robert and many classmates attended the speech at the town hall, and one of those, Marshall Solomon Snow, who would later become a history professor, then dean, and then chancellor at Washington University, recounted as an adult what he saw and thought of Lincoln before the speech:

> His hair was rumpled, his neckwear was all awry, he sat somewhat bent in the chair, and altogether presented a very remarkable and, to us, disappointing appearance.[134]

But just as the crowd at Cooper Union had, Snow and his fellow students found themselves quickly impressed when Lincoln began to speak, as Snow later described:

> Not ten minutes had passed before his uncouth appearance was absolutely forgotten by us boys, and, I believe, by all of that large audience. For an hour and a half he held the closest attention of every person present.[135]

Others who heard Lincoln speak on his northeast tour were similarly impressed, including those on the other side of the political aisle. The editor of a Democratic paper in Providence, Rhode Island, for example, reportedly said that Lincoln's speech in that city was "the finest constitutional argument for a popular audience" that he had ever heard.[136] A newspaper in Concord, New Hampshire similarly wrote that Lincoln's speech there was "one of the ablest, most closely reasoned and eloquent speeches ever listened to" in that city.[137]

Among others whom Lincoln impressed was Edward H. Rollins, a young Republican who would head the New Hampshire delegation at the Republican convention in Chicago three months later, and would announce on the first ballot, with New Hampshire just the second state to vote, that seven of its ten votes were for Lincoln. That vote, as Mike Pride writes, made a most important statement:

> [It] sent a powerful twofold message. [William] Seward [the presumed front-runner going into the convention] did not have a lock on the Northeast, and a majority of at least one open-minded delegation saw Lincoln as the electable alternative to Seward or any other contender.[138]

Doris Kearns Goodwin writes that in Lincoln's midwest swing in the fall of 1859, and his Cooper Union and New England speeches in early 1860, "he had appeared before tens of thousands of people," not to mention the many thousands more who had read or become familiar with his speeches via the newspapers.[139] By the time of the Republican convention in mid-May, he had become at least the popular second choice of delegates, and in the voting that then ensued, received the second highest number of votes on the first two ballots, and won on the third.

As the Republican nominee, he followed the custom of the day and made no new speeches in the general election campaign,[140] but "had surrogates present excerpts from his previous speeches to reinforce his positions,"[141] and won in a tight race against three other opponents, one of whom—Stephen Douglas, his adversary of decades—would be dead by the next June.[142]

In a remarkable *tour de force*, Abraham Lincoln, he of the meager political credentials, education, and looks, had won the Republican nomination for president, and then the general election, over men with eminently more impressive educations and political credentials, but not his ability to make a case.

Yes, his Republican opponents (William Seward, Salmon Chase, and Edward Bates) hurt themselves with statements that came across as too radical, or by not attending to the necessary details of a political campaign, and yes, having the Republican presidential convention in Chicago also undoubtedly helped Lincoln, but it was his six years of speeches—and the power of the case they made—that put him in contention for the nomination. Without those speeches, what the other Republican contenders said, or where the convention was held, would not have mattered. Lincoln would not have been in the race. He would have been just an Illinois lawyer, unknown to the rest of the country.

And yes, the Democratic party's splintering into two factions helped him in the general election, to be sure, but again, it was his past speeches—and the case they made—that made him the Republican beneficiary of that splintering, and that "spoke" for him, and shaped his identity, for voters across the North.

The story of Lincoln's ability to make a case, and how far it carried him, would be extraordinary if it were to stop here, with his election as president. But it does not. His greatest challenges in making a case, and his greatest accomplishments, lay yet ahead.

Chapter 4: Mr. President

WE THINK OF Abraham Lincoln the president as the strong, wartime commander in chief, expanding the powers of the office to the point of controversy. But he was not a dictator or king. He was a democratically elected executive who had to work with a democratically elected Congress, for which—as for him—public opinion was everything. As Lincoln himself put it: "With public sentiment, nothing can fail; without it nothing can succeed."[1]

And public sentiment was a battle for him from the start.

He entered the White House with a lack of presidential "stature" in the eyes of many, because of his "unexceptional political career and little national experience . . . [as well as] his limited education, backwoods stories, peculiar accent, awkward manner, and homely face."[2]

He was also elected by just a plurality—only 39.7 percent of the popular vote. Seven southern states then seceded between his election and inauguration, four more followed when war broke out just thirty-nine days after that inauguration, and four more teetered on the edge, the "border states" of Delaware, Maryland, Kentucky, and Missouri, without which Lincoln thought the Union cause could not be won.

Public opinion was overwhelmingly against him in the South, of course, but he also faced substantial opposition in the North, at one time or another, on:

- his capacity to meet the demands of the presidency, especially in the crisis he faced;
- his authorizing military arrests and trials, and suspending habeas corpus;
- his refusal to make emancipation a war goal;
- his Emancipation Proclamation;
- his acceptance of freed slaves and free blacks into the Union Army and Navy;
- the military draft of 1863;[3] and
- the war itself, with its awful, prolonged, and ever-increasing toll on lives, families, and property.

Public disenchantment showed less than two years into his presidency, in the mid-term elections of 1862, when Republicans lost elections in five states that Lincoln had carried, Democrats increased their seats in the House of Representatives by sixty-three percent (twenty-eight seats),[4] and a Democrat won the governor's office in New York,[5] the country's most populous state. And for much of the two years that followed, Lincoln faced a significant risk of not being re-elected; indeed, at one point, Lincoln thought his defeat, to his former commander of the Union Army, General George McClellan, was all but certain.

In short, as Douglas Wilson writes:

> For most of his [Lincoln's] presidency, he was beset by critics on all sides. He found himself operating in a perpetual cross fire from congressmen, governors, generals, office seekers, ordinary citizens—all dissatisfied, and many sincerely convinced that he was incompetent and leading the nation down the path of destruction.[6]

Lincoln could command the Union military, but not public opinion. He could only try to influence that through persuasion, and did so repeatedly, with carefully crafted public statements, nearly a hundred of them,[7] an unprecedented number for a president up to that time.

Three of these would be formal speeches for which he is remembered, his First and Second Inaugurals and his Gettysburg Address, but most of his presidential statements that sought to influence public opinion were written messages, among them his messages to Congress, his Preliminary and final Emancipation Proclamations, and perhaps as important as anything else, his "public letters," which he wrote to one person[8] knowing they would be published to the country, often by the next day.[9]

This reliance primarily on written messages was a marked departure from his pre-presidential days, in which he had relied almost totally on speeches to make his case. This was likely a function of time: he liked to carefully research and prepare his speeches, and as president, in the midst of a civil war, he had much less time to do that.

He would also refrain, as president, and for most of his time as president-elect, from making informal "stump" speeches or impromptu remarks on important issues, again in contrast to his pre-presidential approach. Historian William Gienapp attributes this to Lincoln's belief that a president should not campaign or make stump speeches,[10] and Harold Holzer concurs, writing that Lincoln thought that a president, when he spoke about a serious subject, should only speak "officially," from a text.[11] But Holzer adds a possible second reason: Lincoln had not done well, in his eyes and others,' with early attempts at impromptu remarks as president-elect, and thereafter avoided any such further efforts, to avoid any such further embarrassments.[12]

Whatever the reason, writing became President Lincoln's primary tool for making his case. Douglas Wilson writes that Lincoln responded with "some act of writing" "to almost every important development during his presidency, and to many that were not so important."[13] Lincoln's pen, Wilson says, became his *"sword."*[14]

But Lincoln's first presidential effort at persuasion *was* a speech, his First Inaugural Address,[15] in which he sought to make three cases:

- that there was no need for civil war;
- that he had a duty—grounded in the Constitution and affirmed in his presidential oath—to preserve the Union, *and he intended to do that* (in contrast to his outgoing predecessor, James Buchanan, who thought, or at least professed, that the president and federal government had no power to prevent secession); and
- that he was up to the job.

Carl Schurz, a Union Army general, United States senator, and Secretary of the Interior, later wrote that Lincoln probably "did not expect his inaugural address" to persuade the South, bent as they were "upon disunion at any cost," and that he aimed his address primarily at "the wavering minds in the North,"[16] even if most of the speech was ostensibly directed to the South. His thoughtful but firm arguments may have been his way of showing the North—and the four border states—that he was committed to preserving the Union, was up to the job, and that if civil war came, it would not be his fault.

He began by repeating what he had already and repeatedly said in his past speeches: he had "no purpose, directly or indirectly, to interfere with the institution of slavery in the States where it exists."[17] He had "no lawful right to do so," he said, and "no inclination to do so."[18]

He reiterated the protection that slaveholders had in the "fugitive slave" provision of the Constitution, which compelled the "delivery" of any "person held to service or labor in one State . . . escaping into another," and said that this law, and all laws "which stand unrepealed," should be obeyed.[19]

He said that while "the laws of the Union" had to "be faithfully executed in all the States," "there needs to be no bloodshed or violence; and there shall be none, unless it be forced upon the national authority."[20] He intended simply "to hold, occupy, and possess the property, and places belonging to the [federal] government, and to collect the duties and imposts."[21] "Beyond what may be necessary for these objects," he said, "there will be no invasion—no using of force against, or among the people anywhere."[22]

Having made these statements to the South in general, he then narrowed his focus, recognizing "that there are persons . . . who seek to destroy the Union at all events" and would not be persuaded no matter what he said, and turning to those in the South "who really love the Union."[23]

He asked them to think "before entering upon so grave a matter as the destruction of our national fabric, with all its benefits, its memories, and its hopes."[24]

He asked them to identify "any right, plainly written in the Constitution, [that] has been denied."[25]

He asked them to consider that disagreements in governing are inevitable, and that the only way to resolve them, if the government is to be maintained, is by majority rule, "held in restraint by constitutional checks, and limitations, and always changing easily, with deliberate changes of popular opinions and sentiments."[26]

> If the minority will not acquiesce, the majority must, or the government must cease. There is no other alternative; for continuing the government, is acquiescence on one side or the other. If a minority, in such case, will secede rather than acquiesce, they make a precedent which, in turn, will divide and ruin them; for a minority of their own will secede from them, whenever a majority refuses to be controlled by such minority.[27]

"Plainly," he said, "the central idea of secession, is the essence of anarchy."[28]

He touched again upon the Supreme Court's *Dred Scott* decision, without identifying it by name, and sought to limit its reach, saying that courts decide disputes for the *parties* in a case, so that even if the court's decision is "erroneous," its "evil effect" is "limited to that particular case."[29] But on questions "affecting the whole people," he said, the government's policy must be set *by the whole people*, not the Supreme Court.[30] To do otherwise would have the people, for all practical purposes, cease "to be their own rulers."[31]

He spoke also of practical reasons not to separate, one being simple geography. "Physically speaking," he said, "we cannot separate. We cannot remove our respective sections from each other, nor build an impassable wall between them."[32]

Another was the inevitability, given that geography, of continued contact between the sections even if the Union should split, and the greater advantage of managing that contact through union.

> They cannot but remain face to face; and intercourse, either amicable or hostile, must continue between them. Is it possible then to make that intercourse more

advantageous, or more satisfactory, *after* separation than *before*? Can aliens make treaties easier than friends can make laws?[33]

He further noted that the people, if "they shall grow weary of the existing government," always have the "*constitutional* right of amending it," and even went so far as to say that he would have "no objection" to a proposed constitutional amendment barring the federal government from ever interfering with slavery in the states.[34]

"My countrymen," he said, "think calmly and *well*, upon this whole subject."[35] There was no need to act in "haste," "no single good reason for precipitate action."[36]

But having clearly made his case against civil war, he just as clearly, in passages much shorter, but no less strong, made the case for his resolve to preserve the Union, whatever that required.

He declared his belief that the Union was "perpetual," that it was "much older than the Constitution," and that "as a contract" among the states it could not "be peaceably unmade, by less than all the parties who made it."[37] "No State, upon its own mere motion, . . . [could] lawfully get out of the Union."[38] With this belief as his foundation, he declared his equal belief that there had been no "secession:" "I therefore consider that, in view of the Constitution and the laws, the Union is unbroken."[39]

He further declared that any "acts of violence, within any State or States, against the authority of the United States"—the unbroken Union—would thus be "insurrectionary or revolutionary," and that "the Constitution itself expressly enjoin[ed]" him to take the necessary measures against any such acts, and to see "that the laws of the Union be faithfully executed in all the States."[40]

And in the penultimate paragraph of his address, he made clear his resolve to honor his constitutional duty: "In *your* hands, my dissatisfied fellow countrymen, and not in *mine*, is the momentous issue of civil war."[41] Those last two words—"*civil war*"—left no doubt that Abraham Lincoln, president of the United States and commander in chief of its armed forces, was willing to use the Union's military force if necessary, willing to go to "war," "civil war," rather than let the Union dissolve.

He then immediately fortified that statement with another that emphasized how solemn the duty was that left him no choice but to preserve the Union:

> The government will not assail *you*. You can have no conflict, without being yourselves the aggressors. *You* have no oath registered in Heaven to destroy the government, while *I* shall have the most solemn one to "preserve, protect and defend" it.[42]

It was an unambiguous message of intent and strength, but having conveyed it, he made one final call for peace. "I am loth to close," he said.[43]

> We are not enemies, but friends. We must not be enemies. Though passion may have strained, it must not break our bonds of affection. The mystic chords of memory, stretching from every battle-field, and patriot grave, to every living heart and hearthstone, all over this broad land, will yet swell the chorus of the Union, when again touched, as surely they will be, by the better angels of our nature.[44]

Lincoln's words reached a national audience eagerly awaiting them. According to Carl Sandburg:

> Never before . . . had such crowds waited at newspaper offices. . . . In its week of delivery it was the most widely read and closely scrutinized utterance that had ever come from an American President.[45]

Lincoln's message, Carl Schurz wrote, "made a profound impression" upon these crowds, and while the "partisan sympathy" for the South that "still existed in the North did indeed not disappear," it nonetheless "diminished perceptibly under the influence of such [Lincoln's] reasoning."[46]

Lincoln's effort found many voices of approval, from both sides. The *National Republican* in Washington, D.C. said:

> The Inaugural was well received on all sides. . . . .

> Judge Douglas remarked, in conversation, that it was a very dignified address, and evinced great wisdom. . . .

> Hon. Edwin H. Webster, of Maryland, stated that he believed it was all that was necessary to set matters right again; and De Witt C. Leach, of North Carolina, remarked that he regarded it as eminently conservative.[47]

The *New York Times:*

> Its conciliatory tone, and frank, outspoken declaration of loyalty to the whole country, captured the hearts of many heretofore opposed to Mr. Lincoln, and its firm enunciation of purpose to fulfil his oath to maintain the Constitution and laws, challenge universal respect.[48]

The opinion of one observer in the *New York Herald*:

> Republicans of all shades express the utmost satisfaction with it. Democrats, while denouncing its treatment of the Southern question, yet give the author credit for honesty, firmness and patriotic intentions.[49]

Governor Edwin D. Morgan of New York, in a letter to Lincoln:

> I cannot let one day pass without expressing to you the satisfaction I have felt in reading and in considering the Inaugural address. None can say, truthfully, they do not understand its meaning. Kind in spirit, firm in purpose, national in the highest degree, the points are all well made, and the call is fairly stated and most honorably met. It cannot fail to command the confidence of the North, and the respect of the South.[50]

But after the First Inaugural, Lincoln would go another *two-and-a-half years*—to November 19, 1863, at Gettysburg—before giving another formal speech to make his case on an important issue. In the meantime, it would be his pen that would make his case.

His first important such message came four months after his inauguration, in his first written message to Congress, which presented his case for military action against the southern "rebellion" and for the men (400,000) and money ($400,000,000) that this would require, not only to prevail but to do so quickly, "making this contest a short, and a decisive one."[51] He also sounded a theme that he would repeat throughout the war and elevate its purpose: that the struggle posed an issue not just for the United States, but for the world.

> This issue embraces more than the fate of these United States. It presents to the whole family of man, the question, whether a constitutional republic, or a democracy—a government of the people, by the same people—can, or cannot, maintain its territorial integrity, against its own domestic foes.[52]

And he offered why, in his view, preserving a "government of the people" was so important.

> This is essentially a People's contest. On the side of the Union, it is a struggle for maintaining in the world, that form, and substance of government, whose leading object is, to elevate the condition of men—to lift artificial weights from all shoulders—to clear the paths of laudable pursuit for all—to afford all, an unfettered start, and a fair chance, in the race of life.[53]

The message was a success: the northern public still thought the war would be over quickly, and as Carl Sandburg later wrote, "the Northern press gave it [the President's message] greater approval than any utterance hitherto" from him.[54]

But not so easy to manage was public opinion on emancipation, an issue driven by equally strong and competing forces. Abolitionists and others, including the more aggressive forces in Congress,[55] wanted Lincoln to make emancipation a war objective, but many in the North—including elements in the Union Army—were not ready to go to war over "the negro," and the four, crucial border states saw emancipation as a tipping point that would drive them into the Confederacy.

Civil War and Lincoln scholar Matthew Pinsker writes that as of the spring of 1862, Lincoln's position on emancipation had three, *stated* "guiding principles"—"that emancipation must be gradual, compensated, and voluntary" (on the part of slave owners)—and one "unspoken" one—that the freed slaves "might be sent abroad or colonized voluntarily."[56] By mid-July, however, Lincoln's thinking had gone beyond these four guidelines,[57] and he had come to believe that the war effort required the immediate, uncompensated, and involuntary emancipation of slaves in those states or portions thereof in rebellion. He saw this as "a military necessity absolutely essential for the salvation of the Union."[58] This would be a compromise: it would not free *all* slaves, but it would free *many* (by Union victories or slave escapes to Union lines), and it would not threaten the slave-holding interests in the four, loyal border states.

By July 22, Lincoln had drafted a "Preliminary Emancipation Proclamation," which would announce when the final proclamation would go into effect, and hopefully might sway some states (or portions thereof) in the Confederacy to withdraw from the rebellion before then. Lincoln had shown it to his cabinet, and wanted to announce it to the public, but was persuaded to wait for a Union victory before doing so, to avoid the impression that it was an act of desperation.[59]

And while he waited, Horace Greeley gave him the perfect opportunity to set the stage.

On August 20, 1862, with the war now in its sixteenth month, Greeley ran an editorial, styled as an "open letter" to Lincoln and titled "The Prayer of Twenty Millions."[60] It took Lincoln to task for "the policy you seem to be pursuing with regard to the slaves of the Rebels," which Greeley said showed "mistaken deference to Rebel Slavery," and for not enforcing the "Second" Confiscation Act, which Lincoln had signed on July 17, 1862, authorizing the emancipation of slaves owned by anyone in rebellion against the Union.[61]

Lincoln responded two days later, with an open letter of his own,[62] which he sent to a Washington, D.C. newspaper[63] to ensure immediate national attention.⁶⁴ While the letter purported to be a reply to Greeley, Lincoln had actually drafted its main section before Greeley's editorial,⁶⁵ and used Greeley's letter as the excuse to publish what he had drafted, and in turn pave the way for the Preliminary, and then final, Emancipation Proclamation.⁶⁶

Lincoln began his reply to Greeley with a cordial but firm introduction, the classic "iron fist in a velvet glove." It spoke of Greeley as an "old friend, whose heart . . . [Lincoln had] always supposed to be right," but suggested nonetheless that Greeley's letter had "erroneous" "assumptions of fact," "inferences" that were "falsely drawn," and "an impatient and dictatorial tone."⁶⁷

With that, Lincoln then went right to his main point: he had *one* objective in the war, and one only—to save the Union—and this, and only this, would guide everything that he did or did not do, as to slavery or anything else. In Lincoln's own words:

> As to the policy I "seem to be pursuing" as you say, I have not meant to leave any one in doubt.
>
> I would save the Union. I would save it the shortest way under the Constitution. The sooner the national authority can be restored; the nearer the Union will be "the Union as it was." If there be those who would not save the Union, unless they could at the same time *save* slavery, I do not agree with them. If there be those who would not save the Union unless they could at the same time *destroy* slavery, I do not agree with them. My paramount object in this struggle *is* to save the Union, and is *not* either to save or to destroy slavery. If I could save the Union without freeing *any* slave I would do it, and if I could save it by freeing *all* the slaves I would do it; and if I could save it by freeing some and leaving others alone I would also do that. What I do about slavery, and the colored race, I do because I believe it helps to save the Union; and what I forbear, I forbear because I do *not* believe it would help to save the Union. I shall do *less* whenever I shall believe what I am

doing hurts the cause, and I shall do *more* whenever I shall believe doing more will help the cause. I shall try to correct errors when shown to be errors; and I shall adopt new views so fast as they shall appear to be true views.[68]

But having so clearly made his case, Lincoln then closed by noting that his position was what he believed his office required, and did not reflect how he personally felt about slavery:

I have here stated my purpose according to my view of *official* duty; and I intend no modification of my oft-expressed *personal* wish that all men every where could be free.[69]

His letter, according to Carl Sandburg, was "widely reprinted," and likely reached "nearly all persons in the country who could read."[70] It was recognized as an "unprecedented" exchange, between a president and a newspaper editor via the popular press,[71] and in some quarters criticized for this as beneath the "dignity" of a president.[72]

But it was also widely praised for its core, anchor point—exactly the point Lincoln wanted to make—that his only objective, his only "agenda," was to save the Union. A Washington correspondent wrote of the "unanimous admiration of the skill and force with which he [Lincoln] has defined his policy."[73] The Wheeling *Daily Intelligencer* wrote that it considered the "letter of Mr. Lincoln . . . the most admirable document of the war."[74] The *New York Herald* wrote that the letter, while "widen[ing] the breach" between abolitionists and Lincoln, would nonetheless "strengthen him and his administration among the honest masses of the people"—and that this is what the paper suspected Lincoln had intended.[75] The *Daily Ohio Statesman* sounded a similar theme, writing that Lincoln's "paramount object" in the war—"that THE UNION IS TO BE SAVED UNDER THE CONSTITUTION"—was "the true and loyal position, the only wise and patriotic position."[76]

Moderate Republicans praised the letter, as did even some Democrats and abolitionists,[77] and Greeley himself, in a modest concession, acknowledged the letter as "a sign of progress."[78]

Looking back years later, Civil War veteran William H. Lambert described the letter as "probably the most important of the many notable letters written by the President,"[79] and the historian Ida Tarbell went much further, writing that the "document challenges comparison with the State papers of all times and all countries for its lucidity and its courage."[80]

Having thus made it clear that his decisions on slavery would be guided solely by his goal of saving the Union, Lincoln *then* issued his Preliminary Emancipation Proclamation a month later, on September 22, after the Union victory at Antietam, and—consistent with his letter to Greeley—couched it as a military measure, necessary to the effort to save the Union.

He opened the proclamation in his capacity as "President of the United States of America, and Commander-in-chief of the Army and Navy thereof."[81] The course he announced was one of those his letter to Greeley had said he would follow if it would help *to save the Union*: free *some* of the slaves and leave *others* alone. He referred to two Acts of Congress[82] that provided for freeing slaves (specifically, not returning them to their owners) as a military move, "an additional article of war" "to suppress Insurrection."[83] He reiterated that the purpose of the war remained that of preserving the Union ("practically restoring the constitutional relation between the United States, and each of the states").[84]

The proclamation received tremendous support in the northern press.

The *New York Herald* called it "one of the most important documents that has emanated from the Executive Department of the republic since the adoption of the federal constitution."[85] The *New-York Daily Tribune* went a large step beyond, heralding the proclamation as "one of those stupendous facts in human history which marks not only an era in the progress of the nation, but an epoch in the history of the world."[86] A Michigan newspaper called it "the grandest proclamation ever issued by man."[87]

Then, on December 1, 1862, while the clock ticked closer to January 1, Lincoln followed the Preliminary Proclamation with yet a bolder case: in his Second Annual Message to Congress,[88] he called for a constitutional amendment providing for *total* and *compensated* emancipation, funded by the federal government. Slave owners would be compensated for each slave, unless the slave owner had been "disloyal" to the Union and his slaves had already escaped to freedom, and each state would have up to thirty-seven years to implement its emancipation.

This plan, Lincoln urged, would solve the slavery issue, stop the war, and let the country get on with its internal growth and relations with other nations. Both sides, South and North, he argued, should bear the cost of the plan because slavery was the cause of the war—"Without slavery the rebellion could never have existed; without slavery it could not continue"[89]—and both South *and North* bore *responsibility* for slavery.

The latter was a point that he had made as far back as his speech in Peoria, and would continue to make to the end of his life. "The people of the South," he said,

> are not more responsible for the original introduction of this property, than are the people of the North; and when it is remembered how unhesitatingly we all use cotton and sugar, and share the profits of dealing in them, it may not be quite safe to say, that the South has been more responsible than the North for its continuance.[90]

The *Philadelphia Inquirer* wrote: "It is universally conceded that the arguments in the President's message in favor of emancipation ... are the strongest ever made."[91] The *Chicago Tribune* said that the message "will commend itself to the careful consideration of honest and loyal men, ... [for] the fairness, candor and thoroughness with which the great truths it conveys are put forward."[92] And Horace Greeley, in a letter to John G. Nicolay, one of Lincoln's two private White House secretaries, asked that Lincoln be told that "his Message" not only "fully satisfies the expectations of his friends," but is also "received with general enthusiasm."[93]

Unfortunately, however, whatever "general enthusiasm" may have existed for Lincoln's proposal, Congress would never act on it. Compensated emancipation would never occur, and the war would drag on for another two-and-a-half brutal years. The Emancipation Proclamation would remain the only emancipation measure that would go into effect until the Thirteenth Amendment abolished slavery on January 31, 1865.

True to his word, Lincoln announced the Emancipation Proclamation on January 1, 1863, couching it consistent with his preceding messages.

He first reiterated his Preliminary Emancipation Proclamation, and then began the "new" proclamation by stating that he was taking the action it announced

- "by virtue of the power in me vested as Commander-in-Chief, of the Army and Navy of the United States"
- "in time of actual armed rebellion against authority and government of the United States, and"
- "as a fit and necessary war measure for suppressing said rebellion," i.e., saving the Union, a theme that he then reiterated later in the proclamation, calling the action it announced "an act of justice, warranted by the Constitution, upon military necessity."[94]

And in the same proclamation, implicitly based upon the same rationale—military necessity, to save the Union—Lincoln announced *another* bold step that he had *not* previewed in his Preliminary Emancipation Proclamation: slaves freed by the Emancipation Proclamation, "of suitable condition, will be received into the armed service of the United States to garrison forts, positions, stations, and other places, and to man vessels of all sorts in said service."[95] Former slaves, now dressed in Union blue, would bear arms against their former masters.

William McKinley later described the document as the "crowning glory of Lincoln's administration and the greatest executive act in American history," saying that it converted the Declaration of Independence from an "empty promise" to a "glorious fulfillment."[96]

Newspapers at the time of the proclamation stretched for words describing its place in history. The *Daily National Republican* called it "the great event of the day and of the century," saying that its "concluding paragraph . . . deserves to be set in letters of gold."[97] A Kansas newspaper described it as "an edict, which, in its results to the human race, and the advancement of civilization, will not have an equal in the history of ages past."[98] The *New York Evening Post* said the event was "the greatest recorded in history since the advent of the Messiah; and saving that alone, the greatest of all events that mark the page of time on earth."[99]

But there was also significant opposition to the proclamation, both for its emancipation and its authorizing the enlistment of blacks into the

Union's armed forces. Lincoln would spend the next two years defending both of these aspects, in large part through two more of his most important public letters.

But before writing either of those, he wrote another, in June of 1863, defending two other of his most controversial moves as president. Nine months before, on September 24, 1862, he had issued a proclamation suspending habeas corpus and making statements that discouraged enlistments, and other disloyal practices, subject to martial law and trial by military commissions.[100] Pursuant to this and seven months later, in April 1863, General Ambrose Burnside, commander of the Military District of Ohio, had issued an order forbidding the expression of "sympathies for the enemy,"[101] and a month after that, on May 1, Burnside arrested Clement Vallandigham for violating this order.

Vallandigham was a Democrat, former two-term Ohio congressman, and leader of the northern Democrats known as "Copperheads," who opposed the war and demanded immediate peace with the Confederacy. Four days before his arrest, Vallandigham made a speech against the war, calling it "wicked, cruel and unnecessary," and contending that it was being waged not "for the preservation of the Union," but "for the purpose of crushing out liberty, and erecting a despotism," and for "the freedom of the blacks, and the enslavement of the whites."[102] Vallandigham was then arrested, and a military court tried and convicted him in the next two days.

The arrest provoked outrage throughout the country, and a protest by New York Democrats in Albany, New York on May 16, organized by Erastus Corning, a prominent New York businessman and former congressman, who then drafted and sent Lincoln a letter and formal resolutions on behalf of the protest, condemning military arrests like that of Vallandigham.

Lincoln was privately chagrined at Vallandigham's arrest, but felt compelled to defend his general, and let Corning know on May 28, 1863 that he, Lincoln, would "make a respectful response."[103] Lincoln then drafted that response between May 28 and June 5, and mailed it to Corning on June 12, with a copy to Horace Greeley, who published it on June 15.[104]

The letter[105] was more than 3,800 words,[106] and nothing short of a legal brief for the public. It noted that the Constitution expressly authorized military arrests and the suspension of habeas corpus "when, in cases of Rebellion or Invasion, the public Safety may require" it, and argued that the country now clearly faced a "Rebellion"—indeed, "a clear, flagrant, and gigantic case of Rebellion."[107]

Lincoln pointed out the reason for this constitutional provision: the inability—indeed, the "utter incompetence"—of "courts of justice" to handle cases of "Rebellion or Invasion."[108] Courts were meant to handle individual cases, he said, not large-scale assaults on the government. England had adopted habeas corpus, he noted, only "*after* years of protracted civil war," not *during* them, and "our constitution" had likewise adopted it "at the *close* of the revolution," not during it.[109] "Sympathizers" of the rebellion now in progress, he said, "pervaded all departments of the government, and nearly all communities of the people," and hoped to use "Liberty of speech[,] 'Liberty of the press[,] and *Habeas corpus*," to shield their efforts and keep the government from stopping them.[110] He said that he had been "slow to adopt the strong measures" now complained of, and had done so only "by degrees" and only because he had been "forced to regard [them] as being within the exceptions of the constitution, and as indispensable to the public Safety."[111]

Lincoln then turned to his understanding of Vallandigham's "particular case," saying that Vallandigham was arrested

> because he was laboring, with some effect, to prevent the raising of troops, to encourage desertions from the army, and to leave the rebellion without an adequate military force to suppress it. He . . . was damaging the army, upon the existence, and vigor of which, the life of the nation depends. He was warring upon the military; and this gave the military constitutional jurisdiction to lay hands upon him.[112]

If these facts were true, Lincoln said, the arrest was justified. "He who dissuades one man from volunteering," he said, "or induces one soldier to desert, weakens the Union cause as much as he who kills a union soldier in battle."[113] "Must I shoot a simple-minded soldier boy who deserts," he continued, "while I must not touch a hair of a wiley agitator who induces him to desert?," to which he answered, "I think that in such a case, to silence the agitator, and save the boy, is not only constitutional, but, withal, a great mercy."[114]

Estimates are that there were at least five hundred thousand copies of the letter, and that more than ten million people read them,[115] and they made their mark. Lincoln's two private White House secretaries, John G. Nicolay and John Hay, later said: "There are few of the President's state papers which produced a stronger impression upon the public mind."[116]

The *Daily National Republican* called the letter a "superlatively grand document" that "speaks in thunder tones for itself," "throws shrapnel, shell, round shot, and grape in every direction," and "is a shot that will be heard round the world."[117]

The *Chicago Tribune* said that Lincoln's explanation was not only "complete and satisfactory," but that it had "never seen the argument put in clearer or more forcible language."[118] And privately, the *Tribune* called Lincoln's argument "a crusher."[119]

Public officials and private citizens concurred in letters to Lincoln. Secretary of the Senate John W. Forney wrote: "God be praised the right word has at last been spoken by the right man, at the right time, and from the right place. It will thrill the whole land."[120] Other public officials wrote that Lincoln's reply was "one of your best State Papers,"[121] or "the best thing of all."[122] Philadelphia lawyer, playwright, and orator David P. Brown wrote:

> You have met them upon every ground of objection assumed by them, and utterly routed them. . . . No document issued since Your inauguration, has done more to satisfy the public mind, and vindicate national rights.[123]

Lincoln then maximized the letter's reach and effect: not content with its appearance just in newspapers, he also cleverly used it as a campaign document, as historian Mark E. Neely, Jr. explains:

> After issuing the public letter, the president then had copies of it printed and mailed across the country on the frank of his private secretary John G. Nicolay. This kept

the president above the appearance of self-promotion and electioneering, but the recipients knew exactly what it meant to receive a copy of a presidential position paper sent to them at tax-payers' expense by the private secretary of the head of the Republican party.[124]

But for all the accolades that his letter to Corning received, Lincoln then authored another public letter, just two months later, that Matthew Pinsker says was "arguably the most important" of all of Lincoln's public letters.[125]

In August of 1863, Lincoln received notice of another public protest, this one to be held in Springfield, Illinois—*his hometown*—by Illinois Republicans—*his supposed supporters*. The protest this time was to be against the Emancipation Proclamation and the acceptance of African Americans into the Union Army, and a friend of Lincoln, James Conkling, invited Lincoln to come and make his case on both measures. This was only a month after the battle at Gettysburg, and Lincoln did not think he could spare the time away from Washington that the trip would entail, so he decided to send a letter instead, for Conkling to read to the gathering on Lincoln's behalf.

Lincoln, the seasoned writer, was confident about the letter even before he wrote it, saying, "I shall send them a letter instead; and it will be a rather good letter."[126] He addressed the letter to the gathering, but it was, as Carl Sandburg noted, "really a paper aimed at the masses of people in America and Europe."[127]

He began the letter—again the iron fist in the velvet glove—by conveying his regret at not being able to "meet my old friends, at my own home," he applauded the gathering as "those who maintain unconditional devotion to the Union," and he thanked as well "those other noble men, whom no partizan malice, or partizan hope, can make false to the nation's life."[128]

He then addressed a preliminary point that he knew was also a source of dissatisfaction, independent of the Emancipation Proclamation and blacks enlisting in the armed forces: it was that peace had not yet been achieved. He posited that there were three ways of achieving this: force of arms, giving up the Union, or compromise. He rejected the second out of hand, and the third because he had received no sign of any desire to compromise by the only entity that mattered: the rebellion's army. "The strength of the rebellion," he said, "is its military—its army,"[129] and without that army's support, any agreement on compromise would be a waste of time. "Now allow me to assure you," Lincoln wrote, "that no word or intimation, from that rebel army, or from any of the men controlling it, in relation to any peace compromise, has ever come to my knowledge or belief."[130]

This left only the first option—force of arms—which he *was* pursuing, and he then wove that into his defense on the group's principal source of dissatisfaction with him: "the negro,"[131] and specifically the Emancipation Proclamation and the enlistment of blacks.

He turned first to the Emancipation Proclamation, and reminded the audience that he had "suggested compensated emancipation" before the Emancipation Proclamation, but to no avail, that he had issued the Emancipation Proclamation under the authority that the Constitution gave him as "commander-in-chief, with the law of war, in time of war," and that the proclamation was a measure consistent with that authority.[132] If Confederate slaves were "property," he asked, as slave owners had always claimed they were, "is there—has there ever been—any question that by the law of war, property, both of enemies and friends, may be taken when needed?"[133]

And he then added a new argument justifying the Emancipation Proclamation as a military measure, an argument that went straight at the protest's objection to the enlistment of blacks: the Emancipation Proclamation had hurt the rebellion not only by taking their slave property, but also by giving the Union forces a much-needed supply of new manpower. "I know," he wrote,

> that some of the commanders of our armies in the field who have given us our most important successes, believe the emancipation policy, and the use of the colored troops, constitute the heaviest blow yet dealt to the rebellion; and that, at least one of those important successes, could not have been achieved when it was, but for the aid of black soldiers. Among the commanders holding these views are

some who have never had any affinity with what is called abolitionism, or with republican party politics; but who hold them purely as military opinions. I submit these opinions as being entitled to some weight against the objections, often urged, that emancipation, and arming the blacks, are unwise as military measures, and were not adopted, as such, in good faith.[134]

And then having noted the military benefit of the Emancipation Proclamation, he couched the proclamation as a necessary—and *permanent*—trade-off for the "negroes'" willingness to fight and die for the Union cause.

Negroes, like other people, act upon motives. Why should they do any thing for us, if we will do nothing for them? If they stake their lives for us, they must be prompted by the strongest motive—even the promise of freedom. And the promise being made, must be kept.[135]

He then turned, on a positive note, to a review of recent victories, his hope that peace was closer, and his view again as to what was at stake in the war, not just for the United States, but for "free men:" the preservation of democratic government:

Peace does not appear so distant as it did. I hope it will come soon, and come to stay; and so come as to be worth the keeping in all future time. It will then have been proved that, among free men, there can be no successful appeal from the ballot to the bullet; and that they who take such appeal are sure to lose their case, and pay the cost.[136]

With this, he returned to the letter's central subject—"the negro"—by linking the worthy cause for which the war was being fought with the brave contributions to that cause of the Army's newly emancipated black troops. When peace does come, Lincoln said, and the cause for which the war was fought has been won, then, there will be some black men who can remember that, with silent tongue, and clenched teeth, and steady eye, and well-poised bayonet, they have helped mankind on to this great consummation; while, I fear, there will be some white ones, unable to forget that, with malignant heart, and deceitful speech, they have strove to hinder it.[137]

His optimism about the letter ("it will be a rather good letter") was correct. Lincoln's two White House secretaries would later say: "Nothing he ever uttered had a more instantaneous success."[138] The *New York Times* wrote:

The President's letter . . . receives the unqualified admiration of loyal men throughout the breadth of the land. . . . nothing could have been more true or more apt. Its hard sense, its sharp outlines, its noble temper, defy malice. Even the Copperhead gnaws upon it as vainly as did the viper upon the file.[139]

"No previous letter, address or state paper of Lincoln's," Carl Sandburg would later write, "received such warmhearted comment."[140] The *Chicago Tribune* said the letter "will take its place among the most important documents of the war, and of itself alone will make the Springfield meeting which has elicited it, long memorable."[141] And in a different article, the same paper wrote that no "sentences . . . more important were ever uttered in this country."[142]

Public officials and private citizens concurred. Massachusetts Senator Charles Sumner praised the letter as "true & noble . . . an historic document. The case is admirably stated, so that all but the wicked must confess its force. It cannot be answered."[143] Merchant and railroad magnate John M. Forbes wrote Lincoln that the letter would "live in History side by side with your Proclamation."[144]

The public's favorable reaction to the letter even prompted a group of abolitionist Republicans, led by the mayor of New York, to abandon their plan to convene a convention the next year to nominate a Republican candidate for president other than Lincoln.[145]

Lincoln's letter to Conkling was his third successful effort in 1863 at making a case to the public—his Emancipation Proclamation and his letter to Corning being the two others—but his achievements in persuasion that year were not yet done: three months after his letter to Conkling, he added perhaps his most famous statement of all, at Gettysburg on November 19.[146] At the site of the bloodiest battle yet fought, in a war that had already taken a horrible cost in lives and treasure, Lincoln sought to make the case, in just 271 words, and only three minutes,[147] for why the Union had to *continue* that war to a successful completion.

At stake, he said, returning again to the theme he had urged from the start of the war, was more than just suppressing a rebellion within the United States: at stake was the experiment in democracy that the United States represented to the world, the experiment based on "the proposition that all men are created equal," the experiment in "government of the people, by the people, for the people," and in the "new birth of freedom" then unfolding under that experiment.[148] The dead being honored had given their lives for this cause, he said, and while the ceremony honoring their sacrifice was "altogether fitting and proper," the only way *truly* to honor them was to *complete* that for which they had made that ultimate sacrifice.[149]

His message, in one way, contrasted with his First Inaugural, in which he had sought to make the case *against* civil war, while he now sought to make the case for *continuing* that war, but both cases had the same reason and goal: *preserving the Union*. And in both messages he invoked the memories of the battles fought for that Union, and the lives given for it, be it the "battle-field[s], and patriot grave[s]" of the Revolution,[150] or the battlefield where he and his audience were now standing, and the patriot graves they were now viewing.

Michael Burlingame notes that while Lincoln's address was a speech, it was, "in effect, another of Lincoln's highly successful public letters,"[151] shorter in fact—by a substantial margin—than many of his actual public letters, which increased the likelihood of its being read when printed in the country's newspapers.

A special correspondent to Washington D.C.'s *Daily Morning Chronicle* said that the address, "glittered with gems . . . and will receive the attention and command the admiration of all of the tens of thousands who will read it."[152] A Vermont newspaper called the speech "a perfect gem; deep in feeling, correct in thought and expression, and tasteful and elegant in every word and comma."[153] A special dispatch to the *Chicago Tribune* said that the speech "will live among the annals of the war,"[154] and the Wheeling *Daily Intelligencer* concurred, three years later, saying that

> Mr. [Daniel] Webster, with all his superior education, never on any occasion of his life made a five minutes' speech so comprehensive as the Gettysburg address of Mr. Lincoln. We believe that little simple speech . . . will stand on the page of history as one of the most remarkable productions of these eventful days.[155]

Private citizens agreed, among them the most "literate" in the country. Charles King Newcomb, a New England critic of Lincoln who had bemoaned Lincoln's "want of eloquence" only three months before, now wrote: "Lincoln is, doubtless, the greatest orator of the age."[156] *Harper's Weekly*, edited by George William Curtis, an American writer and public speaker, called the address "the most perfect piece of American eloquence."[157] Noah Brooks, a journalist and editor, as well as a Lincoln biographer and confidant, went a step beyond, calling the speech "one of the few masterpieces" in *world* oratory.[158] And according to one biographer, Secretary of State William Seward, when asked if he had played a role in Lincoln's address, demurred with the highest compliment to Lincoln, saying that "no one but Abraham Lincoln could have made that address."[159]

But having made so eloquent a case for continuing the war, Lincoln then followed in the months thereafter with efforts to make his case for what the Union should look like *after* the war, and in particular the need to maintain the emancipation that had been achieved.

His first such message was his Proclamation of Amnesty and Reconstruction, which he included in his Third Annual Message to Congress,[160] and which called for restoring a state to the Union after voters equal to ten percent of those who had cast ballots in 1860 took an oath of loyalty to the Union and willingness to accept emancipation. When that level was met, those taking the oath would have all rights restored, except that of owning slaves, and the state could hold elections and rejoin the Union.

The proclamation also called for a state's adopting "any provision" for freed slaves "which shall recognize and declare their permanent freedom, [and] provide for their education, and which may yet be consistent, as a temporary arrangement, with their present condition as a laboring, landless, and homeless class."[161]

And in the annual message that enclosed the proclamation, Lincoln again defended the emancipation that had so far occurred, and again urged, as had his letter to Conkling, that the emancipation so far achieved must be maintained. It was enacted for the purpose of suppressing the rebellion, he said, and preserving that emancipation was the moral thing to do. To renege on it, he said, would be "a cruel and an astounding breach of faith."[162]

Noah Brooks wrote that the message probably gave "more general satisfaction than any Message since the days of Washington."[163] One of Lincoln's private secretaries, John Hay, wrote that he had never "seen such an effect produced by a public document."[164] And according to Michael Burlingame, "members of both houses as well as other politicians considered his message 'the best document yet produced by him [Lincoln].'"[165]

Message after approving message likewise came from individual citizens. Samuel Galloway, a former U.S. representative from Ohio who served as a judge advocate during the Civil War, wrote:

> Your message and Proclamation have strengthened public confidence in you in Ohio—and have rendered any competition for the next Presidential term utterly hopeless and forlorn—It is the best document you have written, always excepting your letter on military arrests to the Albany Committee.[166]

Albert Smith, a former Democratic congressman from Maine, concurred, writing: "you have touched & <u>taken</u> the popular heart—and secured your re-election beyond a peradventure—should you desire it."[167]

John J. Janney, Secretary of the Board of Control of the State Bank of Ohio, wrote that the annual message and proclamation surely speak the truth on the great question before us all. . . . Your firm stand on the "the proclamation" will cheer your friends and make the knees of your, and our enemies shake.[168]

William Dennison, former Ohio governor and (later) U.S. Postmaster General, echoed a similar thought, writing, "I hear but one opinion of the Message and Proclamation, and that is, in each, you have said the right word at the right time."[169]

Several months later, on March 13, 1864, Lincoln then sent another letter seeking to shape the post-war Union, this one to Governor Michael Hahn of Louisiana, with a significant new proposal. Lincoln "suggest[ed]" that Louisiana's upcoming constitutional convention extend the right to vote to "some of the colored people . . . as, for instance, the very intelligent, and especially those who have fought gallantly in our ranks."[170] Hahn recognized that while Lincoln addressed the letter to him as "private,"[171] Lincoln "no doubt intended [it] to be seen by other Union men in Louisiana besides myself, and [it] was consequently shown to many members of our Constitutional Convention and leading free-State men."[172]

But opposition to the Emancipation Proclamation and African Americans in the Union forces was by no means done, and in April of 1864, Lincoln had to write yet another public letter defending these measures—but this time at the request of someone who had come to protest them. Albert Hodges was a prominent Kentucky newspaper editor, and came to the White House with Kentucky's current governor and former United States senator to convey their state's opposition to emancipation and blacks serving in the Union Army. After they presented their case, Lincoln asked if he could present his—"make a little speech,"[173] as he called it—and what he said so impressed Hodges that he later returned to the White House alone and asked Lincoln to put what he had said in a letter that Hodges could publish.

Lincoln did so, noting first in his letter[174] that he had not been quick to invoke military emancipation, that he had overruled attempts at it by two of his generals (Fremont and Hunter) and his Secretary of War (Cameron), and that he had appealed to Kentucky and the other border states—*before* issuing his Emancipation Proclamation—to support compensated emancipation, but they had declined to do so.

With compensated emancipation not an option, Lincoln then said he had faced, in his judgment, a harsh choice: "either surrendering the Union"—i.e., giving up the fight to preserve it, because the Union needed more men than it had to press the war successfully, or "laying strong hand upon the colored element,"[175] i.e., emancipating the slaves and bringing them into the Union forces. Lincoln then said that, faced with these two options, he had chosen "the latter," taking "the colored element" into the Army and Navy, and that

> more than a year of trial now shows no loss by it in our foreign relations, none in our home popular sentiment, none in our white military force,—no loss by it any how or any where.[176]

"On the contrary," he said, the option that he had selected—the "trial" as he called it—

> shows a gain of quite a hundred and thirty thousand soldiers, seamen, and laborers. These are palpable facts, about which, as facts, there can be no cavilling. We have the men; and we could not have had them without the measure.[177]

And having thus made his case for the military necessity of enlisting the "colored" troops, he then closed with this challenge:

> And now let any Union man who complains of the measure, test himself by writing down in one line that he is for subduing the rebellion by force of arms; and in the next, that he is for taking these hundred and thirty thousand men from the Union side, and placing them where they would be but for the measure he condemns. If he can not face his case so stated, it is only because he can not face the truth.[178]

The letter was another success. Horace Greeley praised it effusively, saying:

> few men have ever lived who could have better explained and commended his [Lincoln's] course and attitude with regard to Slavery than he has done in his late letter to Mr. Hodges of Kentucky. . . .
>
> . . .
>
> What the President says of the Military expediency of Emancipation and of Arming the Blacks, is incontrovertible. There is no need of adding a word.[179]

Seven months later, after his re-election in November 1864, Lincoln sent Congress what would become his last annual message,[180] urging several cases, one being that the present Congress should pass the Thirteenth Amendment. He argued that the recent election was a mandate for that passage. The days of partial emancipation were now numbered, he said. It was time to make emancipation complete.

> The next Congress will pass the measure if this does not. Hence there is only a question of *time* as to when the proposed amendment will go to the States for their action. And as it is to so go, at all events, may we not agree that the sooner the better? . . . It is the voice of the people now, for the first time, heard upon the question.[181]

A second case was against negotiating with Jefferson Davis, because the latter "would accept nothing short of severance of the Union—precisely what we will not and cannot give."[182] The war could not end by negotiations, Lincoln said. "Between him and us the issue is distinct, simple, and inflexible," Lincoln said.[183] "It is an issue which can only be tried by war, and decided by victory."[184]

A third case, consistent with the second, was to reject any end to the war short of the Confederacy "laying down their arms and submitting to the national authority under the Constitution."[185]

And his fourth reiterated his refusal to waffle on the emancipation that had already occurred. Indeed, lest there be any doubt about his resolve on this, his concluding sentence made it no less than a line in the sand:

> I repeat the declaration made a year ago, that "while I remain in my present position I shall not attempt to retract or modify the emancipation proclamation, nor shall I return to slavery any person who is free by the terms of that proclamation, or by any of the Acts of Congress." If the people should, by whatever mode or means, make it an Executive duty to re-enslave such persons, another, and not I must be their instrument to perform it.[186]

As Michael Burlingame, quoting the *New York Independent*, writes: "Congress applauded this last statement loud and long. Republican 'Radicals' hailed its 'unblemished moral grandeur' and predicted that it would 'have immortal life' and 'go down as a heritage to future generations.'"[187]

Thaddeus Stevens, a Radical leader who had "never 'believed' in Lincoln," said that Lincoln's statement was "the best message which has been sent to Congress in the past sixty years."[188] Many newspapers hailed Lincoln's message as among his best—the most "well-written,"[189] and the best of *any* president: the "clearest, firmest, and most able and important" that he or any other president had authored.[190] African Americans, of course, hailed the message, with one, a colonel in the U.S. Colored Troops, writing:

> God bless you Abraham Lincoln for these noble words that bring joy to so many thousands of Colored Soldiers and so many hundreds of thousands of women and children; words that would of themselves had you no other claim endear you for all time to all who love Freedom and the Nation.[191]

Four months later, on March 4, 1865, in his Second Inaugural,[192] Lincoln delivered what would be his final major effort at making a case, in speech or writing. His themes were familiar, but this time presented virtually as a sermon. With the war still raging, he echoed his entreaty at Gettysburg that it be brought to a successful conclusion—"to finish the work we are in," "with firmness in the right, as God gives us to see the right."[193] But he then equally made his case for a swift, vengeance-free reunification, reiterating his earlier themes that slavery, as all recognized, was the cause of the war, that both North and South bore responsibility for it, and that the war, with all its horror, might be seen as divine retribution on both sides for slavery's sin on the national soul.

> If we shall suppose that American Slavery is one of those offences which, in the providence of God, must needs come, but which, having continued through His appointed time, He now wills to remove, and that He gives to both North and South, this terrible war, as the woe due to those by whom the offence came, shall we discern therein any departure from those divine attributes which the believers in a Living God always ascribe to Him?[194]

He then further drove this theme, emphasizing the depth of the mutual sin and the atonement it might still require:

> Fondly do we hope—fervently do we pray—that this mighty scourge of war may speedily pass away. Yet, if God wills that it continue, until all the wealth piled by the bond-man's two hundred and fifty years of unrequited toil shall be sunk, and until every drop of blood drawn with the lash, shall be paid by another drawn with the sword, as was said three thousand years ago, so still it must be said "the judgments of the Lord, are true and righteous altogether."[195]

When the war's end finally came, he said, the nation's reconciliation should be mutual, swift, and meaningful. The Union should finish its work "with malice toward none" and "charity for all,"[196] an appeal that circled back to his First Inaugural and its plea for the country to follow "the better angels of our nature," and "swell the chorus of the Union."[197] Now, after four years of horrid civil war, he again appealed to the nation's better angels, to heal and swell that chorus once again.

Noah Brooks wrote that it was "impossible to describe the effect" of the speech "upon those who heard . . . [or] read it:"

> Its lofty tone and grand majesty reminded one of the Hebraic prophecies; and its dispassionate and almost merciless dissection of the issues of the struggle for the preservation of the Union, and the dying contortions of the monster slavery, were received with a feeling of awe. The impression made by the inaugural was profound. It was conclusive of the genius and the intellectual greatness of its author. From that time forth, the world gave among its orators and statesmen a high place to Abraham Lincoln.[198]

Brooks was not alone in seeing the address as a religious work. Author Charles W. Moores wrote: "The poetry and philosophy of a thousand years of Hebrew prophesy was restated in a paragraph of the Second Inaugural."[199] George Haven Putnam, in addition to calling the address "possibly the most impressive utterance ever made by a national leader," said that "Lincoln speaks almost in the language of a Hebrew prophet."[200] And not to slight the New Testament, a Pennsylvania newspaper called the speech a "sacred . . . instrument" comparable to the Apostle Paul's letters to the Colossians, Philippians, and Thessalonians.[201] Bishop William F. MacDowell said that "while liberty lasts, while charity survives among men, while patriotism lives under any flag," the words of the Second Inaugural "will be on men's lips like prophesy, psalm or gospel,"[202] and the *Cleveland Morning Leader* said that the closing words of Lincoln's address "should be engraven on every heart."[203]

Charles Francis Adams, Jr., of the prominent and highly educated Massachusetts family, not only applauded the speech, but said that it could only have come from someone, like Lincoln, *without* formal education in oratory or "the schools:"

> That rail-splitting lawyer is one of the wonders of the day. Once at Gettysburg and now again on a greater occasion he has shown a capacity for rising to the demands of the hour which we should not expect from orators or men of the schools. . . . Not a prince or minister in all Europe could have risen to such an equality with the occasion.[204]

How ironic that his lack of formal education, having been seen his whole life as a *handicap*, would at the end of his life be seen as a source of *praise*.

Adams was not alone in calling the Second Inaugural unsurpassed even at the international level. William Gladstone, later the Prime Minister of England, reportedly said that the Second Inaugural was not only, and "unquestionably[,] a most striking and sublime utterance," but also was "not surpassed by any delivered during the nineteenth century."[205] Gladstone was also not alone in such sentiment: according to Theodore Cuyler, a Presbyterian minister and religious writer, even the ordinarily "hostile" London *Times* agreed with Gladstone's appraisal, calling the address, in Cuyler's account, "the most sublime state paper of this century."[206]

Gladstone and the *Times* thus ranked the Second Inaugural ahead of even the Gettysburg Address, and they, too, were not alone. Lincoln friend and biographer Henry C. Whitney called the Second Inaugural "the most sublime of Mr. Lincoln's utterances," and said, "it exceeds even the Gettysburg speech. It is, and will ever remain, a sacred classic."[207] Carl Schurz agreed, saying that while Lincoln's "Gettysburg speech has been much and justly admired," his Second Inaugural was "far greater, as well as far more characteristic."[208] It was an address

> in which he poured out the whole devotion and tenderness of his great soul. It had all the solemnity of a father's last admonition and blessing to his children before he lay down to die.[209]

Scholar Daniel Kilham Dodge would go even further, writing that the Second Inaugural not only signified "the highest pitch" of Lincoln's "presidential addresses," just as Cooper Union signified "the highest pitch" of his "political addresses," but also that:

> It is not too much to say that in its combined distinction of thought and beauty and perfection of form the Second Inaugural is unexcelled by any other state paper in the English tongue.[210]

In response to a comment that Lincoln's Second Inaugural was "the finest state paper in all history,"[211] another observer, whom it has been suggested was Secretary of State William Seward,[212] reportedly went further in his praise, saying:

> Yes, and as Washington's name grows brighter with time, so it will be with Lincoln's. A century from to-day that inaugural will be read as one of the most sublime utterances ever spoken by man. Washington is the great man of the era of the Revolution. So will Lincoln be of this, but Lincoln will reach the higher position in history.[213]

Opinions like these can be debated, of course, but what cannot is that, in the eyes of so many, in this country and beyond, the Second Inaugural stands among the greatest state papers of any statesman and any time. In a life of great statements, great efforts at public persuasion, Abraham Lincoln arguably may have saved his best for last.

Lincoln himself thought this might be the case. In a letter of March 15 to Thurlow Weed, Lincoln said that he "expect[ed]" his Second Inaugural Address "to wear as well—perhaps better than—any thing I have produced," but cautioned that it might take time for this to be the case, since "men are not flattered by being shown that there has been a difference of purpose between the Almighty and them."[214] He had nonetheless delivered that message, he said, because "it is a truth which I thought needed to be told."[215]

On April 11, 1865, two days after Lee's surrender at Appomattox, Lincoln gave his last speech, from a window on the north side of the White House.[216] He first gave thanks to Him "from Whom all blessings flow," and then to "Gen. Grant, his skilful officers and brave men," whose efforts had given "the cause of rejoicing."[217] After that, he turned to the topic of reconstruction, focusing on the newly adopted constitution and state government of Louisiana. He acknowledged that they were not perfect, but emphasized those points that were good, including the state's ratification of the Thirteenth Amendment, and its new constitution, which not only emancipated all slaves within the state, but also—as Lincoln had suggested in his letter to Governor Hahn—empowered the state legislature "to confer the elective franchise upon the colored man."[218] He advocated accepting what had been put in place, and working to build on that.

> The question is not whether the Louisiana government, as it stands, is quite all that is desirable. The question is, "Will it be wiser to take it as it is, and help to improve it; or to reject, and disperse it?" "Can Louisiana be brought into proper practical relation with the Union *sooner* by *sustaining*, or by *discarding* her new State government?"[219]

He urged similar flexibility, except on "important principles," in reuniting the other states that had rebelled.

> What has been said of Louisiana will apply generally to other States. And yet so great peculiarities pertain to each state; and such important and sudden changes occur in the same state; and, withal, so new and unprecedented is the whole case, that no exclusive, and inflexible plan can safely be prescribed as to details and colatterals. Such exclusive, and inflexible plan, would surely become a new entanglement.[220]

He then closed by saying, "it may be my duty to make some new announcement to the people of the South. I am considering, and shall not fail to act, when satisfied that action will be proper."[221]

What Lincoln may have said in that "new announcement to the people of the South," and what further messages he might have given, to South and North, in guiding reunion and reconstruction, we will never know. Just three days after his speech from the White House window, an assassin ensured that Abraham Lincoln would never give another speech or message of any kind. He would make no further case. He would never again seek to persuade. The world had lost, forever, not only "the foremost *convincer* of his day,"[222] but one of the foremost of *any*.

Abraham Lincoln and Making a Case

The earliest known photograph of Abraham Lincoln (age thirty-seven), taken in 1846, when he was a Springfield lawyer and congressman-elect.[1]

Joseph F. Roda

A page from the first book of Euclid's Elements, six of which Lincoln mastered.[2]

Abraham Lincoln and Making a Case

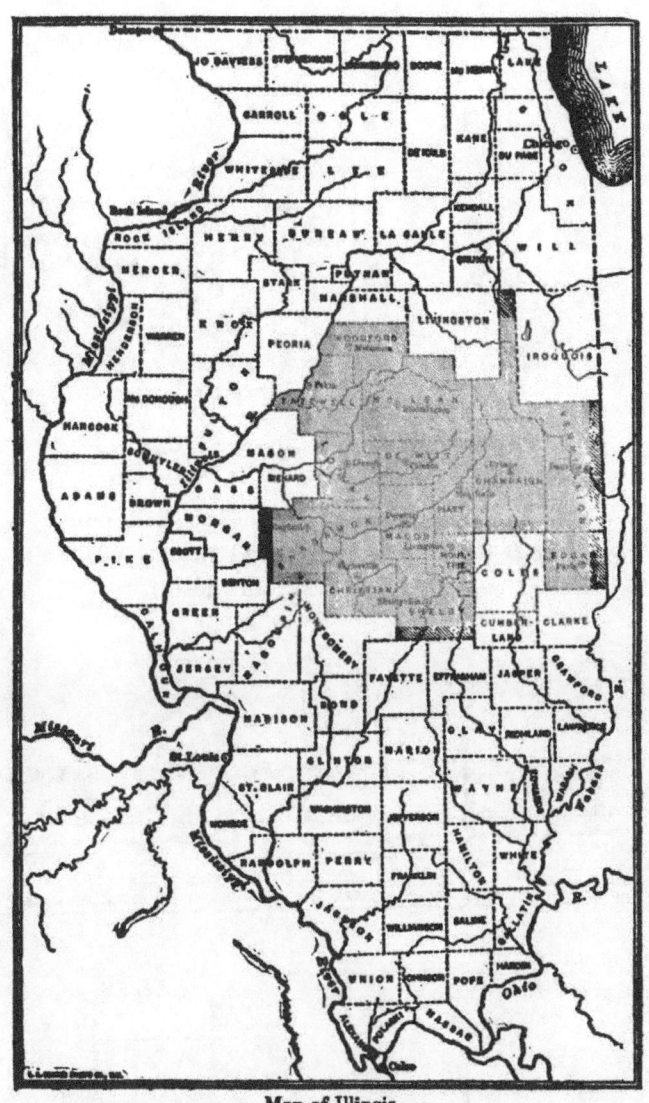

Map of Illinois
The shaded portion indicates the circuit of Lincoln's law practice

The Eighth Circuit, as organized under the provisions of the Illinois Session Laws of 1847, page 31, is shown by the shaded area on the above map. Later (in 1853) it was reduced to Sangamon, Logan, McLean, Woodford, Tazewell, DeWitt, Champaign, and Vermilion counties (Illinois Session Laws, 1853, page 63); and in 1857 it was further reduced to DeWitt, Logan, McLean, Champaign, and Vermilion counties (Illinois Session Laws, 1857, page 12). Even after Sangamon county was transferred to another circuit, Lincoln still continued to travel the Eighth.

Map of Illinois showing the Eighth Judicial Circuit.[3]

Joseph F. Roda

Old State House, which contained the Sangamon County Courthouse, Springfield, Illinois (image circa 1898, after Lincoln's death).[4]

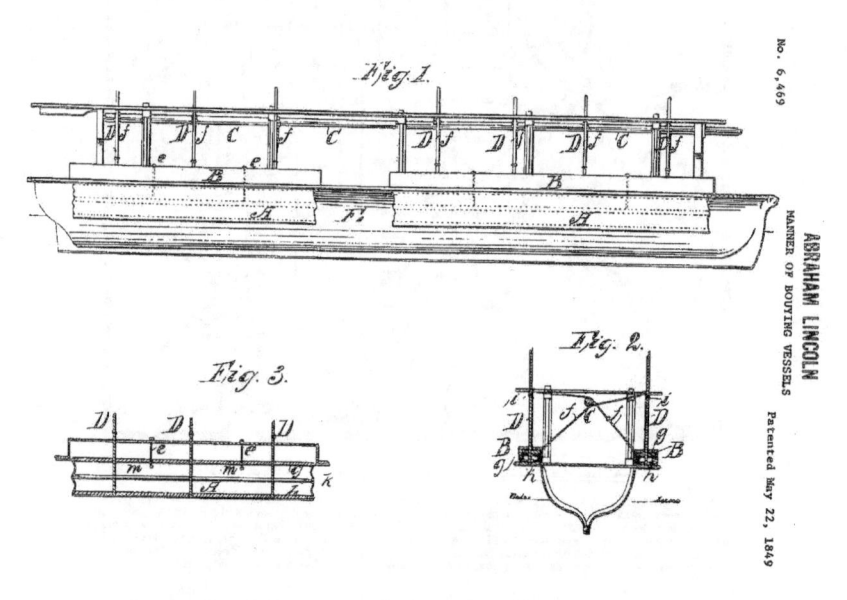

Images from Lincoln's patent of May 22, 1849.[5]

Stephen A. Douglas, Lincoln's frequent
debate opponent (circa 1850-1852).[6]

Lincoln on May 7, 1858, the day he won the
William "Duff" Armstrong trial.[7]

Joseph F. Roda

Lincoln, photographed by Matthew Brady, before his Cooper Union address on February 27, 1860 in New York City.[8]

Lincoln as presidential candidate, June 1860.[9]

Lincoln as presidential candidate in August 1860. This is reported to be the last photograph of Lincoln without a beard.[10]

Lincoln's first presidential inauguration, March 4, 1861.[11]

President Lincoln, August 9, 1863.[12]

Abraham Lincoln and Making a Case

President Lincoln, November 8, 1863, eleven days before the Gettysburg Address.[13]

President Lincoln and his private secretaries, John Nicolay (seated) and John Hay (standing).[14]

President Lincoln, January 8, 1864.[15]

Abraham Lincoln and Making a Case

President Lincoln, February 9, 1864.[16]

Joseph F. Roda

President Lincoln on February 5, 1865, in his last formal photograph sitting.[17]

Abraham Lincoln and Making a Case

The crowd bearing the rainy day to witness Lincoln's second presidential inauguration, March 4, 1865.[18]

Taken on the White House balcony on March 6, 1865, this is the last photograph of President Lincoln.[19]

Joseph F. Roda

Lincoln's funeral, Washington, D.C., April 19, 1865.[20]

PART II

SO WHERE DID Lincoln's "rare powers"[1] of public persuasion come from? What made him, as Greeley called him, the "foremost *convincer* of his day?"[2]

It was a mix of many things.

It was in part his personality and his intellect.

It was in part his knowledge of people, and what did and did not work in persuading them.

It was in part his preparation; his years of practice, in hundreds of speeches in politics and courts; and his timing.

And it was in part—very large part—his command of five keys to persuasion: credibility, clarity, fact, logic, and emotion.

Chapter 5: Personality and Intellect

ABRAHAM LINCOLN HAD a personality especially suited to public speaking and writing.

He was ambitious. He wanted recognition, and public speaking was a key to that in his day, especially in politics, where, as Doris Kearns Goodwin writes, speech was the "principal weapon," and a "gift for oratory was the key to success."[1]

Lincoln also *liked* public speaking. He drew energy from it, and could speak for three to four hours at a time without feeling weary,[2] even after a day in court. He did exactly that on the last day of the Duff Armstrong trial: after giving his closing argument and winning the acquittal, he then gave his favorite lecture that evening, on discoveries and inventions.[3]

He loved a positive reaction to his speeches, and loathed a negative one. When Frederick Douglass visited the White House after Lincoln's second inauguration, Lincoln promptly asked him what he had thought of Lincoln's speech. When Douglass replied, "Mr. Lincoln, that was a sacred effort,"[4] Lincoln was reportedly very pleased. Conversely, Lincoln told an acquaintance in 1856: "I'm one of the thinnest skinned men to any marks of impatience in my audience."[5]

His desire to do well in his speeches (and writings) led him to put in the work that this required (see Chapter 7 on his preparation), but he also enjoyed the creative process in speaking and writing. He was, as Garry Wills writes, "a student of the word,"[6] who thought that "language and its modes of dissemination (writing and printing)" were "the supreme inventions of mankind."[7] Wills notes that even in the depths of the Civil War, Lincoln found time to discuss philology (the study of words) with John Hay, a Brown graduate and one of Lincoln's two White House secretaries.[8]

With his passion for language, Lincoln not surprisingly loved Shakespeare's plays. Lincoln told a famous Shakespearean actor, James Hackett, that he (Lincoln) liked the soliloquy in Hamlet beginning, "O, my offence is rank," more than that beginning, "To be, or not to be."[9] Lincoln also asked questions of Hackett in that discussion, such as why certain lines from Shakespeare's plays, as written, were omitted from those plays when performed, and later pursued the same questions at the White House with another Shakespearean actor, John McDonough.[10]

He also loved poetry, particularly that of Byron, Burns, Cowper, Gray, and Pope.[11] He would read it aloud, or recite it from memory.[12] He also wrote poetry himself,[13] and has been called "our only poet-president."[14]

Also not surprisingly, given his fondness of poetry, he was sensitive not only to the content of words, but also to their sound and rhythm. He had an "ear" for these, as his speeches and writings reflected.[15] He read aloud even when alone, saying that it gave him the benefit of two senses.[16] John Hay recalled debating Lincoln one night during the Civil War, at the soldiers' cottage that Matthew Pinsker has called "Lincoln's Sanctuary,"[17] over whether James Hackett, had properly emphasized the right word in playing Falstaff.[18] Hackett had said "mainly *thrust* at me," while Lincoln thought he should have said "mainly thrust at *me*."[19]

Lincoln's "ear" played a vital role in his speeches and writings. He told one of his law clerks that he wrote "by ear," and that when he had "got . . . [his] thoughts on paper," he "read it aloud" to see "if it sounds all right."[20] He similarly told William O. Stoddard, a young newspaper editor from Illinois who became an assistant secretary in the White House, that he could "always tell more about a thing after I've heard it read aloud, and know how it sounds."[21]

As his love of poetry would further suggest, he was also a man of emotion, which he used to great effect in his speeches, as explored in greater detail in Chapter 12.

But simply being drawn to public speaking, and even working hard at it, does not make one a *good* speaker. Many is the person who likes to speak, but has nothing to say. Lincoln *did* have something to say, because of his mind.

He modestly liked to deprecate his mind, saying, "I am slow to learn and slow to forget that which I have learned—My mind is like a piece of steel, very hard to scratch any thing on it and almost impossible after you get it there to rub it out."[22] But his mind was, in truth, anything but "slow." He could not have accomplished all that he did if it had been. With less than a year of formal schooling, he taught himself grammar, elocution, surveying, law, and classic geometry (discussed below). He became, as noted, the leading courtroom lawyer in his state, for both trials and appeals, a combination not frequently found. He crafted political speeches that surpassed those of his highly educated rivals, speeches that repeatedly drew superlatives even from opponents, speeches—and writings—that are considered classics, in this country and beyond.

His mind was gifted, and he showed signs of this early on. His stepmother, Sarah Bush Johnston Lincoln, said that Lincoln "read all the books he could lay his hands on,"[23] and his schoolmaster, Mentor Graham, echoed that, saying that Lincoln "devoted more time to reading the scripture, books on science and comments on law and to the acquisition of Knowledge of men & things than any man I ever knew."[24]

He also had a superior memory. A Kentucky woman remembered him as the "gawkiest, dullest looking boy you ever saw," but also said "there was one thing remarkable about him. He could always remember things better than any other boy in the neighborhood."[25] J. Rowan Herndon, who owned the general store that Lincoln bought in New Salem, paid a similar compliment, saying that Lincoln "had the Best memory of any man i Ever Knew he Never forgot any thing he Read."[26]

Lincoln's stepmother spoke of how Lincoln trained his memory even as a young boy, saying that when he

> came across a passage that Struck him he would write it down on boards if he had no paper & keep it there till he did get paper—then he would re-write it—look at it repeat it—He had a copy book—a kind of scrap book in which he put down all things and this preserved them.... What he learned and Stowed away was well defined in his own

mind—repeated over & over again & again till it was so defined and fixed firmly & permanently in his Memory.[27]

A former governor of Massachusetts, Henry J. Gardner, recalled that Lincoln, as president, some twelve or more years after the fact, not only could remember an elaborate dinner that Governor Levi Lincoln of Massachusetts had hosted during Lincoln's speaking tour of New England in 1848[28]—a "superb" dinner, Lincoln called it, "by far the finest I ever saw in my life,"—but also could identify, in order, where each of the many dinner guests sat around the table, "without the omission of a single one."[29]

His memory allowed him to quote long passages from the Bible[30] and Shakespeare,[31] his two favorite works,[32] and to try court cases with few or no notes;[33] he relied instead on a "well-trained memory that recorded and indexed every passing detail."[34] Indeed, he reportedly disparaged the use of notes in trials, saying, "Notes are a bother, taking time to make, and more to hunt them up afterward," and that lawyers who relied too much on them "soon get the habit of referring to them so much that it confused and tired the jury."[35]

His memory likewise aided him in his political speeches, allowing him to speak even at great length without reliance on notes.[36]

But his most valuable mental asset was his ability to analyze, to see relationships and reduce an issue to its essence. A friend, Joshua Speed, said that Lincoln "could grasp, exhaust, and quit any subject with more facility than any man I have ever seen or heard of."[37] Another friend, Leonard Swett, said that the "world" to Lincoln "was a question of cause and effect,"[38] and "life . . . a school" in which "he was always studying and mastering every subject which came before him."[39]

He was fascinated with machines, not only handling patent cases as an attorney, but also receiving a patent of his own, the only American president to do so. He received his in 1849, for an invention to lift boats over shallow sandbars or shoals.[40]

He also had a lifelong fascination with astronomy and mathematics,[41] and what Garry Wills calls "analytical exercises."[42] In his forties, with less than a year of formal education in mathematics, and entirely on his own, he worked through the first six books of Euclid's classic text on geometry, proudly finishing at age fifty-one, the year he was elected president.[43]

Abraham Lincoln and Making a Case

His law partner William Herndon found him at one point in this effort surrounded in their office by "a quantity of blank paper, large heavy sheets, a compass, a rule, numerous pencils, several bottles of ink of various colors, and a profusion of stationery and writing appliances generally[,] . . . trying to solve the difficult problem of squaring the circle."[44] Herndon said Lincoln spent "the better part of the succeeding two days" on this, "almost to the point of exhaustion."[45]

His analytical ability was a tremendous asset in the courtroom and out. John P. Frank, in his 1961 study of Lincoln the lawyer, wrote that "the key to Lincoln's [law] practice" was his "directness of thought."[46] Isaac N. Arnold, a lawyer who saw Lincoln try many cases, said that "he had the ability to perceive with almost intuitive quickness the decisive point in the case,"[47] and that "however complicated" the case, Lincoln

> would disentangle it, and present the turning point in a way so simple and clear that all could understand. Indeed, his statement [of the case] often rendered argument unnecessary, and often the Court would stop him and say, "If that is the case, we will hear the other side."[48]

Another lawyer, who heard Lincoln try more than a hundred cases of all types, similarly said that Lincoln

> had a genius for seeing the real point in a case . . . and aiming steadily at it from the beginning of a trial to the end. The issue in most cases lies in very narrow compass, and the really great lawyer disregards everything not directly tending to that issue. . . . Mr. Lincoln instinctively saw the kernel of every case . . ., never lost sight of it, and never let it escape the jury.[49]

Lincoln showed the same ability outside the courtroom, in his rise to national political prominence. At Peoria, while giving a masterful speech of three hours opposing the extension of slavery into the territories, he ultimately reduced the issue to one question: "whether a negro is not or is a man."

> If he is *not* a man, why in that case, he who *is* a man may, as a matter of self-government, do just as he pleases with him. But if the negro *is* a man, is it not to that extent, a total destruction of self-government, to say that he too shall not govern *himself*? . . . If the negro is a *man*, why then my ancient faith teaches me that "all men are created equal;" and that there can be no moral right in connection with one man's making a slave of another.[50]

Six years later, in his ninety minute address at Cooper Union, he again reduced the issue, this time to whether slavery was "right" or "wrong:"

> If slavery is right, all words, acts, laws, and constitutions against it, are themselves wrong, and should be silenced, and swept away. If it is right, we cannot justly object to its nationality—its universality; if it is wrong, they cannot justly insist upon its extension—its enlargement. All they ask, we could readily grant, if we thought slavery right; all we ask, they could as readily grant, if they thought it wrong. Their thinking it right, and our thinking it wrong, is the precise fact upon which depends the whole controversy.[51]

In between these two speeches, a commentator noted how well Lincoln had taken apart and refuted Douglas on the *Dred Scott* decision: "Mr. Lincoln analyzed it—dissected Douglas's idea, and held up to the gaze of the crowd *the skeleton* Douglas would have."[52]

He then showed the same analytical ability as president. John P. Frank credits Lincoln's "capacity to reach the one essential element of his case" as one of Lincoln's talents as president that led to his "extraordinary success" as "a leader of public thought."[53] A contemporary *New York Times* writer, commenting on Lincoln's letter as president to James Conkling, similarly praised Lincoln's "singular faculty of discovering the real relations of things,"[54] and focusing on the point that really mattered. Lincoln, the writer said, invariably gets at the needed truth of the time. When he writes, it is always said that "he hits the nail upon the head," and so he does; but the beauty of it is that the nail which he hits is sure to be the very nail of all others which needs driving.[55]

Edward Everett, the main speaker at the Gettysburg dedication, and originally a Lincoln critic, recognized and complimented the same talent in Lincoln in a note that he sent Lincoln after that ceremony. "I should be glad," Everett said, "if I could flatter myself that I came as near to the central idea of the occasion, in two hours, as you did in two minutes."[56]

Chapter 6: Knowledge of People

LINCOLN'S MIND ALSO gave him another advantage in persuasion: a keen understanding of people.

Robert L. Wilson, who saw Lincoln's efforts to move the capital of Illinois to Springfield in the 1830s, said that even then the young Lincoln had a "practical common Sense, . . . [a] thorough knowledge of human nature, [which] made him an overmatch for his compeers and for any man that I have ever known."[1]

A contemporary attorney echoed this sentiment, saying that Lincoln "understood, almost intuitively, the jury, witnesses, parties, and judges, and how best to address, convince, and influence them."[2] Thurlow Weed, a Republican leader in New York, referred to the same "intuitive knowledge of human nature" after he visited with Lincoln, then the Republican presidential nominee, in 1860.[3]

That intuitive knowledge and understanding came from many sources, starting with Lincoln's first two decades of life, spent with his poor, illiterate family and others of similar circumstances. Many of them asked him to write letters for them, either because they could not write or because they thought he could convey better than they what they wanted to say. Lincoln reportedly told his teacher, Mentor Graham, that writing these letters for other people "sharpened" his "perceptions" and taught him "to see other people['s] thoughts and feelings and ideas."[4]

Lincoln's understanding of people then grew with his modest first years on his own, as a clerk in a general store and a post office, mixing daily with the general public, and then continued in his years on the Eighth Judicial Circuit, where he engaged with people of all levels, both in and out of the courtroom. He interacted with judges, juries, court staff, and clients in his trials, and after the court day gathered with the same persons and townsfolk in the local general store, for meals and storytelling. He also lodged with families, sharing time with them on the weekends and learning their "concerns, struggles, and questions."[5] He talked with the men he would seek to persuade as jurors and voters, and the women who would influence them, as mothers, sisters, wives, and daughters.

This constant immersion with "regular" people was a continuing education into their minds and feelings—what moved them, appealed to them, struck a chord with them—knowledge that he would tap first as a lawyer, and then as a political candidate and president. Horace Greeley, after Lincoln's death, wrote that "no one was ever acquainted and on terms of friendly intimacy with a greater number of human beings of all ranks and conditions."[6] James Russell Lowell, a nineteenth century poet, critic, editor, and diplomat, wrote of the advantage that this "friendly intimacy" gave Lincoln, allowing him to speak "as if the people were listening to their own thinking out loud."[7]

A repeated theme in books about Lincoln's legal career is the "insights" that it gave him "into human nature," the "thought-processes of the people,"[8] and the "foibles and complexities of human affairs,"[9] all of which benefitted him in both court and politics. Frederick Trevor Hill wrote that Lincoln's knowledge of human nature made him "the best all-around jury lawyer of his day in Illinois,"[10] and William McKinley, himself an accomplished trial lawyer who would also become president three decades after Lincoln (and also die by assassination), said that Lincoln's many years on the judicial circuit were "the best training" that he could have had for the presidency.[11]

With his feel for people, Lincoln studied what worked in persuasion and what did not. Beginning in 1832, with his first run for public office, he gave hundreds of political stump speeches, and beginning in 1836, with his admission to the practice of law, he gave hundreds of speeches to juries and judges. Each speech, in court or out, was an exercise in "reading" his audience, crafting the argument most likely to appeal, and delivering that argument as well as possible. Each was also a learning experience, as

Horace Greeley noted in a talk about Lincoln several years after his death. While the public speaker "is teaching his hearers," Greeley said, he also

> can hardly fail to be instructed himself. He is day by day presenting facts and arguments and reading in the faces of his hearers their relative pertinence and effectiveness. If his statement of his case does not seem to produce conviction, he varies, fortifies, reënforces it; giving it from day to day new shapes until he has hit upon that which seems to command the hearty, enthusiastic assent of the great body of his hearers; and this becomes henceforth his model.[12]

"Such was the school," Greeley said, "in which Abraham Lincoln trained himself to be the foremost *convincer* of his day."[13]

The courtroom "school" was especially influential. The courtroom is nothing but persuasion, start to finish. The courtroom lawyer does not speak to a crowd that has come on its own to hear him. He speaks to a jury that may not want to be there, an opponent who wants to beat him, and a judge who wants to control him. The courtroom lawyer does not finish to applause. He finishes to await a decision that will affect his client's money or liberty, and sometimes even determine whether his client will live or die. The courtroom thus has a singular way of identifying what works in persuasion and what does not.

Lincoln's hundreds of efforts in the courtroom left their mark, creating habits that shaped his approach to persuasion not only in the courtroom but also beyond it; he remained the courtroom lawyer even in his political speeches and writings. His speeches against the Kansas-Nebraska Act and the spread of slavery read like a closing argument in a trial: first the issue, then the facts, then his argument, and then—just as a lawyer asks for a specific verdict or ruling—his request for specific action: restore the Missouri Compromise (Springfield and Peoria); stand firm against the efforts to expand slavery (House Divided); "have faith" and do "our duty" (Cooper Union).

His speeches and writings as president were similarly those of a lawyer, based in fact and logic, simple in style and content, and with one exception—his 3,800-word letter to Erastus Corning—short and to the point. (see Chapters 9, 10, and 11 on Lincoln's mastery of clarity, fact, and logic.) Jesse Dunn, himself a lawyer, called Lincoln's short 1862 letter to Greeley "an example of masterful pleading, . . . an embodiment of legal expression."[14] And the letter to Corning, while long, was a legal brief for laypersons—first the facts, then the law (in that case, the Constitution), and then the application of facts to law: "Let us consider the real case with which we are dealing, and apply to it the parts of the constitution plainly made for such cases."[15]

As Mark E. Steiner has noted, biographies of Lincoln, especially those written before the publication in 2000 of the papers from Lincoln's law practice (*The Law Practice of Abraham Lincoln: Complete Documentary Edition*), "have tended to hurry past Lincoln's law practice."[16] Even where it is addressed, Lincoln's career in the courtroom is often treated as a "chapter" in his life, separate from those on his politics and presidency. The relationship is seen as sequential: Lincoln was first a lawyer and then a president.

Books that focus on his law practice go beyond this, note the influence of his law practice on his presidency,[17] and in at least one instance—Albert A. Woldman—raise a possible "causal" link between Lincoln's law practice and his becoming president. Woldman writes that "without his [Lincoln's] twenty-three years of experience at the bar, he might never have become President of the United States."[18]

We can never answer Woldman's question, of course, because we cannot know what would have happened if Lincoln had not been a lawyer. But we do know what *did* happen when he *was* a lawyer, and the causal relationship can be stated more boldly. If Lincoln's career in the courtroom honed his ability to make a case, as it surely did, and his ability to make a case then brought him to national attention and the Republican nomination for president, as it also surely did, it might be said that Abraham Lincoln was not just a courtroom lawyer who became president, but a courtroom lawyer who became president *because* he was a courtroom lawyer.

In any event, from both his knowledge of people and the "schools" of politics and court in which he practiced and studied, Lincoln came to his own principles of persuasion, some of which he mentioned in an early address on temperance in 1842, at the age of thirty-three, just ten years after his first run for office and only six after his admission to the bar.

- "When the conduct of men is designed to be influenced, *persuasion*, kind, unassuming persuasion, should ever be adopted."[19]
- "It is an old and true maxim, that 'a drop of honey catches more flies than a gallon of gall.'"[20]
- "If you would win a man to your cause, *first* convince him that you are his sincere friend."[21]
- A person's "heart, . . . say what he will, is the great high road to his reason," and when the heart is "once gained, you will find but little trouble in convincing his judgment of the justice of your cause, if indeed that cause really be a just one."[22]

By contrast, Lincoln said in the same address, trying to *tell* a person what to do dooms the attempt at persuasion to failure:

> assume to dictate to his judgment, or to command his action, . . . and he will retreat within himself, close all the avenues to his head and his heart; and tho' your cause be naked truth itself, transformed to the heaviest lance, harder than steel, and sharper than steel can be made, and tho' you throw it with more than Herculean force and precision, you shall be no more able to pierce him, than to penetrate the hard shell of a tortoise with a rye straw.[23]

"Such is man," Lincoln said, "and so *must* he be understood by those who would lead him."[24] Those who are successful at persuasion, Lincoln said, do not talk sternly *at* a person. They instead

> glow with a generous and brotherly zeal. . . . Benevolence and charity possess *their* hearts entirely; and out of the abundance of their hearts, their tongues give utterance. . . . In this spirit they speak and act, and in the same, they are heard and regarded. And when such is the temper of the advocate, and such of the audience, no good cause can be unsuccessful.[25]

Lincoln also emphasized the value of simplicity in persuasion, which he emphasized to his third and younger law partner, William Herndon:

> Billy, don't shoot too high—aim lower, and the common people will understand you. . . . The educated and refined people will understand you any way. If you aim too high your ideas will go over the heads of the masses, and only hit those who need no hitting.[26]

And on the same point—helping the ordinary person "understand you"—he emphasized the value of mental images or pictures. "Plain people," he said, "take them as you find them, are more easily influenced through the medium of a broad and humorous illustration than in any other way."[27]

Lincoln also believed in confining his argument to the narrowest point he needed to win. "Never *plead* what you *need* not," he said, "lest you oblige yourself to *prove* what you *can* not."[28] He was practical, not an ideologue. He argued to bar slavery's extension, not abolish it where it already was. He argued that slaves should be free, not equal to whites in all rights. He argued that his goal was to save the Union, not to free the slaves, and based his Emancipation Proclamation on that objective, rather than a humanitarian or moral one.

Lincoln also studied the approaches to persuasion of others. As a new congressman, he went to the Senate to hear Daniel Webster and John Calhoun, who along with Henry Clay formed "the Great Triumvirate" in that age of oratory.[29] He considered Webster's reply to Robert Hayne in 1830 "the grandest specimen of American oratory,"[30] and said that a speech by the Whig congressman Alexander H. Stephens from Georgia, attacking President Polk on the seizure of Mexican territory, was "the very best speech, of an hour's length, I have ever heard."[31]

He also noted—and complimented—a debate tactic of Stephen Douglas, his opponent of decades, saying: "It is impossible to get the advantage of him; even if he is worsted, he so bears himself that the people are bewildered and uncertain as to who has the better of it."[32] He similarly noted a related tactic of effective debaters generally, without limitation to Douglas:

> It was a great trick among some public speakers to hurl a naked absurdity at his audience, with such confidence that they should be puzzled to know if the speaker didn't see some point of great magnitude in it which entirely escaped their observation. A neatly varnished sophism would be readily penetrated, but a great, rough *non sequitur w*as sometimes twice as dangerous as a well polished fallacy.[33]

And in still another comment, Lincoln offered what he thought made the "great" orator:

> It is very common in this country to find great facility of expression, and common, though not so common, to find great lucidity of thought. The combination of the two faculties in one person is uncommon indeed; but whenever you do find it, you have a great man.[34]

He could have been speaking of himself—and perhaps was. "The Lincoln of myth," says Garry Wills, was "a simple and plainspoken fellow."[35] "The real Lincoln," Wills says, was a shrewd and accomplished student of persuasive speech, "the master of a calculated rhetoric."[36]

Chapter 7: Preparation and Timing

"WORK, WORK, WORK," Lincoln said was the key to becoming a successful lawyer,[1] and this described as well his approach to persuasion, in court and out.

He worked, first of all, at learning his case, whatever it involved. His second law partner, Stephen T. Logan, said that Lincoln "would get a case and try to learn all there was connected with it,"[2] and his last law partner, William Herndon, similarly said that Lincoln would express no opinion on a subject until he knew it "inside and outside, upside and downside."[3]

When the defense retained him in Cyrus McCormick's patent case, and the lead lawyers for the defense were slow in sending Lincoln copies of the complaint, answer, and depositions, he went looking for the facts himself, going to the federal courthouse in Chicago to obtain copies of the pleadings, spending half a day investigating the opposition's machine, and asking for "all the material" the defense team could provide.[4]

When he represented the bridge company in the steamboat collision, and ultimately argued that the steamboat captain had been negligent in handling the river's currents, he prepared his defense by visiting the scene, interviewing the designer of the bridge about its construction, questioning that man's teenage son about the river's currents, hiring men to navigate a steamer in the area so that he could see how the vessel responded to winds and currents, and placing various objects in the water to see how they flowed.[5]

When his partner William Herndon asked him why he went to the trouble he did in preparing a brief, Lincoln replied: "I dare not trust this case on presumptions that this court knows all things. I argued the case on the presumption that the court did not know any thing."[6]

He similarly spent months researching and preparing his speeches against the Kansas-Nebraska Act in 1854, his speech against the *Dred Scott* decision in 1857, and his speech at Cooper Union in 1860. The *Chicago Press and Tribune*, writing about him shortly before the Cooper Union speech, noted that he was "laboriously attentive to detail, industrious and conscientious,"[7] as Lincoln's speech then showed.

For both courtroom trials and political speeches, Lincoln worked as hard at learning his opponent's case as he did his own. Fellow attorney Jesse Dunn said that if Lincoln "had any quality in the preparation of his cases superior to others, it was the diligence with which he studied the opposite side of every case."[8] As a result, Dunn continued, "it is said of him that in all his long career, he was never surprised by the testimony of the opposition."[9]

And having mastered his opponent's case, he met it head on. At Peoria, after stating his affirmative case for reinstating the Missouri Compromise, Lincoln then "answered" each of the arguments by which pro-slavery proponents sought to justify the repeal of the Missouri Compromise.[10] He did the same at Cooper Union: after making his case that the "fathers" believed as Republicans did, he then turned to the South, saying, "Bring forward your charges and specifications, and then be patient long enough to hear us deny or justify."[11] A year later, his First Inaugural speech[12] was virtually a rebuttal from start to finish of southern charges against Republicans and the assumption that war was inevitable.

His approach drew compliments. The *New-York Daily Tribune*, in writing about Lincoln's letter as president to James Conkling, said that Lincoln, "in answering his [the opponent's] criticisms and objections . . . is sure to cover all the doubts, if there are any, of his friends.[13]

His preparation for political speeches often involved working through issues in private writings. Garry Wills says that Lincoln used writing "as a way of ordering his thought,"[14] and Doris Kearns Goodwin, quoting John Nicolay, refers to Lincoln's successive writing on an issue as his "cumulative thought," saying:

He would reduce complex ideas to paragraphs and sentences, and then days or weeks later return to the same passage and polish it further "to elaborate or to conclude his point or argument."[15]

A prime example was his effort as president to reconcile the concept of a divinity with the terrible civil war then raging. In his 1862 "Meditation on the Divine Will," he wrote that God, who could have prevented the war or ended it at any point, must have "willed" its continuation:

> The will of God prevails. In great contests each party claims to act in accordance with the will of God. Both *may* be, and one *must* be wrong. God can not be *for*, and *against* the same thing at the same time. In the present civil war it is quite possible that God's purpose is something different from the purpose of either party—and yet the human instrumentalities, working just as they do, are of the best adaptation to effect His purpose. I am almost ready to say this is probably true—that God wills this contest, and wills that it shall not end yet. By his mere quiet power, on the minds of the now contestants, He could have either *saved* or *destroyed* the Union without a human contest. Yet the contest began. And having begun He could give the final victory to either side any day. Yet the contest proceeds.[16]

Two years later, he included the same thought, but now slightly more developed, at the end of his letter to Albert Hodges: he now tied the war's continuation to the concept of divine punishment.

> Now, at the end of three years struggle the nation's condition is not what either party, or any man devised, or expected. God alone can claim it. Whither it is tending seems plain. If God now wills the removal of a great wrong, and wills also that we of the North as well as you of the South, shall pay fairly for our complicity in that

> wrong, impartial history will find therein new cause to attest and revere the justice and goodness of God.[17]

And less than a year later, his Second Inaugural made the same thought, even more fully sharpened, a central theme.

> If we shall suppose that American Slavery is one of those offences which, in the providence of God, must needs come, but which, having continued through His appointed time, He now wills to remove, and that He gives to both North and South, this terrible war, as the woe due to those by whom the offence came, shall we discern therein any departure from those divine attributes which the believers in a Living God always ascribe to Him? Fondly do we hope—fervently do we pray—that this mighty scourge of war may speedily pass away. Yet, if God wills that it continue, until all the wealth piled by the bond-man's two hundred and fifty years of unrequited toil shall be sunk, and until every drop of blood drawn with the lash, shall be paid by another drawn with the sword, as was said three thousand years ago, so still it must be said "the judgments of the Lord, are true and righteous altogether."[18]

Lincoln was not a "natural" writer, according to John Nicolay, one of his two White House clerks. He "*learned* to write—learned to appreciate the value of the pen as an instrument to formulate and record his thought, and the more clearly, forcibly, and elegantly to express it."[19] Lincoln's friend Joshua Speed similarly said that Lincoln studied composition, to learn "to make short sentences & a compact style,"[20] traits for which his compositions would be noted.

Lincoln's law partner William Herndon described the methodical approach that Lincoln used to prepare his House Divided acceptance speech in 1858:

> This speech he wrote on stray envelopes and scraps of paper, as ideas suggested themselves, putting them

into that miscellaneous and convenient receptacle, his hat. As the convention drew near he copied the whole on connected sheets, carefully revising every line and sentence, and fastened them together for reference during the delivery of the speech, and for publication.[21]

For Lincoln's message to Congress of July 4, 1861, John Hay, Lincoln's other White House secretary, said that Lincoln "engaged in constant thought,"[22] and Carl Sandburg called it an unprecedented effort. "No previous manuscript from Lincoln's hand," Sandburg wrote, "had been so carefully written by him, rearranged, modified."[23]

Lincoln *preferred* the opportunity to prepare his speeches and writings. While he lauded the art of extemporaneous speech to young lawyers,[24] he avoided it if he could, particularly after his election as president.[25] Indeed, historians seem to agree that Lincoln was generally not good at, or comfortable with, truly impromptu remarks,[26] which led him frequently, as president, to decline saying anything other than a polite acknowledgement.

When a crowd and brass band came to serenade him at the White House in July 1863 after the victory at Gettysburg, Lincoln told them, "Gentlemen, this is a glorious theme, and the occasion for a speech, but I am not prepared to make one worthy of the occasion."[27]

Similarly, when a crowd assembled outside his hotel in Gettysburg the night before his famous address, he again declined to speak, other than to say:

> I appear before you, fellow-citizens, merely to thank you for this compliment. The inference is a very fair one that you would hear me for a little while at least, were I to commence to make a speech. I do not appear before you for the purpose of doing so, and for several substantial reasons. The most substantial of these is that I have no speech to make. [Laughter.] In my position it is somewhat important that I should not say any foolish things.
>
> [A VOICE—If you can help it.]

> It very often happens that the only way to help it is to say nothing at all. [Laughter.] Believing that is my present condition this evening, I must beg of you to excuse me from addressing you further.[28]

He then returned to his room to work on one of the great speeches in history—American *and* world.

Lincoln would work on a speech right up to giving it. When he learned, upon arriving in New York in February 1860, that he would give his speech not at the Reverend Beecher's church, but at the Cooper Union Institute before a much larger crowd, he told an organizer that he, Lincoln, "must review his address," because "what he had prepared for Mr. Beecher's church folk might not be altogether appropriate to a miscellaneous political audience."[29]

And at the Gettysburg dedication in November 1863, he apparently revised his speech even after composing his final draft, adding to the last sentence the words "under God" (". . . that this nation, under God, shall have a new birth of freedom"),[30] which do not appear in any pre-delivery drafts of the speech.

He paid careful attention to every word. After he gave his House Divided speech, he handed the text to a young reporter, Horace White, to take to the *Illinois State Journal* for publication.[31] When White started to proofread the speech and penned in some revisions, Lincoln looked over the revised proof and told White that he wanted the speech printed without revisions, "exactly as he had delivered it."[32]

Two years later, when Charles Nott, one of the Cooper Union organizers, suggested reprinting Lincoln's speech in a pamphlet with some editorial changes, Lincoln agreed to proofreading for "grammar, and elegance of composition," but emphasized that he did not "wish the sense changed, or modified," not even "to a hair's breadth."[33] He explained why:

> You, not having studied the particular points so closely as I have, can not be quite sure that you do not change the sense when you do not intend it. For instance, . . . you proposed to substitute "Democrats" for "Douglas." But what I am saying there is *true* of Douglas, and is not true of

"Democrats" generally; so that the proposed substitution would be a very considerable blunder.[34]

Lincoln's preparation extended even to the seemingly "extemporaneous" stories and anecdotes that he used to make a point (see Chapter 9, on clarity). Judge Samuel Treat reportedly gave Lincoln the compiled jokes of Joe Miller, only to find later that Lincoln had not only mastered them, but had also "very much embellished and changed" them,[35] presumably to better illustrate the points he wanted to make.

While "many of Lincoln's witticisms and humorous turns of phrase were original," Lincoln himself admitted late in life that only two of his stories were originals.[36] The rest he had heard from others, or had read, and carefully tucked them into his memory (or occasionally wrote them down) for future reference.[37]

Lincoln would accept nothing less: he wanted what he said, even his stories and anecdotes, to hit their mark.

Lincoln then combined his preparation with a shrewd sense of timing.

He waited until he could confront the author of the Kansas-Nebraska Act in person, at a large public gathering, and with the press who routinely followed that author. He had clearly worked for some time on the 16,600-word masterpiece that he delivered, and had just as clearly intended to give it at some point, but waited for the moment that would give maximum exposure.

As president, Lincoln had drafted the main part of his "reply" to Horace Greeley before Greeley ever wrote his editorial, but waited for the right moment to release it, which Greeley then gave him: an unprecedented public "confrontation" between a president and a newspaper editor via public letters in newspapers. Lincoln's message would have been widely read under any circumstances, but the novelty of the circumstances and setting in which he issued it gave it even more prominence.

One newspaper observed that in choosing to issue the Preliminary Emancipation Proclamation when he did, Lincoln "has been neither too soon nor too late,"[38] and Francis Fisher Browne, a Civil War veteran and later an editor, poet, and critic, conveyed the same thought about the later Emancipation Proclamation itself, writing that Lincoln:

> would not be hurried, nor worried, nor badgered, into premature and inoperative measures. He bided his time; and when that time came the deed was done, unalterably and irrevocably: approved by the logic of events, and by the enlightened conscience of the world.[39]

The newspaper and Browne were in good company with their opinions: Lincoln himself agreed. "It is my conviction," he later said, "that, had the proclamation been issued even six months earlier than it was, public sentiment would not have sustained it."[40]

Lincoln similarly showed calculated timing in his response to Erastus Corning. It was 3,800 words, masterfully crafted, and obviously not assembled quickly. Even if Lincoln actually wrote it between just May 28 and June 5, as claimed, he had obviously *thought* long and hard about the issues, which he knew he would likely have to address at some point. He could have done so at any time before Corning's protest, but waited for the "public confrontation" that the prominent protest presented, and the drama of his then giving his "case" in response, which enhanced the public interest in it.

The same was true of his letter to James Conkling. The letter took on issues—the Emancipation Proclamation and the acceptance of blacks into the Union forces—that Lincoln had to know he would have to address, from the moment he issued the proclamation. He would have thought a great deal about what he would say, and was likely ready to say it long before he did. But waiting to do so as a response to a prominent public protest—a protest in his *hometown* and by members of *his own party*—lent drama to what he said, and thereby increased public attention.

He similarly could have conveyed his theme at Gettysburg—that the war effort had to be continued because of what it sought to preserve and secure—at any time or place he wanted, and long before the ceremony on November 19, 1863. But waiting to convey it on the most important battlefield of that war effort to date, honoring the thousands who had given their lives there in support of that effort, lent a power to his message that its utterance at a different time or place likely would not have.

Likewise, the core message of his Second Inaugural, that both South *and* North bore responsibility for slavery and the awful war it had provoked, and that they both, equally humbled by the Almighty, should reunite "with malice toward none . . . [and] charity for all . . . to bind up the nation's wounds,"[41] i.e., the wounds of both North and South, had a special meaning with the toll of the war so great, the country exhausted from it, and a Union victory now finally in sight.

Chapter 8: Credibility

AUDIENCE ACCEPTANCE INVOLVES another all-important element: "credibility," the quality of being believed or trusted. Before the audience will accept the message, the saying goes, they must accept the messenger.

Lincoln won that acceptance in a number of ways.

He adapted to his audience and the occasion. For the Cooper Union audience, he bought a new suit[1] and comported himself much differently than "back home," said Mayson Brayman, a fellow lawyer from Springfield who saw the Cooper Union speech.[2] Brayman said that it was

> somewhat funny, to see a man who *at home,* talks along in so familiar a way, walking up and down, swaying about, swinging his arms, bobbing forward, telling droll stories and laughing at them himself, *here in New-York,* standing up stiff and straight, with his hands quiet, pronouncing sentence after sentence, in good telling english.[3]

Similarly, when Lincoln spoke against the Supreme Court's *Dred Scott* decision in 1857 with a scholarly speech, he set the stage by entering the room "with law books under his arms."[4]

He also won credibility by conveying the impression that he said what was true, or at a minimum what he believed was true. He was "straight" with his audience. He "leveled" with them. "Honest Abe" was one of his several nicknames, and Judge David Davis, who presided over more of Lincoln's trials than anyone else, said that "honesty" was the "framework of his [Lincoln's] mental and moral being."[5] Indeed, Davis said, it affected his ability in court: Lincoln was not good at defending "a wrong case."[6] To be at his best, "he had to be convinced of the right and justice of the matter which he advocated."[7]

Another contemporary attorney, Samuel C. Parks, whom Lincoln as president appointed to the Supreme Court of Idaho in 1862, put it more bluntly: "when he [Lincoln] thought he was wrong he was the weakest lawyer I ever saw."[8] Lincoln reportedly withdrew from one case "because our witnesses have been lying, and I don't believe them,"[9] he said, and he similarly left the courtroom in another case and went to his hotel after opposing counsel produced clear evidence that Lincoln's position was wrong.[10] When the judge sent for him to return, Lincoln replied: "Tell the Judge that I can't come—*my hands are dirty & I came over to clean them.*"[11]

Lincoln also enhanced his impression of honesty in the courtroom by conceding many points,[12] which in turn enhanced his credibility on the points he contested. Ida Tarbell put it thus, based on her research into Lincoln the lawyer and talking with lawyers who had seen Lincoln in action:

> In his desire to keep his case clear he rarely argued points which seemed to him unessential. . . . He would thus give away point after point with an indifferent "I reckon that's so," until the point which he considered pivotal was reached, and there he hung.[13]

He had the same reputation for honesty in his politics and presidency. When Stephen Douglas learned that Lincoln would oppose him in the Senate race in 1858, Douglas not only praised Lincoln as "the best stump speaker . . . in the West," but also added, "he is as *honest* as he is shrewd."[14]

In 1862, the *National Republican* said that Lincoln's Second Annual Message to Congress "permeated throughout with that *honesty*, . . . which is so eminently characteristic of the man."[15] Two years later, the *New York Times* ranked Lincoln with George Washington for honesty as a president, and put them above all other occupants of that office. Lincoln's ability to unify the North, it wrote, came from "his peculiar transparency of character, his remarkable faculty—never equaled in any other President since the first—of inspiring every one . . . that he is a thoroughly *honest* and trustworthy man."[16]

The abolitionist leader William Lloyd Garrison, at one point a harsh critic of Lincoln, went even further, writing that Lincoln was unsurpassed for honesty among *all* American presidents: "no man," Garrison wrote, "has occupied . . . [the office of the presidency] who has more assiduously or more *honestly* endeavored to discharge all its duties."[17]

"Sincerity" was another, similar trait for which Lincoln was noted. Horace White, reporting on Lincoln's speech at Springfield in 1854, wrote that when Lincoln spoke, the crowd "felt that he believed every word he said, and that, like Martin Luther, he would go to the stake rather than abate one jot or tittle of it."[18] Richard McCormick, an organizer and member of the committee that sponsored Lincoln's speech at Cooper Union, wrote that its "tender *sincerity*" was one of the things that made its appeal so great.[19] And an Ohio newspaper wrote similarly about the Gettysburg Address. It was, the paper said, "like all the President does— . . . clothed with a *sincere honesty* of expression."[20]

Consistent with the image of honesty and sincerity, Lincoln did not avoid or evade. He took issues head on, and won credibility for this as well. A colleague in the Illinois legislature, Robert L. Wilson, said that Lincoln "always got right down to the merits of his case, without any nonsense or circumlocution."[21] The *New-York Daily Tribune*, on the eve of Lincoln's Cooper Union speech, said that his "*candor* of statement" was one of the "distinguishing characteristics of his political addresses."[22] And the *New York Sun*, writing of the First Inaugural Address, said that "the reasonableness and *candor* of the whole are such as to invite very little comment beyond general approval."[23]

He was candid about his aversion to slavery, from his first speeches against the Kansas-Nebraska Act. At Peoria, in his opening salvo against that Act, he said: "This *declared* indifference, but as I must think, covert *real* zeal for the spread of slavery, I can not but hate. I hate it because of the monstrous injustice of slavery itself."[24]

As president, he made the same point in his letter to James C. Conkling: "to be plain, you are dissatisfied with me about the negro. . . . I certainly wish that all men could be free, while I suppose you do not."[25] The *New-York Daily Tribune* complimented this candor, saying:

> Disclaiming the arts of the diplomatist, the cunning of the politician, and the graces of rhetoric, he comes straight to the points he wants to discuss, and talks as a plain, earnest man to men anxious to hear what he has to say and to know what he means. He dodges nothing.[26]

The same was true the next year in his letter to Albert Hodges: "I am naturally anti-slavery," he said.[27] "If slavery is not wrong, nothing is wrong. I can not remember when I did not so think, and feel."[28]

When Horace Greeley challenged Lincoln on not making emancipation a war goal, Lincoln's reply likewise went right to the point, in its first sentence after the polite introduction—"As to the policy I 'seem to be pursuing' as you say, I have not meant to leave any one in doubt. I would save the Union"[29]—and then hammered that point throughout its remaining ten sentences.

A Vermont newspaper, in commenting on Lincoln's Second Annual Message to Congress said that it had "the same directness" that had "characterized all his public official papers."[30] The *Chicago Tribune* similarly complimented Lincoln's Third Annual Message to Congress a year later, saying: "He evidently does not believe that language was given to *conceal* ideas."[31] And a Pennsylvania newspaper, writing about the same message to Congress, said that Lincoln was "perhaps more *candid* than any statesman of his time, certainly as *honest* and *straightforward* as any," and that "he never fails to convince even his enemies of his *sincerity*."[32]

Lincoln also won credibility with his modesty. Chief Justice Scott wrote that "no lawyer on the circuit was more unassuming than was Mr. Lincoln," and that he "arrogated to himself no superiority over any one—not even the most obscure member of the bar"[33] or jurors. To the contrary, Scott wrote, Lincoln

> had the happy and unusual faculty of making the jury believe they—and not he—were trying the case. In that mode of presenting a case he had few if any equals. An

attorney makes a grave mistake if he puts too much of <u>himself</u> into his argument before the jury or before the court. Mr. Lincoln kept himself in the back ground, and apparently assumed nothing more than to be an <u>assistant</u> counsel to the court or the jury on whom the primary responsibility for the final decision of the case in fact rested.[34]

John Strong, an Illinois contemporary, said that Lincoln would tell a jury, "This is the way it seems to me," rather than "This is the way it is."[35] He shared his conclusions with the jury, but let them feel they had come to their conclusions on their own. He understood what psychologists say about persuasion: take the audience to the door, but let them feel they have walked in on their own.

He was equally modest in his political speeches, conveying to his political audiences the same impression that he conveyed to his juries: all he cared about was helping them do their job. He began his speech at Cooper Union, the speech that would make him president, with a most modest disclaimer[36] (see the Preface above), and ended his forceful letter to Albert Hodges with a similar one:

> I add a word which was not in the verbal conversation. In telling this tale I attempt no compliment to my own sagacity. I claim not to have controlled events, but confess plainly that events have controlled me.[37]

The editor John Clarke, who heard essentially the Cooper Union speech in Manchester, New Hampshire, wrote that Lincoln "seems to *forget all about himself* while talking, and to be entirely engrossed in the welfare of his hearers."[38]

Lincoln also minimized the word "I" in the speeches of his mature years, and never used it to draw credit or attention to himself. In perhaps his two most famous speeches, the Gettysburg Address and the Second Inaugural, the first does not use "I" at all,[39] and the second uses it only once, in the simple phrase "I trust."[40] By distinct contrast, the young

Lincoln, in an 1839 speech against a Democratic monetary proposal, used the word "I" seven times *in just one sentence* and *eighty-six times* overall.[41]

The Second Inaugural was a picture of modesty even when less than that might have been accepted. With the war now all but over, and success won after so many difficult years, there might have been some tone of triumph, but there was none, and the public noticed. The *New York Herald* wrote that Lincoln's address defied the expectations that "its tone would have been decidedly more congratulatory and sanguine,"[42] and the *New York Times* said that Lincoln had made "no boasts of what he has done," instead offering an address marked by "extreme simplicity," "calmness," "*modesty*," and "reserve."[43]

Lincoln also won credibility by adhering to one of his base principles on persuasion—"If you would win a man to your cause, *first* convince him that you are his sincere friend."[44]

Charles Maltby, a lifelong friend who served with Lincoln in the Black Hawk War and was his business partner in Indiana, said that Lincoln talked to people in a way that made them feel that they had met not only "a friend," but "one near as a brother."[45]

Chief Justice Scott similarly said that Lincoln treated everyone on the judicial circuit "with that simplicity and kindness that friendly neighbors manifest in their relations with each other."[46] James S. Ewing, who was inspired to become a lawyer after watching Lincoln in the courtroom, said that by the time Lincoln finished selecting a jury, "each member . . . felt that the great lawyer was his friend and was relying upon him as a juror to see that no injustice was done."[47] A juror said the same thing about one of Lincoln's closing arguments: "he talked to the jurors, one at a time, like an old friend who wanted to reason it out with them and make it as easy as possible for them to find the truth."[48]

Lincoln conveyed the same sense of friendship even to his opponents. J. Henry Shaw, an assistant prosecutor in the Duff Armstrong trial, wrote that, in the courtroom, the mature Lincoln "never vexed an opponent."[49] To the contrary, Shaw said, Lincoln frequently used "his irresistible *good humour*" to throw his opponent off guard.[50]

This again differed from the younger Lincoln, who often resorted to stories and other methods "for the purpose of rendering his opponents ridiculous."[51] Chief Justice Scott said that even as of 1840, when the young

Lincoln was still in the early years of his political and courtroom careers, he nonetheless "had no equals in the state" in this.[52] One example in particular showed what Scott meant. Another young lawyer and politician, Jesse Thomas, criticized Lincoln at a rally while Lincoln was absent, and Lincoln savagely lit into Thomas upon returning, as Lincoln's law partner William Herndon later described:

> The substance of his [Lincoln's] speech on this occasion was not so memorable as the manner of its delivery. He felt the sting of Thomas's allusions, and for the first time, on the stump or in public, resorted to mimicry for effect. In this, as will be seen later along, he was without a rival. He imitated Thomas in gesture and voice, at times caricaturing his walk and the very motion of his body. Thomas, like everybody else, had some peculiarities of expression and gesture, and these Lincoln succeeded in rendering more prominent than ever. The crowd yelled and cheered as he continued. Encouraged by these demonstrations, the ludicrous features of the speaker's performance gave way to intense and scathing ridicule.[53]

Lincoln's performance devastated Thomas, Herndon said.

> The exhibition goaded him to desperation. He ... actually gave way to tears. ... the next day it was the talk of the town, and for years afterwards it was called the "skinning" of Thomas.[54]

But Herndon also noted that Lincoln's attack was uncharacteristic, and the cause of substantial remorse:

> The whole thing was so unlike Lincoln, it was not soon forgotten either by his friends or enemies. I heard him afterwards say that the recollection of his conduct that evening filled him with the deepest chagrin. He felt that he had gone too far, and to rid his good-nature of a load, hunted up Thomas and made ample apology.[55]

As that apology showed, even though Lincoln could readily "skin" an opponent if he wanted to, his "norm" was good will, even while young, and especially when older. He conveyed it, in part, in his face, which although homely, was seen as "genial and kind."[56] James Garfield, another future president who, like Lincoln, would also suffer assassination, wrote after seeing Lincoln for the first time, in early 1861 on Lincoln's trip east to be inaugurated, that "through all his awkward homeliness there is a look of transparent, genuine *goodness*, which at once reaches your heart, and makes you trust and love him."[57]

Lincoln also conveyed good will in his words. In just the third sentence of his Peoria speech, he said: "I do not propose to question the patriotism, or to assail the motives of any man, or class of men; but rather to strictly confine myself to the naked merits of the question."[58] And in the same speech and others, he did not condemn southerners as bad people. He said instead:

> They are just what we would be in their situation. If slavery did not now exist amongst them, they would not introduce it. If it did now exist amongst us, we should not instantly give it up. . . .
>
> . . . I surely will not blame them for not doing what I should not know how to do myself.[59]

His approach was noticed. Reporting on Lincoln's speeches for Republican John Fremont in the 1856 presidential campaign, a newspaper wrote that Lincoln's "language is pure and respectful, he attacks no man's character or motives, but fights with arguments."[60] Before the Cooper Union speech, the *New-York Daily Tribune* similarly wrote that "a *chivalrous courtesy* to opponents, and a *broad genial humor*" were "distinguishing characteristics of his [Lincoln's] political addresses,"[61] and Lincoln showed that in the speech he then gave, which the next day's edition of the paper called "one of the *happiest* . . . political arguments ever made in this City."[62]

The editor John Clarke wrote of how Lincoln's happy demeanor charmed his audience, even those who disagreed with him:

> So great a vein of *pleasantry* and *good nature* pervades what he says, . . . he keeps his hearers in a *smiling mood* with their mouths open ready to swallow all he says. . . .
>
> He is *never offensive,* and steals away willingly into his train of belief persons who were opposed to him.[63]

Consistent with this, southern sympathizers who heard Lincoln at Cooper Union said, "'I like that man, [even] if I don't agree with him.' 'He is a good fellow. . . .' 'He doesn't make you mad as [the abolitionists] Garrison and Phillips do.'"[64]

Good will then marked President Lincoln's approach to persuasion from his first words. As William McKinley later noted, Lincoln's First Inaugural "addressed the men of the South, as well as the North, as his *'countrymen' one and all.*"[65] Noah Brooks likewise said that "generosity breathed in every line" of that address,[66] and Indiana politician George W. Julian said that its "tone of moderation, tenderness, and good-will . . . made a profound impression in his [Lincoln's] favor."[67]

Carl Schurz wrote in the same vein, saying that the address, rather than the "flaming anti-slavery manifesto" that "the more ardent Republicans" might have wanted, was instead

> the entreaty of a sorrowing father speaking to his wayward children. In the kindliest language he pointed out to the secessionists how ill advised their attempt at disunion was, and why, for their own sakes, they should desist. . . . It was a masterpiece of persuasiveness.[68]

Lincoln conveyed the same good will in his letters to Horace Greeley and Erastus Corning, without sacrificing the strength of what he said. The *New York Times* complimented Lincoln's art at this, writing that the letter to Corning and his fellow protestors "utterly annihilated the case they thought they had made so strong," but did so "in so *genial* a way that the victims themselves felt like joining in the general applause."[69]

Lincoln then conveyed the same good will to his opponents after his re-election in November 1864, notwithstanding the vitriol of the campaign against him:

> Now that the election is over, may not all, having a common interest, re-unite in a common effort, to save our common country? . . .
>
> . . .
>
> May I ask those who have not differed with me, to join with me, in this same spirit towards those who have?[70]

Lydia Marie Child captured the tone of this speech, writing: "A most beautiful spirit pervaded it."[71] Lincoln's Second Inaugural then kept to that spirit with his message of the highest good will, entreating his fellow citizens to act "with malice toward none; with charity for all."[72]

Lincoln also deftly enhanced his credibility with humor. One observer of the lawyer Lincoln said that "his wit and humor . . . added immensely to his power as a jury-advocate,"[73] and Michael Burlingame describes such a case,[74] in which Lincoln defended an affluent, pro-South colonel whom a newspaper editor sued for $10,000 after the colonel physically whipped him. The editor's case went in very well, and the colonel appeared to be in deep trouble when the time came for Lincoln's closing. Moving very deliberately, Lincoln first took his legs off the table in front of him (courtroom demeanor, at least in that court, was apparently more relaxed in those days), and then slowly took off his coat, his tie, and his vest, while three times picking up a piece of paper from his table, looking at it, and laughing. Each such instance of laughter on his part drew more laughter from the jurors and others in the courtroom, even though they had no idea what he was looking at.

When Lincoln finally spoke, he apologized, but pointed out that the original claim for damages—the piece of paper at which he had three times looked and laughed—had been for only $1,000, not the $10,000 the editor was then seeking, and said with continuing humor that the editor must have changed his mind somewhere along the way and decided that his injury was worth ten times more than he had originally thought.

Lincoln's tactic apparently worked: the jury awarded not the $10,000 that the editor sought at trial, nor even the $1,000 that he had originally asked for, but only $300.

Lincoln was equally known for humor on the campaign stump. When he encountered hostile campaign crowds, he responded with humor and jokes to defuse the mood, in contrast to Douglas, who responded angrily to hostile crowds, called them "Black Republicans," and stormed off the stage. And when Douglas called him "two-faced" in their 1858 debates, Lincoln replied: "If I had another face, do you think I'd wear this one?"

In all these many ways—honesty, sincerity, candor, modesty, the sense of friendship, good will, and humor—Lincoln won and enhanced his credibility. His audiences accepted him as a messenger, and listened openly to what he had to say.

Chapter 9: Clarity

THE REVEREND JOHN P. Gulliver heard Lincoln speak in 1860, and told him on a train shortly thereafter that what had most impressed him was "the *clearness*" of Lincoln's statements.[1] What Lincoln reportedly said in response emphasized how important clarity had been to him all his life. He said that even as a child:

> I used to get irritated when any body talked to me in a way I could not understand. . . . I can remember going to my little bedroom . . . and spending no small part of the night walking up and down, and trying to make out . . . the exact meaning. . . . I could not sleep . . . when I got on such a hunt after an idea, until I had caught it; . . . I was not satisfied until I had repeated it over and over, until I had put it in language plain enough, as I thought, for any boy I knew to comprehend. This was a kind of passion with me, and it has stuck by me; for I am never easy now, when I am handling a thought, till I have bounded it North, and bounded it South, and bounded it East, and bounded it West.[2]

Lincoln's stepmother gave a similar account of the young Lincoln, saying that when old folks were at our house, [the young Abe] was a silent & attentive observer—never speaking or asking questions till they were gone and then he must understand Every thing— even to the smallest thing—Minutely & Exactly—: he would then repeat it over to himself again & again—sometimes in one form and then in another & when it was fixed in his mind to suit him he became Easy and he never lost that fact or his understanding of it. Sometimes he seemed pestered to give Expression to his ideas and got mad almost at one who couldn't Explain plainly what he wanted to convey.[3]

This trait would then carry into adulthood, for both lawyer and politician. Lincoln the lawyer would become known for the "clearness of statement" that he brought to his cases—fellow attorneys said that it "was something remarked by all"[4]—and the same would be true of his political and presidential speeches and writings. The *New-York Daily Tribune,* writing of Lincoln's impending visit to Cooper Union, said that "*clearness* . . . of statement" was yet another of his "distinguishing characteristics,"[5] and the *Chicago Tribune,* writing of Lincoln's 1863 letter to James Conkling, similarly said that the letter "is one of those remarkably clear and forcible documents that come only from Mr. Lincoln's pen."[6]

Lincoln achieved his clarity in a number of ways.

One was to identify his topic right up front, giving his audience an anchor, a framework, against which to organize the information that followed. His speech at Peoria began: "The repeal of the Missouri Compromise, and the propriety of its restoration, constitute the subject of what I am about to say."[7] His House Divided speech similarly began with the four points he intended to address—"*where* we are, . . . *whither* we are tending, . . . *what* to do, and *how* to do it."[8] His speech at Cooper Union likewise identified right up front the recent quote of Stephen Douglas that he intended to "adopt . . . as a text for this discourse."[9]

Lincoln achieved clarity also by pace, intentionally speaking more slowly than the ordinary speaker, about two thirds the normal pace,[10] to let the audience better absorb and follow his points. When he sent the letter to his friend James Conkling to read at Springfield in 1863, he gave but one instruction, which he tactfully called a "suggestion:" "Read it very slowly."[11]

To the same end—pace—Lincoln made liberal use of the comma "as a means of regulating pauses and phrasing,"[12] at times to the consternation of those editing his written messages. He knew that many more persons would *read* what he had to say, or hear it read by someone else, than would actually hear *him* say it, and he wanted the reader to read the words, and to speak them if reading aloud, in the phrasings that Lincoln thought would best make his message clear.

Lincoln also clarified by emphasis, through sound and inflection when he spoke, and italics or capital letters when he wrote, so that the listener or reader would catch the emphasis that Lincoln wanted to convey. At Peoria, he put 133 words of his speech in all capital letters, starting at the beginning with: "I wish to MAKE and to KEEP the distinction between the EXISTING institution, and the EXTENSION of it, so broad, and so clear, that no honest man can misunderstand me, and no dishonest one, successfully misrepresent me."[13]

At Cooper Union, he put in italics virtually the entire paragraph that closed the first part of his speech:

> But enough! *Let all who believe that "our fathers, who framed the government under which we live, understood this question just as well, and even better, than we do now," speak as they spoke, and act as they acted upon it. This is all Republicans ask—all Republicans desire—in relation to slavery. As those fathers marked it, so let it be again marked, as an evil not to be extended, but to be tolerated and protected only because of and so far as its actual presence among us makes that toleration and protection a necessity. Let all the guaranties those fathers gave it, be, not grudgingly, but fully and fairly maintained.* For this Republicans contend, and with this, so far as I know or believe, they will be content.[14]

And then, for even more emphasis, he capitalized every letter of his closing sentence: "LET US HAVE FAITH THAT RIGHT MAKES

MIGHT, AND IN THAT FAITH, LET US, TO THE END, DARE TO DO OUR DUTY AS WE UNDERSTAND IT."[15]

In his presidential messages, Lincoln also often achieved clarity by being concise. His entire letter to Horace Greeley, including his introductory "greeting" and "postscript" closing, was only sixteen sentences. His Emancipation Proclamation was only 637 words, his Gettysburg Address only 272, his letter to Albert Hodges only 817, and his Second Inaugural only 701.

Secretary of the Treasury Hugh McCulloch wrote that when it came to being concise, "it would be difficulty to find his [Lincoln's] superior,"[16] and another writer, speaking of the Gettysburg Address, said that it was "probable that no speaker in recorded history ever succeeded in putting into so few words so much feeling, . . . suggestive thought, and . . . high idealism."[17] The Wheeling *Daily Intelligencer* similarly wrote that the "power to condense is held to be the distinguishing characteristic of great intellects," and compared Lincoln with Daniel Webster on that, noting the remarkable combinations of brevity and depth in both the Gettysburg Address and the Second Inaugural.[18]

Lincoln also clarified by repetition. His cross-examination of the key witness in the Duff Armstrong case had the witness repeat, multiple times, the supposed importance of the moon and its position in the sky. His speech at Cooper Union repeated, multiple times, all or part of Stephen Douglas's statement that *"Our fathers, when they framed the Government under which we live, understood the question just as well, and even better, than we do now."*[19] His 1862 letter to Greeley repeated his theme—"save the Union"—ten times in eight sentences.[20]

And at Gettysburg, as Gary Wills notes, Lincoln repeated multiple words multiple times—e.g., "nation," "conceived," "dedicated," "war," "consecrate," "these dead"—and thereby "interlocks his sentences," which emphasized his themes and made it easier for listeners, or readers, to follow his progression of ideas.[21] Virtually every sentence, except the first and last, is linked to the sentence before and the sentence after it by at least one word or a clear word substitute (such as "it" for "this ground").

Lincoln also clarified by "antithesis, the balanced opposition of words or phrases, [which] would stamp nearly all of . . . [his] greatest writings as president,"[22] as well as his speeches before that. It was one of his favorite devices: take any of his important speeches or writings and there will be antithesis.

Peoria:

> Doubtless there are individuals, on both sides, who would not hold slaves under any circumstances; and others who would gladly introduce slavery anew, if it were out of existence. We know that some southern men do free their slaves, go north, and become tip-top abolitionists; while some northern ones go south, and become most cruel slave-masters.[23]

His House Divided speech:

> We shall *lie down* pleasantly dreaming that the people of *Missouri* are on the verge of making their State *free*; and we shall *awake* to the *reality*, instead, that the *Supreme* Court has made *Illinois* a *slave* state.[24]

Cooper Union:

> We [Republicans] stick to, contend for, the identical old policy on the point in controversy which was adopted by "our fathers who framed the Government under which we live;" while you with one accord reject, and scout, and spit upon that old policy, and insist upon substituting something new.[25]

His First Inaugural:

> In *your* hands, my dissatisfied fellow countrymen, and not in *mine*, is the momentous issue of civil war. . . . *You* have no oath registered in Heaven to destroy the government, while *I* shall have the most solemn one to "preserve, protect and defend" it.[26]

His letter to Horace Greeley was a veritable cascade of antitheses in just twelve sentences:[27]

Save the Union versus **save slavery**.
Save the Union versus **destroy slavery**.
Save the Union versus **save or destroy slavery**.
Free **no slaves** versus free **all slaves**.
Free some slaves versus **not free others**.
What I **do** versus what I **forbear**.
Help to save the Union versus **not help**.
Hurt the cause versus **help** the cause.
Do **less** versus do **more**.
Correct versus **adopt**.
Errors versus **new views / true views**.
Official duty versus **personal wish**.

His letter to Erastus Corning: "Must I shoot a simple-minded soldier boy who deserts, while I must not touch a hair of a wiley agitator who induces him to desert?"[28]

His letter to James Conkling: "You say you will not fight to free negroes. Some of them seem willing to fight for you."[29]

His Gettysburg Address: "The world will little note, nor long remember what we say here, but it can never forget what they did here."[30]

His Second Inaugural:

> Both parties deprecated war; but one of them would *make* war rather than let the nation survive; and the other would *accept* war rather than let it perish. . . .
>
> . . . until every drop of blood drawn with the lash, shall be paid by another drawn with the sword."[31]

Lincoln further clarified by "illustrations," in court and out. They were images, conveyed in stories and anecdotes, to make or emphasize a point. "They say I tell a great many stories," he said,

> I reckon I do, but I have found in the course of a long experience that common people, . . . take them as they

run, are more easily influenced and informed through the medium of a broad illustration than in any other way.[32]

Lincoln elaborated on this point on another occasion, when a drunken army major asked him to "tell us one of your good stories."[33] Lincoln replied that "he only told stories to illustrate points or to avoid tedious discussions and never for sheer amusement."[34] Silas Burt recalled Lincoln's words:

> I believe I have the popular reputation of being a storyteller, but I do not deserve the name in its general sense; for it is not the story itself, but its purpose, or effect, that interests me. I often avoid a long and useless discussion by others or a laborious explanation on my own part by a short story that illustrates my point of view.[35]

His approach worked. Robert L. Wilson, a colleague in the Illinois legislature, said that "no one ever forgets, after hearing Mr. Lincoln tell a Story, either the argument of the Story, the Story itself, or the author."[36] A contemporary lawyer similarly said that while Lincoln's "illustrations were often quaint and homely," they were also

> always clear and apt, and generally conclusive.... His... inexhaustible stores of anecdote, always to the point, added immensely to his power as a jury-advocate.[37]

Chief Justice Scott wrote that, in his use of stories, Lincoln was able to do what few others could. For many lawyers, Scott wrote, trying to illustrate a legal argument with a story or anecdote "would be a most dangerous experiment," but Lincoln "never failed" with it.[38] Lincoln, Scott elaborated,

> always seemed to have an apt story on hand for use on all occasions. If he had no story in stock he could formulate one instantly so pertinent it would seem he had brought it into service on many previous occasions.... That is a

talent akin to the power to construct a parable—a talent that few men possess.[39]

Lincoln showed the same talent as president-elect and president. *New-York Tribune* correspondent Henry Villard noted how adept Lincoln was, as the new president-elect, in using stories with his visitors in Springfield, "to explain a meaning or enforce a point, the aptness of which was always perfect."[40]

That "elites" often looked down on his stories did not matter to Lincoln. His priority was clarity: "As to what the hypercritical few may think," he said, "I don't care."[41]

And some of those elites ultimately came to realize the value of Lincoln's approach. One of them, Edward Bates, Lincoln's attorney general, wrote that Lincoln's "illustrations" at first annoyed him, but that he came to appreciate their effectiveness, their "central role," as Doris Kearns Goodwin calls it, in Lincoln's communicating with the public.[42] The "converted" Bates then complimented Lincoln's "illustrations," in words that sounded like Lincoln's own, saying that "this form of illustration . . . invariably brought home" the point that Lincoln wished to make "with a strength and clearness impossible in hours of abstract argument."[43]

Lincoln also clarified by images from analogies. His speech at Peoria in 1854:

> When we voted against extending the Missouri line, little did we think we were voting to destroy the old line, then of near thirty years standing. To argue that we thus repudiated the Missouri Compromise is no less absurd than it would be to argue that . . . because I may have refused to build an addition to my house, I thereby have decided to destroy the existing house![44]

To make the point that while slavery could easily be prevented from going where it was not, but could not so easily be eliminated where it already was, he used the contrasting images of a snake in the road and one in a child's bed.

> If I saw a venomous snake crawling in the road, any man would say I might seize the nearest stick and kill it; but if I found that snake in bed with my children, that would be another question. I might hurt the children more than the snake, and it might bite them. . . . But if there was a bed newly made up, to which the children were to be taken, and it was proposed to take a batch of young snakes and put them there with them, I take it no man would say there was any question how I ought to decide!
>
> . . . The new Territories are the newly made bed to which our children are to go, and it lies with the nation to say whether they shall have snakes mixed up with them or not.[45]

In response to Chief Justice Taney's statement in the *Dred Scott* decision that attitudes towards "the black man" were "better" now than when the Declaration of Independence and Constitution were adopted, Lincoln begged to differ, with this image:

> All the powers of earth seem rapidly combining against him. . . . They have him in his prison house; they have searched his person, and left no prying instrument with him. One after another they have closed the heavy iron doors upon him, and now they have him, as it were, bolted in with a lock of a hundred keys, which can never be unlocked without the concurrence of every key; the keys in the hands of a hundred different men, and they scattered to a hundred different and distant places.[46]

In his House Divided speech, Lincoln used a carpentry image to support his argument that recent actions by Stephen Douglas, Presidents Franklin Pierce and James Buchanan, and Chief Justice Roger Taney were more than coincidental, and instead served a plan to make slavery constitutional in *all* states:

> But when we see a lot of framed timbers, different portions of which we know have been gotten out at different times and places and by different workmen—Stephen, Franklin, Roger and James, for instance—and when we see these timbers joined together, and see they exactly make the frame of a house or a mill, all the tenons and mortices exactly fitting, and all the lengths and proportions of the different pieces exactly adapted to their respective places, and not a piece too many or too few—not omitting even scaffolding—or, if a single piece be lacking, we can see the place in the frame exactly fitted and prepared to yet bring such piece in—in *such* a case, we find it impossible to not *believe* that Stephen and Franklin and Roger and James all understood one another from the beginning, and all worked upon a common *plan* or *draft* drawn up before the first lick was struck.[47]

At Cooper Union, to the South's argument that if it succeeded in separating from the Union, it would nonetheless be the North that would have the Union's "death" on its hands, Lincoln replied: "That is cool. A highwayman holds a pistol to my ear, and mutters through his teeth, Stand and deliver, or I shall kill you, and then you will be a murderer!"[48]

And in response to Erastus Corning's argument that "the government" could not "constitutionally" do "in time of rebellion" what it could not lawfully do "in time of peace," Lincoln said that he could "no more be persuaded" of this than he could be persuaded "that a particular drug is not good medicine for a sick man, because it can be shown to not be good food for a well one."[49]

And through more than any other device, Lincoln achieved clarity through simplicity, in style and content.

Harold Holzer writes that oratory in Lincoln's time was "high entertainment,"[50] with a style that was bombastic, full of grand flourishes and dramatic gestures. The best public speakers were ordinarily "true performers—men, like Thomas Corwin, who could be counted on to roam the platform and discard their outer garments, one by one," or

Stephen Douglas, "who was known for 'clenching his fists, and stamping his feet.' "[51]

Lincoln's style was the opposite. His law partner William Herndon said that Lincoln

> never sawed the air nor rent space into tatters and rags as some orators do. He never acted for stage effect. He was cool, considerate, reflective. . . . His style was clear, terse, and compact. . . . He despised glitter, show, set forms, and shams.[52]

Chief Justice Scott wrote of Lincoln's "simple and natural" style of presenting the facts, which Scott said "seemed to give the impression, [that] the jury were themselves making the statement."[53] He was equally simple in his political speeches. An observer to an 1859 Lincoln speech in Kansas said that Lincoln "began, not to declaim, but to talk," "in a conversational tone,"[54] and the Ohio Unitarian minister Moncure D. Conway, who also heard Lincoln in 1859, said that the "charm" of Lincoln's "manner was that he had no manner," noting among other things the simplicity of Lincoln's style.[55]

John Hill, a newspaper editor of Lincoln's day, wrote that:

> In making a speech, Mr. Lincoln was the plainest man I ever heard—He was not a speaker, but a talker—He talked to juries + to political gatherings plain sensible candid talk, almost as in conversation, no effort whatever in oratory.[56]

And this style, Hill said, "had wonderful effect."[57]

Lincoln was also simple in content. A Pennsylvania newspaper spoke almost poetically of the clarity that Lincoln achieved through this, saying that he had "beyond all question, the power of dealing with grand subjects in noble simplicity, and the unusual merit of divesting statesmanship of its mystery, and truth of its disguise."[58]

William Jones, Lincoln's former employer, said after hearing Lincoln speak about the tariff issue in 1844, that Lincoln "makes his arguments as plain as the nose on your face. You can't miss the point."[59] A key to this was his choice of words. The oratorical style of the day tended to multi-syllable words that were impressive to the audience, but not always understood. Lincoln, seeking to persuade, used plain words that *everyone* understood. Recalling a Lincoln speech of 1840, a fellow attorney and Whig politician, Albert Taylor Bledsoe, praised Lincoln's "simple, terse, plain, direct English," which "goes right home to the point."[60]

Of the twenty-six words in the first sentence of his House Divided speech, twenty-three have only one syllable. In his Gettysburg Address, which drew praise for its "eloquent *simplicity*"[61] from Edward Everett, the main speaker at the Gettysburg dedication, and perhaps the leading "traditional" orator of that time, more than seventy percent of the words *in the entire speech* are only one syllable. The same is true of his Second Inaugural, which ranks with his Gettysburg Address as his greatest speeches.

The *New York Evening Post* similarly wrote of the "sublime simplicity" of the words in the Emancipation Proclamation and the clarity they leant: "No sophistry can pervert them, no distortion change them, no judicial authority misunderstand them."[62] Harriet Beecher Stowe wrote—approvingly—that Lincoln's state papers "more resembled a father's talks to his children than a state-paper,"[63] and Ida Tarbell echoed a similar thought, again based on her research, writing that Lincoln "never used a word which the dullest juryman could not understand."[64]

Writers of Lincoln's day agreed, saying that he spoke "in the language of an average Ohio or New York farmer,"[65] language "that leaves no one in doubt of the meaning,"[66] words that were "so plain and explicit, that the most pro-slavery flunkey cannot mistake their meaning."[67]

The *New-York Daily Tribune*, writing of Lincoln's letter to Albert Hodges, said that Lincoln had a "rare quality, the ability to make a statement which appeals at once, and irresistibly, to the popular apprehension—what we may call the shrewdly homely way of 'putting things.'"[68]

The *New York Times*, in writing about Lincoln's letter to James Conkling, said: "The most consummate rhetorician never used language more pat to the purpose; and still there is not a word in the letter not familiar to the plainest plowman."[69]

And as noted above, the writer James Russell Lowell perhaps put it best: Lincoln, he said, spoke "as if the people were listening to their *own* thinking out loud."[70]

Lincoln was adamant about using words that everyone would understand. When a government printer suggested that he not use the words "sugar-coated" to describe how southern leaders were promoting their rebellion to the general populace, because the printer thought "sugar-coated" was "undignified," Lincoln disagreed.[71] "That word expresses precisely my idea," he said, "and I am not going to change it. The time will never come in this country when the people won't know exactly what *sugar-coated* means!"[72]

Lincoln's simplicity in statement was something to which he *evolved*. He did not start out that way; he instead, as a young man, at times spoke in the "florid style of oratory" then "in vogue."[73] Albert Taylor Bledsoe, who praised the 1840 Lincoln's "simple, terse, plain, direct English" observed that the Lincoln of just three years earlier (in 1837) had been "most woefully given to . . . *highfalutin* bombast."[74]

In 1838, during this period of "highfalutin" tendency, Lincoln, then twenty-nine, heard Daniel Webster speak in Springfield, Illinois, and may have tried to imitate his style in a lecture that year at the Lyceum.[75] The result was not good: Lincoln's speech was criticized as "spread eagle and vapid oratory."[76]

And a year after that, in 1839, Lincoln stayed with the same style when speaking of a monetary system that Democrats proposed:

> I know that the great volcano at Washington, aroused and directed by the evil spirit that reigns there, is belching forth the lava of political corruption, in a current broad and deep, which is sweeping with frightful velocity over the whole length and breadth of the land, bidding fair to leave unscathed no green spot or living thing, while on its bosom are riding like demons on waves of Hell, the imps of that evil spirit, and fiendishly taunting all those who dare resist its destroying course.[77]

But Lincoln gradually retreated from this style of speech, as William Herndon and Jesse Weik recounted: "he became more eloquent but with less gaudy ornamentation. He grew in oratorical power, dropping gradually the alliteration and rosy metaphor of youth."[78] That evolution to simplicity can be seen in the contrast between Lincoln's descriptions—twenty-five years apart—of the nation's founding fathers and what they achieved.

At the Lyceum, in 1838, age twenty-nine:

> Their's was the task (and nobly they performed it) to possess themselves, and through themselves, us, of this goodly land; and to uprear upon its hills and its valleys, a political edifice of liberty and equal rights.[79]

At Gettysburg, in 1863, age fifty-four:

> Four score and seven years ago our fathers brought forth on this continent, a new nation, conceived in Liberty, and dedicated to the proposition that all men are created equal.[80]

What caused this evolution to simplicity in statement? A leading candidate has to be his more than two decades in the courtroom. Standing daily in front of ordinary citizens, and trying to persuade them, would lead the speaker to use the words those citizens would best understand, since understanding is the first step in persuasion. In any event, whatever the cause, the benefit to his persuasion is clear. As Robert G. Ingersoll—a lawyer, Civil War veteran, political leader, and orator—later said of the Gettysburg Address "the greatest statues need the least drapery."[81]

Chapter 10: Facts

"EVERYONE IS ENTITLED to his own opinion," Daniel Patrick Moynihan said, "but not to his own facts."[1] Facts are objective, and that gives them their power. Lincoln made facts a cornerstone of his cases, in court and out. He researched and mastered them, led with them, argued from them, and challenged his opponents to produce facts to the contrary—*true* facts. And when they failed to do so, he pounced.

Chief Justice Scott wrote, Lincoln's statement of the facts lent "much of the force of his argument" in a case.[2] "When he had in that way secured a clear understanding of the facts," Scott said, "the jury and the court would seem naturally to follow him in his conclusions as to the law of the case."[3]

In his defense of the bridge company in the case involving the steamer and bridge collision on the Mississippi, Lincoln emphasized two sets of facts. One was the importance of "east-west travel"—"now enhanced by the railroad"—to the "astonishing growth" of communities west of the Mississippi.[4] The other consisted of the facts of the accident in question.

As to the importance of east-west travel, Ronald White, Jr. describes Lincoln's approach: "Lincoln, the master of facts, told them that from September 6, 1856, to August 8, 1857, 12,586 freight cars and 74,179 passengers had passed over the rebuilt Rock Island Bridge."[5] By contrast, White further notes, Lincoln "pointed out that during this same time period river traffic was closed 'four days short of four months' due to ice in the river."[6]

As to why the accident in question had happened, Lincoln showed that there had been no less than 959 boat passings under the bridge since that accident, with only seven other cases of any kind of damage, and he explained in detail why the one in question had occurred.[7] Again, Ronald White, Jr.:

> He appeared with a wooden model of [the steamer] the *Effie Afton*. . . . he spoke to the jury of the angular position of the piers, the course of the river, the speed of the currents, the depth of the channel, and the speed of the boat, all to demonstrate that the boat crashed into the pier of the bridge because of the pilot's carelessness and because her starboard wheel had not been working.[8]

Lincoln was just as fact-reliant in his political and presidential speeches and writings. In Congress, Lincoln challenged President Polk to provide proof—*hard facts*—of the "spot" on which American blood had first been shed, and that Mexico, not the United States, had been the aggressor. "Let him answer with *facts*, and not arguments," Lincoln said.[9]

In challenging the Kansas-Nebraska Act in 1854, Lincoln devoted the first twenty percent of his speeches to a factual history of slavery in the colonies and states, and then used further facts to rebut each of the arguments that pro-slavery forces offered in support of the Act. He constantly returned to facts that he had presented and those that Douglas had *not*. In the pattern he would follow in the next six years, through his Cooper Union speech, Lincoln—again the courtroom lawyer—would identify a claim that Douglas had made, "deny" it, and demand that Douglas back it with "proof" or "evidence"—i.e., *facts*. And when Douglas would fail to do so, Lincoln would quickly point that out and claim that Douglas had "defaulted" and was "estopped."

- "That is the fact," he would say.[10]
- "Let the facts be the answer to the argument."[11]
- "The facts of this proposition are not true as stated."[12]
- "What are the facts upon which this bold assertion is based?"[13]
- "That is a mistake, in point of fact."[14]

Lincoln similarly wielded facts in his 1857 speech rebutting Douglas on the *Dred Scott* decision.[15] A writer commenting on that speech said that Lincoln had taken on the *Dred Scott* case "as only Lincoln can," using his skilled presentation of facts to undermine Douglas's argument.[16]

One year later, Lincoln was even more fact-heavy in his House Divided speech,[17] devoting the *first two-thirds* of the speech to the history of pro-slavery efforts, between 1854 and 1858, to extend slavery not only to the territories, but to the free states as well.

Lincoln then leaned just as hard on facts in his seven debates with Douglas that year, using the word "fact" or "facts" sixty-seven times, and its synonym, "evidence," sixty-eight times.[18] And two years later, in his all-important appearance at Cooper Union,[19] Lincoln devoted roughly *the first half* of his speech to his detailed, factual account of how the founding fathers had voted on whether to allow slavery in the territories.

Facts would remain the anchor of his presidential efforts at persuasion. In his June 1863 letter to Erastus Corning, he pointed out that the Constitution expressly allowed the suspension of habeas corpus in times of "rebellion;" the country now faced a "rebellion;" habeas corpus had been adopted both in England and the United States only *after* wars, not during them; and civilian courts were not able to deal with active, simultaneous efforts by thousands of people against the Union.[20]

In his letter two months later to James Conkling and the gathering at Springfield, Illinois, facts were likewise central to his argument. There were only three options for achieving peace, he said: force of arms, abandoning the war effort to save the Union, or compromise. A meaningful compromise could be made only with the "rebellion's" army, which had the only power to enforce any compromise with the North, and that army had communicated *no* interest in a "peace compromise." As for objections to the Emancipation Proclamation:

- under the law of war, "property" can be taken;
- slaves were considered "property" by the South itself; and
- Union commanders had credited the "emancipation policy and the use of colored troops" as "the heaviest blow yet dealt to the rebellion," and with "at least one" of "our most important successes."[21]

Even the short Gettysburg Address led with facts: the nation had been founded eighty-seven years before, on the proposition that all men are created equal; the nation was now in a civil war testing whether that nation, or any founded on that principle, could endure; a great battle in that war had taken place where they now stood; and a portion of that field was now being dedicated to honor those who had died there. Then, on this base of facts, Lincoln offered the "argument" in his address, that the only way truly to honor those who had died there would be to complete the effort for which they had given their lives.

Five months later, Lincoln used nothing but facts, from start to end in his letter to Albert Hodges, making his case for the Emancipation Proclamation and the acceptance of blacks into the Union Army. He noted his early rejection of military emancipation and his unsuccessful effort for compensated emancipation, his judgment that if the Union were to be preserved, its Army needed more men, and that it had received 130,000 additional such men because of the Emancipation Proclamation, with no "loss" to the Union in foreign relations or domestic sentiment. And having so set the stage with facts, he then *emphasized* them as such—"These are palpable facts, about which, as facts, there can be no cavilling. We have the men; and we could not have had them without the measure."[22]

And in his final message to a large audience, his Second Inaugural, Lincoln again led with facts, through more than the first half of the address:

- the scene four years before, with "all thoughts . . . anxiously directed to an impending civil-war;"[23]
- the dread that all had had for such a prospect, and the efforts of all "to avert it;"[24]
- the efforts at that time of those "seeking to *destroy* it [the Union] without war . . . by negotiation;"[25]
- the number of "colored slaves" then in the nation, and their location;[26]
- the "peculiar and powerful interest" that the slaves "constituted;"[27]
- the recognition by all "that this interest was, somehow, the cause of the war;"[28]

- the objective of one side, the South, to "strengthen, perpetuate, and extend this interest," and the government's claimed right to do no "more than to restrict the territorial enlargement" of slavery;[29]
- the expectations of neither side for a war of the "magnitude, or the duration," that had then occurred;[30]
- the expectation of both sides "for an easier triumph, and a result less fundamental and astounding," than had actually occurred;[31]
- the absence of any expectation, by either side, "that the *cause* of the conflict might cease with, or even before, the conflict itself should cease;"[32]
- each side's "read[ing] the same Bible, . . . pray[ing] to the same God," and invoking "His aid against the other;"[33]
- the inability of the prayers of both sides to be "answered;"[34] and
- the failure of the prayers of either side to be "answered fully."[35]

Only then, against such a sobering factual setting, did he offer his suggestion that the war be seen as divine retribution on both sides for a mutually created evil, and that both sides, each now so humbled, should move with "charity for all" and "malice toward none," to reconcile and achieve "a just, and a lasting peace."[36] Tragically, the nation would all too soon thereafter lose his ability to marshal and present facts, his ability to persuade, and the nation's best chance of achieving the post-war peace and reconciliation that he wanted.

Chapter 11: Logic

AND THEN THERE was Lincoln's logic, a staple of his argument noted time and again by observers.

Journalist and Lincoln confidant Noah Brooks called it "sledgehammer."[1] Another journalist, Gideon Welles, called it "clear as crystal,"[2] and yet another, Horace Greeley, said that Lincoln's "command of logic was as perfect as his reliance on it was unqualified," and that Lincoln "was the cleverest logician for the masses that America has yet produced."[3] Lincoln's White House secretary John Hay, educated at Brown, echoed the same thought, saying that Lincoln could "snake a sophism out of its hole, better than all the trained logicians of all schools."[4]

Logic was a staple of Lincoln in the courtroom. He impeached the prosecution's key witness in the Duff Armstrong case with logic: the witness said he could see the alleged blow only because of the light cast by a high moon, but the moon was in fact *not* high at the time of the blow—it was within an hour of setting—and the witness, contrary to what he had testified, thus could *not* have seen the alleged blow.

Logic was likewise a staple of Lincoln's political positions and speeches.

After the election of 1844, a Liberty party member told Lincoln that even though he, the Liberty party member, was against the spread of slavery into Texas, as was the Whig candidate for president, Henry Clay, the Liberty party member could not vote for Clay because Clay was a slaveholder, and because of the religious principle, "We are not to do *evil* that *good* may come."[5] Lincoln responded with logic:

> This general, proposition is doubtless correct; but did it apply? If by your votes you could have prevented the *extention,* &c. of slavery, would it not have been *good* and not *evil* so to have used your votes, even though it involved the casting of them for a slaveholder? By the *fruit* the tree is to be known. An *evil* tree can not bring forth *good* fruit. If the fruit of electing Mr. Clay would have been to prevent the extension of slavery, could the act of electing [him] have been *evil*?[6]

Ten years later, Lincoln's personal notes show him privately and logically testing the arguments for slavery in 1854, and thereby forming his rebuttals to them, months before he included them in his Peoria speech.

> If A. can prove, however conclusively, that he may, of right, enslave B.—why not B. snatch the same argument, and prove equally, that he may enslave A.?
>
> You say A. is white, and B. is black. It is *color* then; the lighter, having the right to enslave the darker? Take care. By this rule, you are to be slave to the first man you meet, with a fairer skin than your own.[7]

He also showed the logical contradiction between slave owners' saying how "good" slavery was for the slaves, and the slave owners' own conduct: "Although volume upon volume is written to prove slavery a good thing, we never hear of the man who wishes to take the good of it, *by being a slave himself.*"[8]

He likewise exposed the logical flaws of the pro-slavery arguments:

- that "equal justice to the south" meant giving slave owners the same right to move slaves into new territories that they had to move hogs, which could be true only if "there is no difference between hogs and negroes;"[9]
- that the unqualified statement in the Declaration of Independence that *all men* are created equal really meant a watered-down, far smaller proposition, i.e., only that "British subjects on this

continent . . . [were] equal to British subjects born and residing in Great Britain;"[10]
- that to oppose the extension of slavery was necessarily to want interracial marriage and "amalgamation," when there was another, readily available option—just leaving the black woman alone;[11] and
- that because the Declaration of Independence, which spoke of aspirations and goals, did not immediately place blacks on an actual equality in all respects with whites, that meant the authors of that document did not intend to include blacks in *any* of the rights with which it said *all* men were endowed.[12]

Carl Schurz recounted the skill with which Lincoln "thrust the sword of his logic through Douglas's adroit sophistries."[13] In his seven debates with Douglas in 1858, Lincoln emphasized the logical inconsistency between Douglas's accepting the *Dred Scott* decision, which held that slavery could not legally be kept from the territories and Douglas's concept of popular sovereignty, under which the people of each territory had the right to decide for themselves whether or not to accept slavery. This, as Noah Brooks noted, was a "glaring inconsistency . . . made conspicuous by Lincoln's merciless logic."[14]

In his fifth debate with Douglas, Lincoln also logically undercut the supposed constitutional argument upon which pro-slavery forces were relying to bring slavery into *all* states, even the free. The pro-slavery argument:

> Nothing in the Constitution or laws of any State can destroy a right distinctly and expressly affirmed in the Constitution of the United States;
>
> The right of property in a slave is distinctly and expressly affirmed in the Constitution of the United States;
>
> Therefore, nothing in the Constitution or laws of any State can destroy the right of property in a slave.[15]

Lincoln, however, pointed out the fault in the minor premise of this argument, and thus the flaw in the argument's logic:

the right of property in a slave *is not* distinctly and expressly affirmed in the Constitution. . . . the Supreme Court and the advocates of that decision may search in vain for the place in the Constitution where the right of property in a slave is distinctly and expressly affirmed.[16]

Even those who disagreed with Lincoln complimented his logic. A prominent slaveholder who heard Lincoln speak in Troy, Kansas in 1859 said that even though he disagreed with Lincoln's conclusions, Lincoln's speech was "the most able and the most logical" that the slaveholder had ever heard.[17]

At Cooper Union, Lincoln brought the issue of slavery to this logical essence:

If slavery is right, all words, acts, laws, and constitutions against it, are themselves wrong, and should be silenced, and swept away. If it is right, we cannot justly object to its nationality—its universality; if it is wrong, they cannot justly insist upon its extension—its enlargement. All they ask, we could readily grant, if we thought slavery right; all we ask, they could as readily grant, if they thought it wrong. Their thinking it right, and our thinking it wrong, is the precise fact upon which depends the whole controversy.[18]

William Cullen Bryant's *New York Evening Post* wrote that the logic in Lincoln's Cooper Union speech enhanced even what was already known: "All this may not be new," the newspaper said, "but it is most *logically* . . . stated in the speech—and it is wonderful how much a truth gains by a certain mastery of clear and impressive statement."[19]

In his letter of August 22, 1862 to Horace Greeley, Lincoln was pure logic. Major premise: I will save the Union. Minor premise: X will or will not save the Union. Conclusion: I will or will not do X.

Lincoln's letter to Erastus Corning in 1863 similarly relied on logic: the Constitution allows the suspension of habeas corpus in times of "Rebellion;"

the country is now in the throes of a "Rebellion;" the Constitution thus now allows the suspension of habeas corpus.

Two months later, in his letter to James Conkling, Lincoln logically showed that "compromise" was not an option for attaining peace, since the only entity with whom discussions of compromise would be meaningful would be the rebellion's army which had shown no evidence whatsoever of inclination to compromise. He then also logically dismantled the argument against the Emancipation Proclamation: enemy "property" may be taken in war; slaves are "property;" slaves may thus be taken.

His letter of April 4, 1864 to Albert Hodges was likewise logic: the Union's armed forces needed more men; the Emancipation Proclamation provided 130,000 more men; the Emancipation Proclamation was thus a good thing. He *defied* anyone to say—logically—that he was *for* the Union cause but *against* the all-important—indeed, essential—boost that the enlistment of freed slaves had given the Union.

Logic commanded even Lincoln's private thoughts. In his 1862 Meditation on the Divine Will, Lincoln logically tried to reconcile the concept of God with the terrible war then raging: "In great contests each party claims to act in accordance with the will of God. Both *may* be, and one *must* be wrong. God can not be *for,* and *against* the same thing at the same time."[20]

Lincoln also enhanced the power of his logic by presenting it in questions, which soften the point, draw the listener in, and let him feel that he has come to the answer on his own, which psychologists say gives a sense of ownership. Lincoln's speeches, as candidate and president, redound with logic by question.

At Peoria in 1854, to make the point that southerners show, by their actions, that they know that "something" is morally wrong about slavery, Lincoln presented facts in declarative sentences, but the logic in questions:

> In 1820 you joined the north, almost unanimously, in declaring the African slave trade piracy, and in annexing to it the punishment of death. Why did you do this? If you did not feel that it was wrong, why did you join in providing that men should be hung for it? . . .

. . .

> And yet again; there are in the United States and territories, including the District of Columbia, 433,643 free blacks. At $500 per head they are worth over two hundred millions of dollars. How comes this vast amount of property to be running about without owners? We do not see free horses or free cattle running at large. How is this? All these free blacks are the descendants of slaves, or have been slaves themselves, and they would be slaves now, but for SOMETHING which has operated on their white owners, inducing them, at vast pecuniary sacrifices, to liberate them. What is that SOMETHING? Is there any mistaking it?[21]

He then gave, in further questions, the logical answer that his questions required, and that his southern listeners already knew:

> And now, why will you ask us to deny the humanity of the slave? and estimate him only as the equal of the hog? Why ask us to do what you will not do yourselves? Why ask us to do for *nothing*, what two hundred million of dollars could not induce you to do?[22]

He similarly used logic by question in his Cooper Union speech. Immediately after the passage quoted above reducing the issue of slavery to one of "right and wrong," for example, he conveyed in three questions his logical argument that Republicans *must* do what is right:

> Thinking it [slavery] right, as they [southerners] do, they are not to blame for desiring its full recognition, as being right; but, thinking it wrong, as we do, can we yield to them? Can we cast our votes with their view, and against our own? In view of our moral, social, and political responsibilities, can we do this?[23]

These are but three of *thirty-four* sentences in the Cooper Union speech that end in a question mark. His House Divided speech has twenty-two, as does his First Inaugural, and the first of his major speeches against the Kansas-Nebraska Act in 1854, the longest of his major speeches (as president or before), has *ninety-nine*.

Turn to any effort by Lincoln at persuasion, and logic will be found at its heart.

Chapter 12: Emotion

BUT AS LOGICAL as Lincoln was, he relied just as much—or more—on emotion, which he believed trumped reason. Indeed, he called emotion "the great high road to . . . [a man's] reason."[1]

He used emotion as a courtroom lawyer: in Duff Armstrong's murder case, he relied not only on the almanac that contradicted the prosecution's key witness, but also on a tearful closing that observers said was so effective that some believed it was that, rather than Lincoln's cross-examination, that won the acquittal.

William Walker, Lincoln's co-counsel in the case, described this part of Lincoln's closing:

> He told of his kind feelings toward the Mother of the Prisoner, a widow, That she had been kind to him when *he* was young, lone, & without friends.[2]

J. Henry Shaw, one of the prosecuting attorneys, likewise described it:

> He told the jury of his once being a poor, friendless boy; that Armstrong's father took him into his house, fed and clothed him & gave him a home &c. the particulars of which were told so pathetically that the jury forgot the guilt of the boy in their admiration of the father.[3]

John T. Brady, one of the jurors in the case, similarly said this:

> Lincoln made a speech which visibly affected everyone in the court room—judge, jury, lawyers and people—relating what a debt of gratitude he was under to Mr. and Mrs. Armstrong for a home when he was homeless and in need, and that Mrs. Armstrong had been a mother to him, and he was only trying to partially repay a debt of gratitude in defending her son.[4]

J. Henry Shaw again, in a different writing:

> There were tears in Mr. Lincoln's eyes while he spoke. But they were genuine. His sympathies were fully enlisted in favor of the young man, and his terrible sincerity could not help but arouse the same passion in the jury. I have said it a hundred times, that it was Lincoln's *speech* that saved that criminal from the Gallows.[5]

Lincoln's ability to use emotion in his persuasion as a lawyer ran the gamut: it was not all "soft" emotion. Chief Justice Scott wrote in 1896 that, when appropriate, Lincoln could exhibit emotion from the other end of the spectrum: "much impatience and at times vehement anger," Scott said, "but . . . always a just indignation."[6] By way of example, Scott singled out a case in which Lincoln represented "an orphan girl that had been betrayed to her ruin," and against whom a witness had given "most disgusting testimony."[7] Scott said that Lincoln "did not believe" that there was "a word of truth" in what the witness said, and that in his closing argument Lincoln "turned upon the offending witness a torrent of invective and denunciation of such severity as rarely ever falls from the lips of an advocate at the bar."[8]

But when Lincoln then spoke of the girl, he did a complete turnabout:

> He suddenly changed his manner of speech and became as tender and gentle as he had just been severe and violent. . . . His words in defence of that friendless girl as she sat alone

in the midst of strangers were gentle, beautiful, and full of tenderest pathos.[9]

Lincoln likewise relied on emotion in his political speeches. Daniel Kilham Dodge wrote that emotion underlay all of Lincoln's best speeches: they

> were always the expression of intense feeling, suggested by some special circumstance. He not only found it difficult to speak when he had nothing to say, but he was unable to find anything to say unless his sympathies were engaged. All of Mr. Lincoln's real contributions to literature are of this occasional class, . . . inspired by devotion to his country and by joy at the prospect of renewed peace and prosperity.[10]

Lincoln's speech at Bloomington in 1856 stirred enormous emotion, as did his speech at Cooper Union in 1860. Carl Sandburg wrote that "reason *and emotion* wove through" Lincoln's Second Inaugural,[11] and General William Tecumseh Sherman wrote that when Lincoln visited the Union soldiers who had just fought the Battle of Bull Run, in July 1861, "Mr. Lincoln stood up in the carriage, and made one of the neatest, best, and *most feeling* addresses I ever listened to."[12]

Addressing the emotion in Lincoln's speeches, Harriet Beecher Stowe wrote that his state papers "have had that relish and smack of the soil, that appeal to the simple human heart and head, which is a greater power in writing than the most artful devices of rhetoric."[13] A reporter at Gettysburg wrote that Lincoln's address "stirred the deepest fountains of feeling and emotion in the hearts of the vast throng before him; . . . scarcely could an untearful eye be seen, while sobs of smothered emotion were heard on every hand."[14] Francis Fisher Browne similarly wrote:

> The simple and sublime words of this short address shook the hearts of listeners. . . . They stood hushed, awed, and melted, as the speaker enforced the solemn lesson of the

hour, and brought home to them, in plain, unvarnished terms, the duty which remained for them to do.[15]

Harper's Weekly contrasted the emotion in Lincoln's speech at Gettysburg with the *lack* of emotion in Edward Everett's. "The oration by Mr. Everett was smooth and cold," *Harper's* said, while

> the few words of the President were from the heart to the heart. They can not be read, even, without kindling emotion. "The world will little note nor long remember what we say here, but it can never forget what they did here." It was as simple and felicitous and earnest a word as was ever spoken.[16]

The Second Inaugural brought similar praise, with Carl Schurz writing that "no American President had ever spoken words like these to the American people. America never had a President who found such words in the depth of his heart."[17]

Lincoln appealed to a variety of emotions. One was the patriotic, which he repeatedly called up in his references to the country's founding fathers and core documents (the Declaration of Independence and the Constitution). Doris Kearns Goodwin writes that Lincoln had the talent of "transporting his listeners back to *their roots* as a people, to the *founding of the nation*—a story that still retained its power to arouse strong emotion and thoughtful attention."[18]

Lincoln leaned heavily on the founding fathers and the nation's history in his pre-presidential speeches at Peoria, Columbus, and Cooper Union, and his speeches as president did the same. His First Inaugural closed with an emotional image of the Revolution: "The mystic chords of memory, stretching from every battle-field, and patriot grave."[19] His speech at Gettysburg opened with the words, "Four score and seven years ago," i.e., eighty-seven years ago, which in November 1863 meant 1776, and then spoke of what the nation's "fathers" had done.[20]

Lincoln also appealed to American pride in what their country meant to the world. His speech at Peoria in 1854:

> Let north and south—let all Americans—let all lovers of liberty everywhere—join in the great and good work. If we do this, we shall not only have saved the Union; but we shall have so saved it . . . that the succeeding millions of free happy people, the world over, shall rise up, and call us blessed, to the latest generations.[21]

His speech at Philadelphia in 1861, on Washington's birthday, spoke of the "great principle or idea" in the Declaration of Independence:

> It was not the mere matter of the separation of the colonies from the mother land; but something in that Declaration giving liberty, not alone to the people of this country, but hope to the world for all future time. It was that which gave promise that in due time the weights should be lifted from the shoulders of all men, and that *all* should have an equal chance.[22]

He closed at Gettysburg with a hope not just for the United States, but for the world: that "government of the people, by the people, for the people, shall not perish from the earth."[23]

Lincoln also evoked emotion by appealing to strongly felt secular concepts, such as justice, simple fairness, freedom, liberty, right and wrong, and duty. At Peoria in 1854:

> Slavery is founded in the selfishness of man's nature—opposition to it, is [in?] his love of justice. . . . Repeal the Missouri compromise—repeal all compromises—repeal the declaration of independence—repeal all past history, you still can not repeal human nature. It still will be the abundance of man's heart, that slavery extension is wrong; and out of the abundance of his heart, his mouth will continue to speak.[24]

And in the same speech, he equated the principle underlying the Kansas-Nebraska Act with the universally hated "Divine right of Kings," under which the King is to do just as he pleases with his white subjects, being responsible to God alone. By the former the white man is to do just as he pleases with his black slaves, being responsible to God alone. The two things are precisely alike.[25]

In his debates with Douglas in 1858, Lincoln attacked the fundamental unfairness of taking from a man the fruits of his labor—without any compensation whatsoever. He said that while "the negro" was not his equal "in many respects," he *was* his equal in the right to reap what he sows.

But in the right to eat the bread, without leave of anybody else, which his own hand earns, *he is my equal and the equal of Judge Douglas, and the equal of every living man.*[26]

A reporter who attended some of the Lincoln-Douglas debates later wrote in his memoirs that "there was nothing at all in Douglas's powerful effort that appealed to the higher instincts of human nature, while Lincoln always touched sympathetic chords."[27]

Lincoln also appealed to emotion with emotion-laden words. In his House Divided speech, Lincoln spoke of "not failing," "standing firm," and gaining "the victory," no matter how long it takes.

We shall not fail—if we stand firm, we shall not fail.

Wise councils may *accelerate* or *mistakes delay* it, but, sooner or later the victory is *sure* to come.[28]

At Cooper Union, his closing similarly invoked a bevy of words designed to evoke emotion: "faith," "right," "might," "dare," "to the end," and "duty."[29]

General William Tecumseh Sherman, in his praise of Lincoln's moving address to the Union soldiers after their defeat at Bull Run, noted how compellingly Lincoln referred to "the *high duties* that still devolved on us,"[30] and Lincoln spoke again of such "duty" at Gettysburg, without using that word itself:

It is for us the living, rather, to be dedicated here to the unfinished work which they who fought here have thus far so nobly advanced. It is rather for us to be here dedicated to the great task remaining before us—that from these honored dead we take increased devotion to that cause for which they gave the last full measure of devotion.[31]

Lincoln also appealed to emotion with heroic images.

At Peoria in 1854, he spoke in valiant terms of those who had risen to meet the surprise and threat of the Kansas-Nebraska Act:

> He [Stephen Douglas] . . . took us by surprise—astounded us—by this measure. We were thunderstruck and stunned; and we reeled and fell in utter confusion. But we rose each fighting, grasping whatever he could first reach—a scythe—a pitchfork—a chopping axe, or a butcher's cleaver. We struck in the direction of the sound; and we are rapidly closing in upon him.[32]

He then invoked a similar image in his House Divided speech of 1858, calling on the memory of how Republicans had "gathered from the four winds, and *formed* and fought the battle through."[33]

His letter to James Conkling in September 1863 abounded in heroic images: the recent capture of Vicksburg ("The Father of Waters again goes unvexed to the sea"); the heroic sacrifices at "Antietam, Murfreesboro, Gettysburg, and on many fields of lesser note;" the many contributions of "Uncle Sam's Web-feet;" and finally the valiant contributions of the Army's recently added "black men" ("with silent tongue, and clenched teeth, and steady eye, and well-poised bayonet").[34]

And Lincoln also appealed to emotions based on the most popular book of the day, the Bible, from which Lincoln borrowed liberally.

He invoked the Bible (John 1:11 and Acts 13:46) in his 1854 speech at Peoria, saying, "He came to his own, and his own received him not, and Lo! He turns unto the Gentiles,"[35] and ending that speech with a religious image: that if those who sought to save the Union succeeded, later generations the world over would call them "blessed."[36]

Joseph F. Roda

In his House Divided speech, his theme sentence, "A house divided against itself cannot stand,"[37] echoed Matthew 12:25 ("Every kingdom divided against itself is brought to desolation; and every city or house divided against itself shall not stand."). And later in the speech, he quoted Ecclesiastes 9:4 when referring to Douglas: "A *living dog* is better than a *dead lion*."[38]

His First Inaugural Address, when addressing the South, invoked the religious sanctity of oaths. "*You* have no oath registered in heaven to destroy the government," he said, "while *I* shall have the most solemn one to 'preserve, protect and defend' it," and he then closed with an appeal to South and North to remain united, under the guidance of "the better angels of our nature."[39]

And after taking his oath of office, he kissed the Bible,[40] silently expressing another religious image.

At Gettysburg, he opened with the words "four score and seven years ago," which spoke of time as the Bible does (Psalm 90:10, which defines a life as "threescore years and ten"), and then immediately followed that with further biblical images, in his words "consecrate" and "hallow," and in his reference to "our fathers," which has a religious symbolism as well as a patriotic one.[41]

In his letter of 1864 to Alfred Hodges, he added a religious postscript, which he had not mentioned in his discussion with Hodges and his two companions earlier that day: that "God alone" could claim control over what lay ahead with the war.[42]

His appeal to religious emotions then reached its zenith in his Second Inaugural Address, the last major speech of his life, and nothing short of a sermon. In its 701 words, he cast the war as punishment from God, on South and North, for two centuries of slavery. He invoked "God," or the synonyms "He," "His," "Him," "the Almighty," or "the Lord" fourteen times; the words "pray" or "prayer" three times;[43] the "Bible" once; and six quotes or paraphrases from the Bible:

- "wringing their bread from the sweat of other men's faces."[44] (Genesis 3:19: "In the sweat of thy face shalt thou eat bread, till

thou return unto the ground; for out of it wast thou taken: for dust thou art, and unto dust shalt thou return.");
- "but let us judge not that we be not judged."[45] (Matthew 7:1: "Judge not, that ye be not judged.");
- "Woe unto the world because of offences! For it must needs be that offences come; but woe to that man by whom the offence cometh!"[46] (Matthew 18:7);
- "the judgments of the Lord, are true and righteous altogether."[47] (Psalm 19:9: "The fear of the Lord is clean, enduring for ever: the judgments of the Lord are true and righteous altogether.");
- "let us strive on to finish the work we are in; to bind up the nation's wounds."[48] (Psalm 147:3: "He healeth the broken in heart, and bindeth up their wounds."); and
- "to care for him who shall have borne the battle, and for his widow, and his orphan."[49] (James 1:27 "Pure religion and undefiled before God and the Father is this, To visit the fatherless and widows in their affliction, and to keep himself unspotted from the world.").

He called for the chastened and redeemed country to go forth "with firmness in the right, as God gives us to see the right," and with the religiously inspired "malice toward none . . . [and] charity for all."[50]

And perhaps most of all, Lincoln appealed to others' emotion through his *own*, especially his passion and conviction, which were also often referred to as his "earnestness." Passion and conviction are contagious: people want to believe, and are drawn to someone who does. Lincoln was such a person. His partner Herndon said that when Lincoln's "gray eye," "face," and "features were lit up by the inward soul in fires of emotion," his

> apparently ugly features sprang into organs of beauty or disappeared in the sea of inspiration that often flooded his face. Sometimes it appeared as if Lincoln's soul was fresh from its Creator.[51]

By contrast, Herndon said, it was the *absence* of emotion that hurt Lincoln on the lecture circuit, the one area of public speaking at which Lincoln failed, by his own admission. "Mr. Lincoln had not the fire . . .

no emotion"[52] as a lecturer, Herndon wrote, in contrast to the passion that characterized his courtroom and political speeches.

Lincoln had entered the lecture circuit in 1838, at the age of twenty-nine, while a young lawyer and in his third term in the Illinois House. His first presentation was to the Young Men's Lyceum in Springfield, Illinois on January 27, 1838, and was entitled "The Perpetuation of Our Political Institutions."[53] He also lectured on temperance, agriculture, and "discoveries and inventions," the latter perhaps being his favorite.[54]

But despite two decades of trying, Lincoln never succeeded as a lecturer. A person who heard him debate Stephen Douglas in 1858 and was much impressed had the opposite reaction to Lincoln's lecture on discoveries and inventions later that year. "People generally were disappointed in his lecture," this person said, "as it was on no particular subject and not well connected."[55] Lincoln was, the person continued, "decidedly inferior to many a lecturer I have heard."[56]

Lincoln himself candidly agreed. "I am not a professional lecturer," he said in 1860, before his election as president.[57] I "never got up but one lecture," he said, presumably referring to his on discoveries and inventions, and even that, he thought, was "rather a poor one."[58]

In any event, while the *absence* of emotion—specifically passion and conviction—may have hurt him in his lectures, the *presence* of it without question helped him in court and politics.

Lawyers who worked with and against Lincoln consistently noted his "earnestness" and "conviction." Attorney William Walker, who assisted Lincoln in the defense of Duff Armstrong, wrote of "the power, & earnestness" in Lincoln's closing speech, and how the "jury & all, Sat as if Entranced" as a result.[59] "I have never Seen," Walker said, "Such mastery Exhibited over the feelings and Emotions of men, as on that occasion."[60] The speech, he said on another occasion, "was the Most Eloquent & Impressive" he had ever heard.[61]

J. Henry Shaw similarly wrote of Lincoln's closing:

> But when he came to talk to the jury (that was always his forte) he resembled Gulliver again; . . . he raised himself in his full power & shook the arguments of his opponent

from him as though they were cobwebs. He took the jury by storm.[62]

In the political arena, an opponent said that even though Lincoln "did not possess the poetry and pathos" that some of his political opponents had, he nonetheless "had an *earnestness* which denoted the strength of his inward convictions and the warmth of his heart."[63]

Lincoln himself put a high value on being "earnest" in speech, and conveying passion and conviction. In his 1844 eulogy of Henry Clay, Lincoln said that Clay's eloquence consisted not of

> elegant arrangement of words and sentences; but rather of that deeply earnest and impassioned tone, and manner, which can proceed only from great sincerity and a thorough conviction, in the speaker of the justice and importance of his cause. This it is, that truly touches the chords of human sympathy.[64]

Lincoln's law partner Herndon wrote that, in Lincoln's captivating closing speech in 1856 at Bloomington, "he had the fervor of a new convert; the smothered flame broke out; enthusiasm unusual to him blazed up; his eyes were aglow with an inspiration; he felt justice."[65]

Chief Justice Scott similarly wrote that when Lincoln came forth to give his speech, "there was an expression on his face of intense emotion seldom if ever seen upon any one before. It was the emotion of a great soul."[66]

A year later, a witness of the emotion that Lincoln conveyed in his speech against the *Dred Scott* decision wrote:

> There was no rant—no fustian—no bombast, but there was something in it of more force and power than these; *the heart felt*, and he gave utterance to *the heart inspirations*, clothed in the eternal maxims of the purest reason.[67]

Henry Villard, a German immigrant who covered the Lincoln-Douglas debates in 1858, gave Douglas higher marks for voice, gestures and rhetorical arts, but Lincoln higher marks for *persuasion*, because of the *conviction* that Lincoln conveyed:

> Yet the unprejudiced mind felt at once that, while there was on the one side a skillful dialectician and debater arguing a wrong and weak cause, there was on the other a thoroughly earnest and truthful man, inspired by sound convictions in consonance with the true spirit of American institutions.[68]

Another reporter, for the *New York Evening Post*, wrote that when Lincoln's emotions became engaged on an issue, "the fire of his genius plays on every feature. . . . you have before you a man of rare power and of strong magnetic influence."[69] Joseph Choate, who heard Lincoln at Cooper Union, similarly wrote: "When he spoke he was transfigured before us. His eye kindled, his voice rang, his face shone and seemed to light up the whole assembly as by an electric flash."[70]

George S. Boutwell, a Republican party founder, politician from Massachusetts, and Secretary of the Treasury under Ulysses S. Grant, recalled that what made Lincoln's First Inaugural in 1861 so memorable was "his simple, *earnest*, persuasive appeals to the South."[71]

A Vermont newspaper wrote in similar terms of Lincoln's Second Annual Message to Congress:

> The *earnestness* and solemnity of the President's closing words cannot fail to reach the heart of every reader. They deserve to be written as the motto of every man who is working to save his country. . . . They are solemn utterances of truth and soberness.[72]

William O. Stoddard, the young newspaper editor from Illinois who became an assistant secretary to Lincoln in the White House, wrote that that Lincoln's passion in speech came through even to an audience of one:

> He is quickly warmed up to the place where his voice rises and his long right arm goes out, and he speaks to you somewhat as if you were a hundred thousand people

of an audience, and as if he believes that something like fifty thousand of you do not at all agree with him. He will convince that half of you, if he can, before he has done with it.[73]

Horace White, the newspaper reporter, wrote that as Lincoln hit stride in his speeches,

> his words began to come faster and his face to light up with the rays of genius and his body to move in unison with his thoughts.... Sometimes his manner was very impassioned, and he seemed transfigured with his subject.... Then the inspiration that possessed him took possession of his hearers also. His speaking went to the heart because it came from the heart. I have heard celebrated orators who could start thunders of applause without changing any man's opinion. Mr. Lincoln's eloquence was of the higher type, which produced conviction in others because of the conviction of the speaker himself.[74]

White, who had "listened at times to nearly all the public speakers of considerable reputation in this country," said in a letter just a month after Lincoln's death that "on those occasions when he [Lincoln] rose to impassioned eloquence," White had "never heard his equal."[75]

Lincoln then further appealed to emotion by combining his passion and conviction with cadence and rhythm, especially in his perorations, which were calls to action that depended on emotion.[76] In this, Lincoln relied heavily on one-syllable words, which when grouped in short phrases lend themselves to a strong beat—BOOM, BOOM, BOOM, BOOM—the cadence to which armies have long marched into battle.

In the penultimate sentence of his House Divided speech, Lincoln used twelve, one-syllable words that stirred emotion: "We shall not fail—if we stand firm, we shall not fail."[77] Similarly, at Dunkirk, New York, in 1861, he grasped the pole of an American flag and uttered fourteen one-syllable words that brought down the house: "I ASK YOU TO STAND BY ME SO LONG AS I STAND BY IT."[78] His secretary John Hay said that it was

Joseph F. Roda

"impossible to describe the applause and the acclamation" that followed this sentence.[79]

At Cooper Union, where he had a similar effect, twenty-four of the twenty-six words in his closing sentence were one syllable, and he put them in all capital letters for even *further* emphasis. "LET US HAVE FAITH THAT RIGHT MAKES MIGHT, AND IN THAT FAITH, LET US, TO THE END, DARE TO DO OUR DUTY AS WE UNDERSTAND IT."[80]

Lincoln's passion and conviction, combined with his emotion-laden words and shortened, rhythmic, and stirring cadence, became the crescendo of a verbal symphony. They did what Lincoln wanted them to do. They touched their target: the heart.

Chapter 13: Conclusion

ABRAHAM LINCOLN MAY be the most *accomplished* advocate the country has ever produced. There have been many Americans adept at making a case, to be sure, but who has *accomplished* more at this than Abraham Lincoln? Who has dealt more successfully, in speech or pen, with issues of the magnitude he faced, much less the *number* of such issues? Who has left speeches more eloquent or lasting than the Gettysburg Address or the Second Inaugural? Who has been a better model of how to make a case?

When Abraham Lincoln took his last breath, his Secretary of War reportedly said, "Now he belongs to the ages."[1] So also do his lessons in persuasion.

Think about your case. Think *hard*. What is its essence, its key issue? What are your best arguments, and as important or more, what are your opponent's?

Avoid the unimportant. Keep your focus on what matters. Let your audience feel that when *you* speak, they should pay attention to every word.

Speak and write with modesty, not self-acclamation. Present your case, not yourself.

Convey honesty, sincerity, and candor.

Be direct. Take the issue head on.

Convey good will, friendship, and humor. Avoid personal attacks.

Be clear. Be simple in manner and content. Use words that everyone understands, words the audience would use in talking about the same thing.

Convey and sharpen your message through images, contrast, and repetition.

Control your pace: let your audience absorb your thoughts.

Know the facts. Lead with the facts. Argue from the facts. Let the facts lead to the conclusions you want, before any conclusions are even mentioned. And if you voice conclusions at all, "share" them with your audience. Do not "impose" them.

Use reason and logic. Test your premises and conclusions. Do they hold together? And do your opponent's?

Remember emotion: you are addressing human beings, not computers. First win the heart. Evoke feeling. Convey *your* emotion, through passion and conviction.

And finally, appeal to the better angels of your audience. Inspire for the good.

These are lessons that Lincoln practiced, and lessons he has left behind, for the ages, and for everyone, in any time, place, or field, who seeks, as did he, to move and shape minds. To persuade. To make a case.

Notes

WORKS FREQUENTLY CITED in these notes have been identified by the following abbreviations:

ALPLC *Abraham Lincoln Papers at the Library of Congress*, Manuscript Division (Washington, D.O.: American Memory Project, [2000-2002], available at http://memory.loc.gov/ammem/alhtml/malhome.html.

CW Abraham Lincoln, *The Collected Works of Abraham Lincoln*, Edited by Roy P. Basler. 8 vols. New Brunswick, NJ: Rutgers University Press, 1953.

HI Douglas L. Wilson and Rodney O. Davis, eds., *Herndon's Informants: Letters, Interviews, and Statements About Abraham Lincoln* (Urbana: University of Illinois Press, 1998).

Part I

Preface

1. Abraham Lincoln, "Address at Cooper Institute, New York City," February 27, 1860, *CW*, 3:522.
2. Doris Kearns Goodwin, *Team of Rivals: The Political Genius of Abraham Lincoln* (New York: Simon and Schuster, 2005).
3. Matthew Pinsker, *Lincoln's Sanctuary: Abraham Lincoln and the Soldiers' Home* (Oxford: Oxford University Press, 2003).

Prologue

1. Abraham Lincoln, "Autobiography Written for John L. Scripps," [c. June, 1860], *CW*, 4:62.
2. Abraham Lincoln, "To Jesse W. Fell, Enclosing Autobiography," December 20, 1859, *CW*, 3:511.
3. *New York Times,* May 7, 1865.
4. George B. McClellan to Mary Ellen McClellan, November 17, 1861, in Stephen W. Sears, ed., *The Civil War Papers of George B. McClellan: Selected Correspondence, 1860-1865* (New York: Ticknor & Fields, 1989), 135.
5. Ward Hill Lamon, *Recollections of Abraham Lincoln 1847-1865* (Chicago: A. C. McClurg and Co., 1895), 231.
6. *Memphis Daily Appeal,* August 30, 1862.
7. Goodwin, *Team of Rivals,* 6.
8. Henry Villard, *Memoirs of Henry Villard, Journalist and Financier: 1835-1900* (Boston: Houghton, Mifflin and Co., 1904), 1:93.
9. Eleanor Atkinson, *The Boyhood of Lincoln* (New York: McClure Co., 1908), 9.
10. *Illinois Journal* (Springfield), October 28, 1847.
11. Villard, *Memoirs of Henry Villard,* 1:93.
12. *New-York Daily Tribune,* June 12, 1860, quoting *Houston Telegraph,* n.d.
13. J. B. McClure, ed., *Abraham Lincoln's Stories and Speeches* (Chicago: Rhodes & McClure Publishing Co., 1896), 78.
14. Horace Greeley, "Greeley's Estimate of Lincoln: An Unpublished Address by Horace Greeley," *Century Magazine* 42, July 1891, 373 (italics in original).

Chapter 1: Born to Speak

1. Sarah Bush Lincoln to William H. Herndon, September 8, 1865, *HI*, 107.
2. Dennis F. Hanks to William H. Herndon, June 13, 1865, *HI*, 42.
3. Douglas L. Wilson, *Honor's Voice: The Transformation of Abraham Lincoln,* 1st Vintage Books ed. (New York: Vintage Books, 1999), 144.
4. "Conversation with Hon. Wm Butler, Springfield, June 13, 1875," in Michael Burlingame, ed., *An Oral History of Abraham Lincoln: John G. Nicolay's Interviews and Essays,* paperback ed. (Carbondale: Southern Illinois University Press, 2006), 20.
5. John Hanks to William H. Herndon, [1865-1866], *HI*, 456.
6. Michael Burlingame, *Abraham Lincoln: A Life,* Johns Hopkins paperback ed. (Baltimore, MD: Johns Hopkins University Press, 2013), 1:65.
7. Robert B. Rutledge to William H. Herndon, [c. November 1, 1866], *HI*, 384-385. Robert B. Rutledge was the son of James Rutledge.
8. Robert B. Rutledge to William H. Herndon, [c. November 1, 1866], *HI*, 384.
9. Burlingame, *Abraham Lincoln: A Life,* 1:74.

10 "Conversation with Hon. J. T. Stuart, June 23, 1875," in Burlingame, ed., *Oral History*, 10.
11 Burlingame, *Abraham Lincoln: A Life*, 1:96.
12 Burlingame, *Abraham Lincoln: A Life*, 1:112.
13 Burlingame, *Abraham Lincoln: A Life*, 1:105.
14 Robert L. Wilson to William H. Herndon, February 10, 1866, *HI*, 202-203.
15 Henry C. Whitney, *Life and Works of Abraham Lincoln,* Vol. 1, *Lincoln the Citizen (February 12, 1809, to March 4, 1861)* (New York: Current Literature Publishing Co., 1907), 127.
16 Old Salem Lincoln League, *Lincoln and New Salem* (Petersburg, IL: Old Salem Lincoln League, 1918), 85.
17 Burlingame, *Abraham Lincoln: A Life*, 1:106.
18 John Locke Scripps, *Life of Abraham Lincoln* (Chicago: Chicago Press and Tribune Co., 1860), 12.
19 Joshua F. Speed (Statement for William H. Herndon), [1865-1866], *HI*, 477.
20 Joshua F. Speed (Statement for William H. Herndon), [1865-1866], *HI*, 478.
21 Joshua F. Speed (Statement for William H. Herndon), [1865-1866], *HI*, 478.
22 Joshua F. Speed (Statement for William H. Herndon), [1865-1866], *HI*, 478.
23 Joshua F. Speed (Statement for William H. Herndon), [1865-1866], *HI*, 478.
24 Joshua F. Speed (Statement for William H. Herndon), [1865-1866], *HI*, 478.
25 Robert L. Wilson, quoted in Whitney, *Lincoln the Citizen*, 140.
26 "Conversation with Hon. Wm. Butler, Springfield, June 13, 1875," in Burlingame, ed., *Oral History*, 21.
27 Ronald C. White, Jr., *A. Lincoln: A Biography* (New York: Random House, 2009), 70.
28 Burlingame, *Abraham Lincoln: A Life*, 1:143.
29 Burlingame, *Abraham Lincoln: A Life*, 1:143.
30 Joseph Gillespie to William H. Herndon, January 31, 1866, *HI*, 181.
31 Burlingame, *Abraham Lincoln: A Life*, 1:150.
32 "Oration of Hon. John M. Palmer, Delivered at Galesburg, Ill., October 7, 1896," in John M. Palmer, *Personal Recollections of John M. Palmer: The Story of an Earnest Life* (Cincinnati: Robert Clarke Co., 1901), 604-605.
33 John M. Scott, "Lincoln on the Stump and at the Bar" December 31, 1896, Ida M. Tarbell Collection of Lincolniana, Allegheny College Pelletier Library, 1.
34 Burlingame, *Abraham Lincoln: A Life,* 1:157, citing *Quincy Whig,* May 23, 1840.
35 Burlingame, *Abraham Lincoln: A Life*, 1:224-225.
36 Elihu B. Washburne in Allen Thorndike Rice, ed., *Reminiscences of Abraham Lincoln by Distinguished Men of His Time* (New York: North American Publishing Co., 1886), 15.

37 James C. Veatch, quoted in *Indianapolis Journal,* November 22, 1896. Sixteen years after that speech, Veatch would play a key role in helping Lincoln win the Republican presidential nomination.
38 Joseph J. Lewis, "The First Published Life of Abraham Lincoln," *Chester County Times* (Westchester, Pennsylvania), February 11, 1860, in William E. Barton, "The Lincoln of the Biographers," *Transactions of the Illinois State Historical Society for the Year 1929*, no. 36 (1929): 83.
39 D. W. Bartlett, *The Life and Public Services of Hon. Abraham Lincoln With a Portrait on Steel* (New York: H. Dayton, 1860), 26.
40 Burlingame, *Abraham Lincoln: A Life,* 1:226, citing David Davis to William P. Walker, Decatur, Illinois, May 4, 1844, David Davis Papers.
41 Lincoln's resolutions would earn the nickname, the "spot" or "spotty" resolutions, because they challenged Polk to establish the "particular spot of soil" on which United States blood had first been shed, and Polk's assertion that Mexico, rather than the United States, was the aggressor. Abraham Lincoln, "'Spot' Resolutions in the United States House of Representatives," December 22, 1847, *CW,* 1:420-422; White, *A. Lincoln,* 150.
42 Burlingame, *Abraham Lincoln: A Life,* 1:270.
43 *Boston Courier,* September 23, 1848.
44 *Boston Daily Advertiser,* September 14, 1848.
45 Governor Henry J. Gardner (statement for Edward L. Pierce), [February-May 1890], *HI,* 699.
46 *Lowell Daily Journal,* September 18, 1848, reprinted in "Speech at Lowell Massachusetts," September 16, 1848, *CW,* 2:7.
47 White, *A. Lincoln,* 159-160, citing *Old Colony Republican* (Taunton, Massachusetts), September 23, 1848.

Chapter 2: Best in the State

1 Lincoln, "Autobiography Written for John L. Scripps," [c. June 1860], *CW,* 4:65.
2 Wilson, *Honor's Voice,* 105.
3 Frederick Trevor Hill, *Lincoln the Lawyer* (New York: Century Co., 1906), 60-61.
4 Lincoln's partnership with John Todd Stuart went from 1837 to 1841, that with Stephen T. Logan went from 1841 to 1844, and that with William H. Herndon went from 1844 until he left for the White House.
5 He "was involved in at least 340 cases in the federal district and circuit courts." Mark E. Steiner, "Abraham Lincoln, Esq.: A Docket That Reflects Then and Now," *ABA Journal* 95 (February 2009): 40.
6 John A. Lupton, "Abraham Lincoln, Esq.: The Common Touch at Trial," *ABA Journal* 95 (February 2009): 41.

7   Daniel W. Stowell, ed., *The Papers of Abraham Lincoln: Legal Documents and Cases* (Charlottesville: University of Virginia Press, 2008), 1:xxxix.
8   Stowell, ed., *The Papers of Abraham Lincoln*, 1:xii.
9   Douglas Brinkley, Foreword to Julie M. Fenster, *The Case of Abraham Lincoln: A Story of Adultery, Murder, and the Making of a Great President* (New York: Palgrave Macmillan, 2007), 16.
10 Stowell, ed., *The Papers of Abraham Lincoln*, 1:xxxvi-xxxvii.
11 Guy C. Fraker, *Lincoln's Ladder to the Presidency: The Eighth Judicial Circuit* (Carbondale, Southern Illinois University Press, 2012), 10.
12 Hill, *Lincoln the Lawyer*, 167; Stephen B. Oates, *With Malice Toward None: A Biography of Abraham Lincoln*, paperback ed. reissued 2011 (New York: Harper Perennial, 2011), 102; Stowell, ed., *The Papers of Abraham Lincoln*, 1:xxxvii-xxxix.
13 Hill, *Lincoln the Lawyer*, 202.
14 Steiner, "Abraham Lincoln, Esq.: A Docket That Reflects Then and Now," 39.
15 Allen D. Spiegel, *A Lincoln, Esquire: A Shrewd, Sophisticated Lawyer in His Time* (Macon, Georgia, Mercer University Press, 2002), 105, 116-151.
16 Hill, *Lincoln the Lawyer*, 259-260.
17 Steiner, "Abraham Lincoln, Esq.: A Docket That Reflects Then and Now," 40.
18 Steiner, "Abraham Lincoln, Esq.: A Docket That Reflects Then and Now," 40.
19 Harry E. Pratt, "Abraham Lincoln's First Murder Trial," *Journal of the Illinois State Historical Society* 37 (September 1944): 245 (on *People v. Truett*).
20 Pratt, "Abraham Lincoln's First Murder Trial," 247.
21 Stephen T. Logan, quoted in Pratt, "Abraham Lincoln's First Murder Trial," 247.
22 Stowell, ed., *The Papers of Abraham Lincoln*, 4:137-192 (on *People v. Harrison*).
23 Stowell, ed., *The Papers of Abraham Lincoln*, 4:1-2.
24 Indictment of William Armstrong and James H. Norris [c. November 1857], reprinted in Stowell, ed., *The Papers of Abraham Lincoln*, 4:4.
25 Indictment of William Armstrong and James H. Norris [c. November 1857], reprinted in Stowell, ed., *The Papers of Abraham Lincoln*, 4:4-5.
26 J. Henry Shaw to William H. Herndon, September 5, 1866, *HI*, 334.
27 Stowell, ed., *The Papers of Abraham Lincoln*, 4:10, citing Judgement, November 5, 1857, Mason County, Illinois Circuit Court Record B, 272-73 and Order, November 5, 1857, Mason County, Illinois Circuit Court Record B, 278.
28 Stowell, ed., *The Papers of Abraham Lincoln*, 4:10.
29 Stowell, ed., *The Papers of Abraham Lincoln*, 4:12.
30 One juror, for example, recalled that Lincoln's questioning elicited testimony from the witness as to the location of the moon "about a half a dozen times." John T. Brady to J. McCan Davis, May 12, 1896, Ida M. Tarbell Collection of Lincolniana, Allegheny College Pelletier Library, 1.
31 Stowell, ed., *The Papers of Abraham Lincoln*, 4:13-14.

32 William Walker to William H. Herndon, June 3, 1865, *HI,* 22-23; J. Henry Shaw to William H. Herndon, August 22, 1866, *HI,* 316.
33 John T. Brady to J. McCan Davis, May 12, 1896, Ida M. Tarbell Collection of Lincolniana, Allegheny College Pelletier Library, 2.
34 William H. Herndon and Jesse W. Weik, *Herndon's Lincoln: The True Story of a Great Life* (Chicago: Belford-Clarke Co., 1890), 2:335.
35 Lawrence Weldon in Rice, ed., *Reminiscences of Abraham Lincoln,* 200.
36 Hugh McCulloch in Rice, ed., *Reminiscences of Abraham Lincoln,* 413.
37 Scott, "Lincoln on the Stump," 11.
38 John T. Richards, "Abraham Lincoln at the Bar of Illinois," in Nathan William MacChesney, ed., *Abraham Lincoln: The Tribute of a Century 1809-1909* (Chicago: A. C. McClurg & Co., 1910), 162.
39 Isaac N. Arnold, "Reminiscences of the Illinois-Bar Forty Years Ago: Lincoln and Douglas as Orators and Lawyers," paper read before the Bar Association of the State of Illinois, Springfield, January 7, 1881 (Chicago: Fergus Printing Co., 1881), 20.
40 Hill, *Lincoln the Lawyer,* 208.
41 Herndon and Weik, *Herndon's Lincoln,* 2:338.
42 Hill, *Lincoln the Lawyer,* 222.
43 Scott, "Lincoln on the Stump," 12.
44 Arnold, "Reminiscences of the Illinois-Bar," 20.
45 White, *A. Lincoln,* 178, citing *Illinois Citizen* (Danville, Illinois), May 29, 1850.
46 Scott, "Lincoln on the Stump," 14.
47 Hill, *Lincoln the Lawyer,* 249-250.
48 White, *A. Lincoln,* 211.
49 White, *A. Lincoln,* 212. When the case was transferred to Cincinnati for trial, however, the defense team unceremoniously dumped Lincoln without telling him, and then ignored him when he showed up in Cincinnati for the trial, even in the hotel where they all stayed. Among the members of that defense team, and a leader in the insulting behavior toward Lincoln, was Edwin Stanton, Goodwin, *Team of Rivals,* 174-175, later one of Lincoln's opponents for the Republican presidential nomination in 1860, thereafter Lincoln's Secretary of War, and ironically the person who would bestow the compliment to Lincoln—"Now he belongs to the ages"—when Lincoln died. John Hay and John George Nicolay, "Abraham Lincoln: The Fourteenth of April," *Century Magazine* 39, January 1890, 436.
50 Burlingame, *Abraham Lincoln: A Life,* 1:337; White, *A. Lincoln,* 241-242.
51 John J. Duff, *A. Lincoln, Prairie Lawyer* (New York: Rinehart & Co., 1960), 129, citing Lionel P. Lacey to John Williams, July 27, 1858. *Black-Williams Papers,* Illinois State Historical Library.
52 Steiner, "Abraham Lincoln, Esq.: A Docket That Reflects Then and Now," 39.

53 Burlingame, *Abraham Lincoln: A Life*, 1:311, 338.
54 Steiner, "Abraham Lincoln, Esq.: A Docket That Reflects Then and Now," 40.
55 Douglas Wilson writes: Lincoln "lives in legend as a trial lawyer... but his skills as an appeals lawyer, whose arguments were submitted in writing to a panel of judges, though less recognized, may have been more impressive." Douglas L. Wilson, *Lincoln's Sword: The Presidency and the Power of Words* (New York: Alfred A. Knopf, 2006), 4-5. Michael Burlingame similarly notes: "For all his acknowledged skill as a jury-trial lawyer, Lincoln was even more successful on the appellate level." Burlingame, *Abraham Lincoln: A Life*, 1:334.
56 David Herbert Donald, *Lincoln* (New York: Simon & Schuster, 1995), 144.
57 White, *A. Lincoln*, 169.
58 Oates, *With Malice Toward None*, 104.
59 Duff, *A. Lincoln, Prairie Lawyer*, 243.
60 Donald, *Lincoln*, 155.
61 Donald, *Lincoln*, 155.
62 Donald, *Lincoln*, 143.

Chapter 3: The Road to the White House

1 36 degrees, 30 minutes north latitude.
2 White, *A. Lincoln*, 196.
3 *Illinois Journal*, September 2, 1854, reprinted in "Speech at Winchester, Illinois," August 26, 1854, *CW*, 2:227.
4 *Weekly Pantagraph* (Bloomington, Illinois), September 20, 1854, reprinted in "Speech at Bloomington, Illinois," *CW*, 2:230-233.
5 White, *A. Lincoln*, 197-198.
6 White, *A. Lincoln*, 198.
7 White, *A. Lincoln*, 198-199.
8 *Illinois Journal*, October 5, 1854, reprinted in "Speech at Springfield, Illinois," October 4, 1854, *CW*, 2:240-247.
9 Horace White, *The Lincoln and Douglas Debates: An Address Before the Chicago Historical Society, February 17, 1914* (Chicago: University of Chicago Press, 1914), 12.
10 Goodwin, *Team of Rivals*, 164.
11 Abraham Lincoln, "Speech at Peoria, Illinois," October 16, 1854, *CW*, 2:247-283. Lincoln also added to his Peoria speech a rebuttal to the reply that Douglas had given to Lincoln's Springfield speech.
12 Burlingame, *Abraham Lincoln: A Life*, 1:370; Eric Foner, *The Fiery Trial: Abraham Lincoln and American Slavery* (New York: W.W. Norton & Co., 2010), 65; Wilson, *Lincoln's Sword*, 37. It is because the speech was published after it was given in Peoria that it has become known as Lincoln's "Peoria" speech, even

though he first gave the main part of it in Springfield. "Speech at Springfield, Illinois," October 4, 1854, *CW*, 2:240 n.1; Oates, *With Malice Toward None*, 114.
13 Which ultimately became Illinois, Indiana, Michigan, Ohio, Wisconsin, and part of Minnesota.
14 Which ultimately became all or part of Arkansas, Colorado, Iowa, Kansas, Louisiana, Minnesota, Missouri, Montana, Nebraska, North Dakota, Oklahoma, South Dakota, and Wyoming. Some sources also include parts of Texas and New Mexico in this list.
15 Lincoln, "Speech at Peoria, Illinois," October 16, 1854, *CW*, 2:255.
16 Lincoln, "Speech at Peoria, Illinois," October 16, 1854, *CW*, 2:255 (italics in original).
17 Lincoln, "Speech at Peoria, Illinois," October 16, 1854, *CW*, 2:256.
18 Lincoln, "Speech at Peoria, Illinois," October 16, 1854, *CW*, 2:257.
19 Lincoln, "Speech at Peoria, Illinois," October 16, 1854, *CW*, 2:261.
20 Lincoln, "Speech at Peoria, Illinois," October 16, 1854, *CW*, 2:262.
21 Lincoln, "Speech at Peoria, Illinois," October 16, 1854, *CW*, 2:262 (italics in original).
22 Lincoln, "Speech at Peoria, Illinois," October 16, 1854, *CW*, 2:264.
23 Lincoln, "Speech at Peoria, Illinois," October 16, 1854, *CW*, 2:264.
24 Lincoln, "Speech at Peoria, Illinois," October 16, 1854, *CW*, 2:264.
25 Lincoln, "Speech at Peoria, Illinois," October 16, 1854, *CW*, 2:264 (capitalization in original).
26 Lincoln, "Speech at Peoria, Illinois," October 16, 1854, *CW*, 2:264.
27 Lincoln, "Speech at Peoria, Illinois," October 16, 1854, *CW*, 2:264.
28 Lincoln, "Speech at Peoria, Illinois," October 16, 1854, *CW*, 2:265 (capitalization in original).
29 Lincoln, "Speech at Peoria, Illinois," October 16, 1854, *CW*, 2:264-265.
30 Lincoln, "Speech at Peoria, Illinois," October 16, 1854, *CW*, 2:275.
31 Lincoln, "Speech at Peoria, Illinois," October 16, 1854, *CW*, 2:276.
32 Lincoln, "Speech at Peoria, Illinois," October 16, 1854, *CW*, 2:276.
33 Hill, *Lincoln the Lawyer*, 264.
34 Hill, *Lincoln the Lawyer*, 267.
35 Reportedly at the root of Lincoln's opposition were the protests of his wife, who thought he deserved to be a candidate for the United States Senate seat that would be up for election in February of the next year. Whitney, *Lincoln the Citizen*, 150.
36 White, *A. Lincoln,* 205.
37 Goodwin, *Team of Rivals,* 186; White, *A. Lincoln,* 220.
38 Burlingame, *Abraham Lincoln: A Life*, 1:420; Joseph Medill to the editor of *McClure's Magazine,* May 15, 1896, in "'Lincoln's Lost Speech,'" *McClure's Magazine* 7, September 1896, 322.

39 Herndon and Weik, *Herndon's Lincoln*, 2:384.
40 Scott, "Lincoln on the Stump," 19-20.
41 Jesse K. Dubois, quoted in Jesse W. Weik, *The Real Lincoln: A Portrait* (Boston: Houghton Mifflin Co., 1922), 257.
42 The convention selected New Jersey's United States Senator William Dayton for the vice presidential spot.
43 White, *A. Lincoln*, 228.
44 White, *A. Lincoln*, 228.
45 Oates, *With Malice Toward None*, 128-129.
46 Abraham Lincoln, "Speech at Kalamazoo, Michigan," August 27, 1856, *CW*, 2:361-366.
47 Lincoln, "Speech at Kalamazoo, Michigan," August 27, 1856, *CW*, 2:361.
48 *Dred Scott v. Sanford*, 60 U.S. 393 (1857).
49 The court split along party lines, seven Democrats voting for the decision, and the two Republicans dissenting. While each of the nine justices wrote his own opinion, the opinion by Chief Justice Taney, with which the other six Democrats concurred, became the opinion for which the case is known. Oates, *With Malice Toward None*, 131.
50 White, *A. Lincoln*, 237.
51 Abraham Lincoln, "Speech at Springfield, Illinois," June 26, 1857, *CW*, 2:398-410.
52 Oates, *With Malice Toward None*, 135.
53 Lincoln, "Speech at Springfield, Illinois," June 26, 1857, *CW*, 2:403.
54 Lincoln, "Speech at Springfield, Illinois," June 26, 1857, *CW*, 2:403.
55 Lincoln, "Speech at Springfield, Illinois," June 26, 1857, *CW*, 2:403 (italics in original).
56 Lincoln, "Speech at Springfield, Illinois," June 26, 1857, *CW*, 2:403.
57 Lincoln, "Speech at Springfield, Illinois," June 26, 1857, *CW*, 2:404.
58 Lincoln, "Speech at Springfield, Illinois," June 26, 1857, *CW*, 2:406.
59 Lincoln, "Speech at Springfield, Illinois," June 26, 1857, *CW*, 2:407 (italics in original).
60 Lincoln, "Speech at Springfield, Illinois," June 26, 1857, *CW*, 2:405.
61 Lincoln, "Speech at Springfield, Illinois," June 26, 1857, *CW*, 2:405 (italics in original).
62 Lincoln, "Speech at Springfield, Illinois," June 26, 1857, *CW*, 2:406.
63 Lincoln, "Speech at Springfield, Illinois," June 26, 1857, *CW*, 2:406 (italics in original).
64 Lincoln, "Speech at Springfield, Illinois," June 26, 1857, *CW*, 2:407-408.
65 Lincoln, "Speech at Springfield, Illinois," June 26, 1857, *CW*, 2:405 (italics in original).
66 Lincoln, "Speech at Springfield, Illinois," June 26, 1857, *CW*, 2:408.

67 Lincoln, "Speech at Springfield, Illinois," June 26, 1857, *CW*, 2:408.
68 Oates, *With Malice Toward None*, 135.
69 Correspondence, June 30, 1857, in *New-York Daily Tribune*, July 6, 1857.
70 Abraham Lincoln, "'A House Divided:' Speech at Springfield, Illinois," June 16, 1858, *CW*, 2:461-469.
71 Lincoln, "'A House Divided:' Speech at Springfield, Illinois," June 16, 1858, *CW*, 2:465 (italics in original).
72 Lincoln, "'A House Divided:' Speech at Springfield, Illinois," June 16, 1858, *CW*, 2:467 (italics in original).
73 Lincoln, "'A House Divided:' Speech at Springfield, Illinois," June 16, 1858, *CW*, 2:467 (italics in original).
74 Lincoln, "'A House Divided:' Speech at Springfield, Illinois," June 16, 1858, *CW*, 2:468 (italics in original).
75 Lincoln, "'A House Divided:' Speech at Springfield, Illinois," June 16, 1858, *CW*, 2:468-469 (italics in original).
76 Oates, *With Malice Toward None*, 144.
77 Oates, *With Malice Toward None*, 144.
78 Stephen Douglas, quoted in Archibald L. Bouton, introduction to Abraham Lincoln, *The Lincoln and Douglas Debates* (New York: Henry Holt and Co., 1905), xxxviii.
79 As Illinois and the midwest were then known. Stephen Douglas, quoted in Bouton, introduction to Abraham Lincoln, *The Lincoln and Douglas Debates*, xxxviii (italics added).
80 Stephen Douglas, quoted in Bouton, introduction to Abraham Lincoln, *The Lincoln and Douglas Debates*, xxxviii.
81 Mike Pride, "The First N.H. Primary?," *Boston Globe*, July 11, 2010.
82 Francis Lynde Stetson to Horace White, December 7, 1908, in Horace White, *The Life of Lyman Trumbull* (Boston: Houghton Mifflin Co., 1913), 40 n.1.
83 White, *A. Lincoln*, 262.
84 "The Campaign in Illinois," *Boston Daily Advertiser,* August 28, 1858, as quoted in Edwin Erle Sparks, ed., *The Lincoln-Douglas Debates of 1858* (Springfield: Illinois State Historical Library, 1908), 1:130-131. Illinois had nine congressional districts, the other two being Chicago and Springfield, where Douglas and Lincoln had each recently spoken.
85 Bouton, introduction to Abraham Lincoln, *The Lincoln and Douglas Debates*, xliv.
86 White, *A. Lincoln*, 289, quoting *Chicago Press & Tribune*, November 10, 1858.
87 Goodwin, *Team of Rivals*, 224.
88 Burlingame, *Abraham Lincoln: A Life*, 1:565.

89   Stephen A. Douglas, "Popular Sovereignty in the Territories: The Dividing Line Between Federal and Local Authority," *Harper's New Monthly Magazine* 19, September 1959, 527.
90   Stephen A. Douglas, Speech at Columbus, Ohio, September 7, 1959, in Harry V. Jaffa and Robert W. Johannsen, eds., *In the Name of the People: Speeches and Writings of Lincoln and Douglas in the Ohio Campaign of 1859* (Columbus: Ohio State University Press, 1959), 135.
91   Abraham Lincoln, "Speech at Columbus, Ohio," September 16, 1859, *CW*, 3:400-425.
92   Lincoln first refuted a statement in the local newspaper that he, Lincoln, was for black suffrage, and then went squarely at Douglas's recent article and speech.
93   Lincoln, "Speech at Columbus, Ohio," September 16, 1859, *CW*, 3:405.
94   Lincoln, "Speech at Columbus, Ohio," September 16, 1859, *CW*, 3:409.
95   Lincoln, Speech at Columbus, Ohio," September 16, 1859, *CW*, 3:410.
96   Lincoln, "Speech at Columbus, Ohio," September 16, 1859, *CW*, 3:416.
97   Francis P. Blair, Jr. to Abraham Lincoln, October 18, 1859, *ALPLC*.
98   Burlingame, *Abraham Lincoln: A Life*, 1:569, citing Indianapolis *Daily State Sentinel*, September 26, 1859, quoted in Elmer Duane Elbert, "Southern Indiana Politics on the Eve of the Civil War, 1858-1861" (Ph.D. dissertation, Indiana University, 1967), 103-104.
99   Daniel Webster Wilder to George W. Martin, April 22, 1902, in *Transactions of the Kansas State Historical Society, 1901-1902* 7 (1902): 536-537 n. The reported speaker was Benjamin F. Stringfellow, who would later become an officer in the Confederate Army.
100 *Randolph County Journal* (Winchester, Indiana), September 22, 1959.
101 *Cincinnati Gazette*, reprinted in *Illinois State Journal* (Springfield, Illinois), October 7, 1859.
102 Harriet Beecher Stowe famously authored *Uncle Tom's Cabin*.
103 Herndon and Weik, *Herndon's Lincoln*, 3:454.
104 Weldon in Rice, ed., *Reminiscences of Abraham Lincoln*, 207.
105 Burlingame, *Abraham Lincoln: A Life*, 1:582-583.
106 "Lincoln's Life Work: Lecture by Mr. Choate at Edinburgh Philosophical Institution," *New York Times*, November 14, 1900.
107 *New-York Daily Tribune*, February 28, 1860.
108 Henry B. Rankin, *Intimate Character Sketches of Abraham Lincoln* (Philadelphia: J. B. Lippincott Co., 1924), 179-180. This account was conveyed to Mr. Rankin by the son of Henry C. Bowen, the committee member.
109 R. C. McCormick, quoted in Francis Fisher Browne, *The Every-Day Life of Abraham Lincoln* (New York: N. D. Thompson Publishing Co., 1886), 314.
110 Russell H. Conwell, "Personal Glimpses of Celebrated Men and Women," quoted in Wayne Whipple, *The Story-Life of Lincoln: A Biography Composed of*

Five Hundred True Stories Told by Abraham Lincoln and His Friends (Philadelphia: John C. Winston Co., 1908), 308.

111 Noah Brooks, *Abraham Lincoln: The Nation's Leader in the Great Struggle Through Which Was Maintained the Existence of the United States* (New York: G. P. Putnam's Sons, 1888), 186.

112 Brooks, *Abraham Lincoln: The Nation's Leader*, 186 (italics in original).

113 Harold Holzer, *Lincoln at Cooper Union: The Speech That Made Abraham Lincoln President* (New York: Simon & Schuster, 2004), 111.

114 Conwell, "Personal Glimpses," in Whipple, *The Story-Life of Lincoln*, 308.

115 Lincoln, "Address at Cooper Institute, New York City," February 27, 1860, *CW*, 3:522-550.

116 Lincoln, "Address at Cooper Institute, New York City," February 27, 1860, *CW*, 3:522 (italics in original).

117 Lincoln, "Address at Cooper Institute, New York City," February 27, 1860, *CW*, 3:522.

118 Lincoln, "Address at Cooper Institute, New York City," February 27, 1860, *CW*, 3:536.

119 Lincoln, "Address at Cooper Institute, New York City," February 27, 1860, *CW*, 3:536.

120 Lincoln, "Address at Cooper Institute, New York City," February 27, 1860, *CW*, 3:536-537.

121 Lincoln, "Address at Cooper Institute, New York City," February 27, 1860, *CW*, 3:538.

122 Lincoln, "Address at Cooper Institute, New York City," February 27, 1860, *CW*, 3:543.

123 Lincoln, "Address at Cooper Institute, New York City," February 27, 1860, *CW*, 3:547 (italics in original).

124 Lincoln, "Address at Cooper Institute, New York City," February 27, 1860, *CW*, 3:550 (capitalization in original).

125 Burlingame, *Abraham Lincoln: A Life*, 1:586.

126 Brooks, *Abraham Lincoln: The Nation's Leader*, 186-187.

127 Brooks, *Abraham Lincoln: The Nation's Leader*, 187.

128 R. C. McCormick, "Abraham Lincoln's Visit to New York in 1860," April 29, 1865 in *New York Evening Post,* reprinted in *Littell's Living Age*, May 20, 1865, 328.

129 Edward K. Spann, *Ideals & Politics: New York Intellectuals and Liberal Democracy 1820-1880* (Albany: State University of New York Press, 1972), 185.

130 Greeley, "Greeley's Estimate of Lincoln," 373.

131 *New-York Daily Tribune,* February 28, 1860.

132 William Safire, ed., *Lend Me Your Ears: Great Speeches in History*, updated and expanded edition (New York: W. W. Norton & Co., 2004), 35 (italics added).

133 Carl Sandburg, *Abraham Lincoln: The Prairie Years and the War Years*, Reader's Digest ill. ed. (Pleasantville, NY: Reader's Digest Association, 1970), 146.
134 Marshall Solomon Snow, "Abraham Lincoln: A Personal Reminiscence," *Washington University Record* 4, no. 5 (March 1909): 13.
135 Snow, "Abraham Lincoln: A Personal Reminiscence," 13.
136 Welcome B. Sayles, quoted in James B. Angell, *The Reminiscences of James Burrill Angell* (New York: Longmans, Green, and Co., 1912), 117.
137 Burlingame, *Abraham Lincoln: A Life*, 1:590, citing Concord *Independent Democrat*, March 8, 1860.
138 Pride, "The First N.H. Primary?," *Boston Globe*, July 11, 2010.
139 Goodwin, *Team of Rivals*, 9.
140 Burlingame, *Abraham Lincoln: A Life*, 1:650. This was in contrast to Douglas, who broke with tradition and drew criticism for doing so. Burlingame, *Abraham Lincoln: A Life*, 1:651.
141 Goodwin, *Team of Rivals*, 272.
142 Some historians say that Douglas's death may have been due to alcohol abuse. Fraker, *Lincoln's Ladder to the Presidency*, 254; Goodwin, *Team of Rivals*, 348; White, *A. Lincoln*, 425.

Chapter 4: Mr. President

1 Abraham Lincoln's Reply, "First Debate with Stephen A. Douglas at Ottawa, Illinois," August 21, 1858, *CW*, 3:27.
2 William E. Gienapp, "Abraham Lincoln and Presidential Leadership," in James M. McPherson, ed., *"We Cannot Escape History:" Lincoln and the Last Best Hope of Earth* (Urbana: University of Illinois Press, 1995), 80-81.
3 The draft in 1863—the country's first—provoked riots in Boston, Troy, Newark, and New York City, the latter resulting in five hundred or more deaths, many of them African-American, and requiring weary troops from Gettysburg to quash it. Goodwin, *Team of Rivals*, 537; Oates, *With Malice Toward None*, 357.
4 Democrats increased their number of seats in the House of Representatives from 44 to 72.
5 Sandburg, *Abraham Lincoln: The Prairie Years and the War Years*, 277.
6 Wilson, *Lincoln's Sword*, 7.
7 Ronald C. White, Jr., *The Eloquent President* (New York: Random House, 2005), 123.
8 Strictly speaking, his letter to Erastus Corning was addressed to "Erastus Corning and Others." Abraham Lincoln to Erastus Corning and Others, [June 12,] 1863, *CW*, 6:260.
9 Newspapers now had wires strung across the country and an unprecedented ability to get a president's words almost immediately to the American people. As one magazine writer of the era described it: "To-day, newspapers multiplied

by millions whiten the whole country every morning like the hoar-frost." "Man Under Sealed Orders," *Atlantic Monthly* 9, May 1862, 532.
10. Gienapp, "Abraham Lincoln and Presidential Leadership," in McPherson, ed., *"We Cannot Escape History,"* 77.
11. Harold Holzer, "Avoid Saying 'Foolish Things:' The Legacy of Lincoln's Impromptu Oratory," in McPherson, ed., *"We Cannot Escape History,"* 109.
12. Holzer, "Avoid Saying 'Foolish Things,'" in McPherson, ed., *"We Cannot Escape History,"* 109-110, 113, 121.
13. Wilson, *Lincoln's Sword*, 6.
14. Wilson, *Lincoln's Sword* (italics added).
15. Abraham Lincoln, "First Inaugural Address—Final Text," March 4, 1861, *CW*, 4:262-271.
16. Carl Schurz, *Abraham Lincoln: An Essay* (Boston: Houghton Mifflin Co., 1891), 66.
17. Lincoln, "First Inaugural Address—Final Text," March 4, 1861, *CW*, 4:263.
18. Lincoln, "First Inaugural Address—Final Text," March 4, 1861, *CW*, 4:263.
19. Lincoln, "First Inaugural Address—Final Text," March 4, 1861, *CW*, 4:263-264.
20. Lincoln, "First Inaugural Address—Final Text," March 4, 1861, *CW*, 4:265-266.
21. Lincoln, "First Inaugural Address—Final Text," March 4, 1861, *CW*, 4:266.
22. Lincoln, "First Inaugural Address—Final Text," March 4, 1861, *CW*, 4:266.
23. Lincoln, "First Inaugural Address—Final Text," March 4, 1861, *CW*, 4:266.
24. Lincoln, "First Inaugural Address—Final Text," March 4, 1861, *CW*, 4:266.
25. Lincoln, "First Inaugural Address—Final Text," March 4, 1861, *CW*, 4:267.
26. Lincoln, "First Inaugural Address—Final Text," March 4, 1861, *CW*, 4:268.
27. Lincoln, "First Inaugural Address—Final Text," March 4, 1861, *CW*, 4:267.
28. Lincoln, "First Inaugural Address—Final Text," March 4, 1861, *CW*, 4:268.
29. Lincoln, "First Inaugural Address—Final Text," March 4, 1861, *CW*, 4:268.
30. Lincoln, "First Inaugural Address—Final Text," March 4, 1861, *CW*, 4:268.
31. Lincoln, "First Inaugural Address—Final Text," March 4, 1861, *CW*, 4:268.
32. Lincoln, "First Inaugural Address—Final Text," March 4, 1861, *CW*, 4:269.
33. Lincoln, "First Inaugural Address—Final Text," March 4, 1861, *CW*, 4:269 (italics in original).
34. Lincoln, "First Inaugural Address—Final Text," March 4, 1861, *CW*, 4:269-270 (italics in original).
35. Lincoln, "First Inaugural Address—Final Text," March 4, 1861, *CW*, 4:270 (italics in original).
36. Lincoln, "First Inaugural Address—Final Text," March 4, 1861, *CW*, 4:270-271.
37. Lincoln, "First Inaugural Address—Final Text," March 4, 1861, *CW*, 4:265.
38. Lincoln, "First Inaugural Address—Final Text," March 4, 1861, *CW*, 4:265.
39. Lincoln, "First Inaugural Address—Final Text," March 4, 1861, *CW*, 4:265.
40. Lincoln, "First Inaugural Address—Final Text," March 4, 1861, *CW*, 4:265.

41　Lincoln, First Inaugural Address—Final Text, March 4, 1861, *CW*, 4:271 (italics in original).
42　Lincoln, First Inaugural Address—Final Text, March 4, 1861, *CW*, 4:271 (italics in original).
43　Lincoln, "First Inaugural Address—Final Text," March 4, 1861, *CW*, 4:271.
44　Lincoln, "First Inaugural Address—Final Text," March 4, 1861, *CW*, 4:271.
45　Sandburg, *Abraham Lincoln: The Prairie Years and the War Years*, 186.
46　Schurz, *Abraham Lincoln: An Essay*, 66.
47　*National Republican* (Washington, D.C.), March 5, 1861.
48　*New York Times,* March 5, 1861.
49　"Opinions of Mr. Lincoln's Inaugural," March 4, 1861, in *New York Herald,* March 5, 1861.
50　Edwin D. Morgan to Abraham Lincoln, March 5, 1861, *ALPLC*.
51　Abraham Lincoln, "Message to Congress in a Special Session," July 4, 1861, *CW*, 4:431-432.
52　Lincoln, "Message to Congress in a Special Session," July 4, 1861, *CW*, 4:426.
53　Lincoln, "Message to Congress in a Special Session," July 4, 1861, *CW*, 4:438.
54　Sandburg, *Abraham Lincoln: The Prairie Years and the War Years*, 218.
55　Pinsker, *Lincoln's Sanctuary*, 27.
56　Pinsker, *Lincoln's Sanctuary*, 26-27.
57　Pinsker, *Lincoln's Sanctuary*, 26-27.
58　Entry for July 13, 1862, Gideon Welles, *Diary of Gideon Welles: Secretary of the Navy Under Lincoln and Johnson* (Boston: Houghton Mifflin Co., 1911), 1:70.
59　Lincoln had already presented an early version of the Preliminary Emancipation Proclamation to his cabinet on July 22, 1862. Donald, *Lincoln*, 365.
60　Horace Greeley, "The Prayer of Twenty Millions," *New-York Daily Tribune,* August 20, 1862.
61　Greeley, "The Prayer of Twenty Millions," *New-York Daily Tribune,* August 20, 1862.
62　Abraham Lincoln to Horace Greeley, August 22, 1862, *CW*, 5:388-389.
63　*National Intelligencer* (Washington, D.C.), August 23, 1862.
64　Burlingame, *Abraham Lincoln: A Life*, 2:401.
65　Special Dispatch to *Cincinnati Gazette,* August 24, 1862, reprinted in *Daily Intelligencer* (Wheeling, Virginia [West Virginia]), August 27, 1862.
66　Brooks, *Abraham Lincoln: The Nation's Leader*, 305.
67　Abraham Lincoln to Horace Greeley, August 22, 1862, *CW*, 5:388.
68　Abraham Lincoln to Horace Greeley, August 22, 1862, *CW*, 5:388-389 (italics in original).
69　Abraham Lincoln to Horace Greeley, August 22, 1862, *CW*, 5:389 (italics in original).
70　Sandburg, *Abraham Lincoln: The Prairie Years and the War Years*, 267.

71 Burlingame, *Abraham Lincoln: A Life*, 2:401.
72 The *Wyandot Pioneer* remarked that in answering Greeley as he had, Lincoln was "departing from all precedent set him by those who have preceded him in the chair of State." *Wyandot Pioneer* (Upper Sandusky, Ohio), August 29, 1862. "So novel a thing" was how the correspondent to the *Cincinnati Gazette* referred to this extraordinary public exchange of letters. Special Dispatch to *Cincinnati Gazette*, August 24, 1862, reprinted in *Daily Intelligencer* (Wheeling, Virginia [West Virginia]), August 27, 1862. More pointedly, the *Daily Ohio Statesman* opined that it "was hardly worth while, perhaps, for the President to reply to Mr. Greeley at all," noting that "many will question the propriety of such action." *Daily Ohio Statesman* (Columbus, Ohio), August 29, 1862. Even more critically, the *North Branch Democrat* said that the "President . . ., to the astonishment of almost every one, condescended to notice this miserable abolition brawler," referring of course to Greeley. *North Branch Democrat* (Tunkhannock, Pennsylvania), August 27, 1862.
73 Washington Correspondence, August 23, 1862, in *New York Times*, August 24, 1862.
74 *Daily Intelligencer* (Wheeling, Virginia [West Virginia]), August 26, 1862.
75 *New York Herald,* August 24, 1862.
76 *Daily Ohio Statesman* (Columbus, Ohio), August 29, 1862.
77 Burlingame, *Abraham Lincoln: A Life*, 2:401-402.
78 Burlingame, *Abraham Lincoln: A Life*, 2:402, citing Horace Greeley to George W. Wright, August 27, 1862, Horace Greeley Papers, Library of Congress.
79 William H. Lambert, "Preserver of the Union—Saviour of the Republic: Reminiscences of Abraham Lincoln," in MacChesney, ed., *Abraham Lincoln: The Tribute of a Century*, 448.
80 Ida M. Tarbell, *The Life of Abraham Lincoln* (New York: Lincoln Historical Society, 1907), 3:117.
81 Abraham Lincoln, "Preliminary Emancipation Proclamation," September 22, 1862, *CW,* 5:433.
82 Approved March 13, 1862 and July 17, 1862.
83 Lincoln, "Preliminary Emancipation Proclamation," September 22, 1862, *CW,* 5:434-435.
84 Lincoln, "Preliminary Emancipation Proclamation," September 22, 1862, *CW,* 5:433-434.
85 *New York Herald,* September 23, 1862 (italics in original).
86 *New-York Daily Tribune,* September 24, 1862.
87 *Cass County Republican* (Dowagiac, Michigan), September 25, 1862.
88 Abraham Lincoln, "Annual Message to Congress," December 1, 1862, *CW,* 5:518-537.
89 Lincoln, "Annual Message to Congress," December 1, 1862, *CW,* 5:530.

90 Lincoln, "Annual Message to Congress," December 1, 1862, *CW*, 5:531-532.
91 *Philadelphia Inquirer,* December 2, 1862.
92 *Chicago Tribune,* December 3, 1862.
93 Horace Greeley to John G. Nicolay, January 10, 1863, *ALPLC*.
94 Abraham Lincoln, "Emancipation Proclamation," January 1, 1863, *CW*, 6:29-30 (bullet points added).
95 Lincoln, "Emancipation Proclamation," January 1, 1863, *CW*, 6:30.
96 J. S. Ogilvie, ed., *Life and Speeches of William McKinley* (New York: J.S. Ogilvie Publishing Co., 1896), 212-213.
97 *Daily National Republican* (Washington, D.C.), January 2, 1863.
98 *Smoky Hill and Republican Union* (Junction City, Kansas), January 3, 1863.
99 *New York Evening Post*, January 7, 1863.
100 Abraham Lincoln, "Proclamation Suspending the Writ of Habeas Corpus," September 24, 1862, *CW*, 5:436-437.
101 General Order No. 38, quoted in Augustus Woodbury, *Major General Ambrose E. Burnside and the Ninth Army Corps* (Providence, RI: Sidney S. Rider & Brother, 1867), 266.
102 *Cincinnati Commercial*, May 9, 1863, reprinted in *New York Times*, May 11, 1863.
103 Abraham Lincoln to Erastus Corning, May 28, 1863, *CW*, 6:235.
104 White, *A. Lincoln*, 564.
105 Abraham Lincoln to Erastus Corning and Others, [June 12,] 1863, *CW*, 6:260-269.
106 White, *A. Lincoln*, 564.
107 Abraham Lincoln to Erastus Corning and Others, [June 12,] 1863, *CW*, 6:262, 264. Lincoln avoided, however, taking on the question of *which* branch of government had the constitutional authority to suspend habeas corpus. The provision that authorizes that suspension appears in Article I of the Constitution, which defines the powers of Congress, and not Article II, which defines the powers of the president.
108 Abraham Lincoln to Erastus Corning and Others, [June 12,] 1863, *CW*, 6:264.
109 Abraham Lincoln to Erastus Corning and Others, [June 12,] 1863, *CW*, 6:262 (italics in original).
110 Abraham Lincoln to Erastus Corning and Others, [June 12,] 1863, *CW*, 6:263 (italics in original).
111 Abraham Lincoln to Erastus Corning and Others, [June 12,] 1863, *CW*, 6:264.
112 Abraham Lincoln to Erastus Corning and Others, [June 12,] 1863, *CW*, 6:266.
113 Abraham Lincoln to Erastus Corning and Others, [June 12,] 1863, *CW*, 6:264.
114 Abraham Lincoln to Erastus Corning and Others, [June 12,] 1863, *CW*, 6:266-267.
115 William A. Hall to Abraham Lincoln, June 15, 1863, *ALPLC*.

116 John G. Nicolay and John Hay, "Abraham Lincoln: A History," *Century Magazine* 38, May 1889, 133.
117 *Daily National Republican* (Washington, D.C.), June 15, 1863.
118 *Chicago Tribune,* June 16, 1863.
119 Chicago Daily Tribune Company to John G. Nicolay, June 16, 1863, *ALPLC* (underlining in original).
120 John W. Forney to Abraham Lincoln, June 14, 1863, *ALPLC.*
121 Edwin D. Morgan to Abraham Lincoln, June 15, 1863, *ALPLC.*
122 Mark W. Delahay to Abraham Lincoln, June 19, 1863, *ALPLC.*
123 David P. Brown to Abraham Lincoln, June 15, 1863, *ALPLC.*
124 Mark E. Neely, Jr., "The Civil War and the Two-Party System," in McPherson, ed., *"We Cannot Escape History,"* 93-94.
125 Pinsker, *Lincoln's Sanctuary,* 116.
126 Nicolay and Hay, "Abraham Lincoln: A History," 145.
127 Sandburg, *Abraham Lincoln: The Prairie Years and the War Years,* 353.
128 Abraham Lincoln to James C. Conkling, August 26, 1863, *CW,* 6:406.
129 Abraham Lincoln to James C. Conkling, August 26, 1863, *CW,* 6:407.
130 Abraham Lincoln to James C. Conkling, August 26, 1863, *CW,* 6:407.
131 Abraham Lincoln to James C. Conkling, August 26, 1863, *CW,* 6:407.
132 Abraham Lincoln to James C. Conkling, August 26, 1863, *CW,* 6:407-408.
133 Abraham Lincoln to James C. Conkling, August 26, 1863, *CW,* 6:408.
134 Abraham Lincoln to James C. Conkling, August 26, 1863, *CW,* 6:408-409.
135 Abraham Lincoln to James C. Conkling, August 26, 1863, *CW,* 6:409.
136 Abraham Lincoln to James C. Conkling, August 26, 1863, *CW,* 6:410.
137 Abraham Lincoln to James C. Conkling, August 26, 1863, *CW,* 6:410.
138 Nicolay and Hay, "Abraham Lincoln: A History," 145 n.2.
139 "The Right Man in the Right Place," *New York Times,* September 7, 1863.
140 Sandburg, *Abraham Lincoln: The Prairie Years and the War Years,* 354.
141 *Chicago Tribune,* September 3, 1863.
142 *Chicago Tribune,* September 3, 1863.
143 Charles Sumner to Abraham Lincoln, September 7, 1863, *ALPLC.*
144 John M. Forbes to Abraham Lincoln, September 8, 1863, *ALPLC.*
145 White, *A. Lincoln,* 589.
146 Abraham Lincoln, "Address Delivered at the Dedication of the Cemetery at Gettysburg, Final Text," November 19, 1863, *CW,* 7:22-23.
147 Garry Wills writes: "Read in a slow, clear way to the farthest listeners, the speech would take about three minutes." Garry Wills, *Lincoln at Gettysburg: The Words That Remade America* (New York: Simon & Schuster, 1992), 36.
148 Lincoln, "Address Delivered at the Dedication of the Cemetery at Gettysburg, Final Text," November 19, 1863, *CW,* 7:23.

149 Lincoln, "Address Delivered at the Dedication of the Cemetery at Gettysburg, Final Text," November 19, 1863, *CW*, 7:23.
150 Abraham Lincoln, "First Inaugural Address—Final Text," March 4, 1861, *CW*, 4:271.
151 Burlingame, *Abraham Lincoln: A Life*, 2:577.
152 Special Correspondence, November 19, 1863, in *Daily Morning Chronicle* (Washington, D.C.), November 21, 1863.
153 *Rutland Weekly Herald* (Rutland, Vermont), November 26, 1863.
154 Special Dispatch, November 19, 1863, in *Chicago Tribune,* November 20, 1863.
155 *Daily Intelligencer* (Wheeling, Virginia [West Virginia]), March 6, 1865.
156 Entries of August 21, 1863 and November 23, 1863 in Judith Kennedy Johnson, ed., *The Journals of Charles King Newcomb* (Providence, RI: Brown University Press, 1946), 194, 196.
157 "Autograph Leaves," *Harper's Weekly* 8, April 23, 1864, 259.
158 Brooks, *Abraham Lincoln: The Nation's Leader*, 379.
159 John M. Taylor, *William Henry Seward: Lincoln's Right Hand Man* (New York: Harper Collins, 1991), 224, citing W. Farquhar to — Boos, May 26, 1921, ADS Catalog, 1990.
160 Abraham Lincoln, "Annual Message to Congress," December 8, 1863, *CW*, 7:36-53; Abraham Lincoln, "Proclamation of Amnesty and Reconstruction," December 8, 1863, *CW*, 7:53-56.
161 Abraham Lincoln, "Proclamation of Amnesty and Reconstruction," December 8, 1863, *CW*, 7:55.
162 Lincoln, "Annual Message to Congress," December 8, 1863, *CW*, 7:51.
163 Dispatch of December 12, 1863, in Michael Burlingame, ed., *Lincoln Observed: Civil War Dispatches of Noah Brooks* (Baltimore: Johns Hopkins University Press, 1998), 94.
164 Entry for December 9, 1863, Michael Burlingame and John R. Turner Ettlinger, eds., *Inside Lincoln's White House: The Complete Civil War Diary of John Hay* (Carbondale: Southern Illinois University Press, 1997), 121.
165 Burlingame, *Abraham Lincoln: A Life*, 2:596, citing Washington Correspondence, December 10, 1863, Cincinnati *Commercial*, December 11, 1863.
166 Samuel Galloway to Abraham Lincoln, December 19, 1863, *ALPLC*. The letter to which Galloway referred was Lincoln's of June 12, 1863 to Erastus Corning.
167 Albert Smith to Abraham Lincoln, December 12, 1863, *ALPLC* (underlining in original).
168 John J. Janney to Abraham Lincoln, December 10, 1863, *ALPLC*.
169 William Dennison to Abraham Lincoln, December 10, 1863, *ALPLC*.
170 Abraham Lincoln to Michael Hahn, March 13, 1864, *CW*, 7:243.
171 Abraham Lincoln to Michael Hahn, March 13, 1864, *CW*, 7:243.

172 "The Late President Lincoln on Negro Suffrage: A Letter from him to Governor Hahn of Louisiana," *New York Times*, June 23, 1865.
173 Abraham Lincoln to Albert G. Hodges, April 4, 1864, *CW*, 7:283 n.1.
174 Abraham Lincoln to Albert G. Hodges, April 4, 1864, *CW*, 7:281-282.
175 Abraham Lincoln to Albert G. Hodges, April 4, 1864, *CW*, 7:282.
176 Abraham Lincoln to Albert G. Hodges, April 4, 1864, *CW*, 7:282.
177 Abraham Lincoln to Albert G. Hodges, April 4, 1864, *CW*, 7:282.
178 Abraham Lincoln to Albert G. Hodges, April 4, 1864, *CW*, 7:282.
179 *New-York Daily Tribune*, April 29, 1864.
180 Abraham Lincoln, "Annual Message to Congress," December 6, 1864, *CW*, 8:136-153.
181 Lincoln, "Annual Message to Congress," December 6, 1864, *CW*, 8:149 (italics in original).
182 Lincoln, "Annual Message to Congress," December 6, 1864, *CW*, 8:151.
183 Lincoln, "Annual Message to Congress," December 6, 1864, *CW*, 8:151.
184 Lincoln, "Annual Message to Congress," December 6, 1864, *CW*, 8:151.
185 Lincoln, "Annual Message to Congress," December 6, 1864, *CW*, 8:151.
186 Lincoln, "Annual Message to Congress," December 6, 1864, *CW*, 8:152.
187 Burlingame, *Abraham Lincoln: A Life*, 2:742, quoting *New York Independent*, December 8, 1864.
188 Noah Brooks to George Witherle, December 10, 1864, in Burlingame, ed., *Lincoln Observed*, 155.
189 *Chicago Tribune*, December 7, 1864.
190 *Daily National Republican* (Washington, D.C.), December 6, 1864.
191 Reuben D. Mussey to Abraham Lincoln, December 9, 1864, *ALPLC*.
192 Abraham Lincoln, "Second Inaugural Address," March 4, 1865, *CW*, 8:332-333.
193 Lincoln, "Second Inaugural Address," March 4, 1865, *CW*, 8:333.
194 Lincoln, "Second Inaugural Address," March 4, 1865, *CW*, 8:333.
195 Lincoln, "Second Inaugural Address," March 4, 1865, *CW*, 8:333.
196 Lincoln, "Second Inaugural Address," March 4, 1865, *CW*, 8:333.
197 Lincoln, "First Inaugural Address—Final Text," March 4, 1861, *CW*, 4:271.
198 Brooks, *Abraham Lincoln: The Nation's Leader*, 413-414.
199 Charles W. Moores, "Abraham Lincoln, Lawyer," *Indiana Historical Society Publications* 7 (1922, reprinted from the Proceedings of the American Bar Association, 1910): 525.
200 George Haven Putnam, *Abraham Lincoln: The People's Leader in the Struggle for National Existence* (New York: G.P. Putnam's Sons, 1909), 169-170.
201 *Democrat and Sentinel* (Ebensburg, Pennsylvania), March 8, 1865.
202 William F. McDowell, "Abraham Lincoln – An Appreciation," in MacChesney, ed., *Abraham Lincoln: The Tribute of a Century*, 369.
203 *Cleveland Morning Leader*, March 6, 1865.

204 Charles Francis Adams, Jr. to Charles Francis Adams, Sr., March 7, 1865, in Worthington Chauncey Ford, ed., *A Cycle of Adams Letters 1861-1865* (Boston: Houghton Mifflin Co., 1920), 2:257-258.
205 James Grant Wilson, "Abraham Would have Enjoyed a Wrestling Match with George," in Rufus Rockwell Wilson, *Intimate Memories of Lincoln* (Elmira, NY: Primavera Press, 1945), 424.
206 Theodore L. Cuyler, "Lincoln – After Thirty Years," in William Hayes Ward, ed., *Abraham Lincoln: Tributes from His Associates* (New York: Thomas Y. Crowell & Co., 1895), 128.
207 Whitney, *Lincoln the Citizen*, 205.
208 Schurz, *Abraham Lincoln: An Essay*, 103.
209 Schurz, *Abraham Lincoln: An Essay*, 103.
210 Daniel Kilham Dodge, "Abraham Lincoln: The Evolution of His Literary Style," *University of Illinois University Studies* 1 (May 1900): 53.
211 Isaac N. Arnold, *The Life of Abraham Lincoln* (Chicago: Jansen, McClurg, & Co., 1885), 404.
212 Goodwin, *Team of Rivals*, 701.
213 Arnold, *The Life of Abraham Lincoln*, 404-405.
214 Abraham Lincoln to Thurlow Weed, March 15, 1865, *CW*, 8:356.
215 Abraham Lincoln to Thurlow Weed, March 15, 1865, *CW*, 8:356.
216 Abraham Lincoln, "Last Public Address," April 11, 1865, *CW*, 8:399-405.
217 Abraham Lincoln, "Last Public Address," April 11, 1865, *CW*, 8:399-400.
218 Lincoln, "Last Public Address," April 11, 1865, *CW*, 8:403.
219 Lincoln, "Last Public Address," April 11, 1865, *CW*, 8:403 (italics in original).
220 Lincoln, "Last Public Address," April 11, 1865, *CW*, 8:404-405.
221 Lincoln, "Last Public Address," April 11, 1865, *CW*, 8:405.
222 Greeley, "Greeley's Estimate of Lincoln," 373 (italics in original).

Photographs and Images

1   Courtesy of the Library of Congress, Prints and Photographs Division, LC-USZC4-2439 (color film copy transparency post-1992) LC-USZ6-2095 (b&w film copy neg. post-1992) LC-USZ6-299 (b&w film copy neg. pre-1992, after 1959 cleaning and restoration?) LC-USZ62-12457 (b&w film copy neg. pre-1992, after 1959 cleaning and restoration, copy of retouched print) LC-USZ62-4377 (b&w film copy neg. made from old photographic print), (digital file from color film copy transparency post-1992) cph 3g02439 http://hdl.loc.gov/loc.pnp/cph.3g02439, Daguerreotype Collection 95861318, DAG no. 1224.
2   Image from I. Todhunter, ed., *The Elements of Euclid for the Use of Schools and Colleges, Books I, II, III* (Toronto: Copp, Clark Co. Ltd., 1876), 4, courtesy of archive.org, https://archive.org/details/elementsof76west00todhuoft.

3   Courtesy of http://www.lookingforlincoln.com/8thcircuit/maps/Map 8th Whimple 1908.jpg.
4   Courtesy of the Library of Congress, Prints and Photographs Division, HABS ILL,84-SPRIF,1—1, (None) hhh il0202.photos.064076p http://hdl.loc.gov/loc.pnp/hhh.il0202/photos.064076p.
5   Courtesy of Google Patents, U.S. Patent no. 6,469 A, May 22, 1849, https://www.google.com/patents/US6469.
6   Courtesy of the Library of Congress, Prints and Photographs Division, LC-USZ62-1754 (b&w film copy neg. post-1992), (b&w film copy neg. post-1992) cph 3a05504 http://hdl.loc.gov/loc.pnp/cph.3a05504, Daguerreotype Collection.
7   Courtesy of https://www.awesomestories.com/asset/view/WARNINGS-AND-OMENS-Assassination-of-Abraham-Lincoln.
8   Courtesy of the Library of Congress, Prints and Photographs Division, LC-USZ62-5803 (b&w film copy neg.) LC-BH8277-242 (b&w film copy neg.), (digital file from b&w film copy neg.) cph 3a09102 http://hdl.loc.gov/loc.pnp/cph.3a09102, Illus. in E457.6 M58 [P&P].
9   Courtesy of the Library of Congress, Prints and Photographs Division, LC-DIG-ppmsca-19200 (digital file from original photograph) LC-USZ62-15303 (b&w film copy neg.), (digital file from original item) ppmsca 19200 http://hdl.loc.gov/loc.pnp/ppmsca.19200, LOT 5908 [item].
10 Courtesy of the Library of Congress, Prints and Photographs Division, LC-DIG-ppmsca-17159 (digital file from original item) LC-USZ62-7728-A (b&w film copy neg.), (digital file from b&w film copy neg.) cph 3a10370 http://hdl.loc.gov/loc.pnp/cph.3a10370, LOT 12559, no. 3.
11 Courtesy of the Library of Congress, Prints and Photographs Division, LC-DIG-ppmsca-07636 (digital file from original) LC-USZ62-48090 (b&w film copy neg.), (digital file from original) ppmsca 07636 http://hdl.loc.gov/loc.pnp/ppmsca.07636, LOT 12251, p.59.
12 Courtesy of the Library of Congress, Prints and Photographs Division, LC-DIG-ppmsca-19206 (digital file from original), (digital file from original) ppmsca 19206 http://hdl.loc.gov/loc.pnp/ppmsca.19206, Unprocessed in PR 13 CN 1972:018 [item].
13 Courtesy of the Library of Congress, Prints and Photographs Division, LC-USZ62-14258 (b&w film copy neg.), (digital file from b&w film copy neg.) cph 3a16523 http://hdl.loc.gov/loc.pnp/cph.3a16523.
14 Courtesy of the Library of Congress, Prints and Photographs Division, LC-DIG-ppmsca-19421 (digital file from original item) LC-USZ62-9708 (b&w film copy neg.), (digital file from original item) ppmsca 19421 http://hdl.loc.gov/loc.pnp/ppmsca.19421, PRES FILE - Lincoln, Abraham--Portraits--Meserve no. 56 [item].

15 Courtesy of the Library of Congress, Prints and Photographs Division, LC-DIG-ppmsca-19211 (digital file from original recto) LC-DIG-ppmsca-19212 (digital file from original verso), (digital file from original recto) ppmsca 19211 http://hdl.loc.gov/loc.pnp/ppmsca.19211, Unprocessed in PR 13 CN 1972:018 [item].
16 Courtesy of the Library of Congress, Prints and Photographs Division, LC-DIG-ppmsca-19190 (digital file from original), (digital file from original) ppmsca 19190 http://hdl.loc.gov/loc.pnp/ppmsca.19190, Unprocessed in PR 13 CN 1995:149 [item] [P&P].
17 Courtesy of the Library of Congress, Prints and Photographs Division, LC-DIG-ppmsca-19215 (digital file from original recto) LC-DIG-ppmsca-19216 (digital file from original verso), (digital file from original recto) ppmsca 19215 http://hdl.loc.gov/loc.pnp/ppmsca.19215, Unprocessed in PR 13 CN 1972:018 [item].
18 Courtesy of the Library of Congress, Prints and Photographs Division, LC-DIG-ppmsc-02927 (digital file from original item) LC-USZ62-7812 (b&w film copy neg.), (digital file from original) ppmsc 02927 http://hdl.loc.gov/loc.pnp/ppmsc.02927, LOT 5908 [item].
19 Courtesy of the Library of Congress, Prints and Photographs Division, LC-DIG-ppmsca-19192 (digital file from original) LC-USZ62-7542 (b&w film copy neg.), (digital file from original) ppmsca 19192 http://hdl.loc.gov/loc.pnp/ppmsca.19192, PH - Warren (H.), no. 1.
20 Courtesy of the Library of Congress, Prints and Photographs Division, LC-DIG-cwpbh-03254 (digital file from original neg.), (digital file from original neg.) cwpbh 03254 http://hdl.loc.gov/loc.pnp/cwpbh.03254, LC-BH823- 145

Part II

1 *New-York Daily Tribune,* February 28, 1860.
2 Greeley, "Greeley's Estimate of Lincoln," 373 (italics in original).

Chapter 5: Personality and Intellect

1 Goodwin, *Team of Rivals,* 140.
2 Charles S. Zane, "Lincoln as I Knew Him," *Pacific Monthly Sunset* 29, October 1912, 435.
3 Hannah Armstrong to William H. Herndon, [1866], *HI,* 526.
4 Frederick Douglass, *The Life and Times of Frederick Douglass* (Hartford, CT: Park Publishing Co., 1881), 445.
5 "Lincoln as a Speaker," speech of "Judge Park" at a banquet in Joliet, Illinois, reprinted in *Washington Post,* April 1, 1883.
6 Wills, *Lincoln at Gettysburg,* 149.
7 Wills, *Lincoln at Gettysburg,* 153.

8   Wills, *Lincoln at Gettysburg*, 149-150.
9   Abraham Lincoln to James H. Hackett, August 17, 1863, *CW*, 6:392.
10 William D. Kelley, in Rice, ed., *Reminiscences of Abraham Lincoln*, 265-266.
11 Burlingame, *Abraham Lincoln: A Life*, 1:64.
12 Goodwin, *Team of Rivals*, 53.
13 Burlingame, *Abraham Lincoln: A Life*, 1:241; Wills, *Lincoln at Gettysburg*, 149.
14 Goodwin, *Team of Rivals*, 52.
15 In the practice of the day, people would often read aloud, to themselves or others, Lincoln's speeches and written public messages, thus making the sound and rhythm of the latter just as important as in the delivered speeches.
16 William H. Herndon to Jesse W. Weik, October 21, 1885, in Emanuel Hertz, ed., *The Hidden Lincoln: From the Letters and Papers of William H. Herndon* (New York: Blue Ribbon Books, 1940), 95; Donald, *Lincoln*, 145, citing William H. Herndon to Jesse W. Weik, February 18, 1887, Herndon-Weik Collection, Library of Congress.
17 Pinsker, *Lincoln's Sanctuary*.
18 William Roscoe Thayer, *The Life and Letters of John Hay* (Boston: Houghton Mifflin Co., 1915), 1:209.
19 Thayer, *The Life and Letters of John Hay*, 1:209.
20 Gibson William Harris, "My Recollections of Abraham Lincoln," *Woman's Home Companion*, January 1904, 13.
21 William O. Stoddard, *Inside the White House in War Times* (New York: Charles L. Webster & Co., 1890), 227.
22 Joshua F. Speed to William H. Herndon, December 6, 1866, *HI*, 499.
23 Sarah Bush Lincoln to William H. Herndon, September 8, 1865, *HI*, 107.
24 Mentor Graham to William H. Herndon, July 15, 1865, *HI*, 76.
25 Springfield, Illinois Correspondence, November 29, 1860, in *New York Herald*, December 4, 1860.
26 J. Rowan Herndon to William H. Herndon, May 28, 1865, *HI*, 7.
27 Sarah Bush Lincoln to William H. Herndon, September 8, 1865, *HI*, 107-108.
28 Gardner himself would become governor in 1855.
29 Governor Henry J. Gardner (Statement for Edward L. Pierce), [February-May, 1890], *HI*, 699.
30 Goodwin, *Team of Rivals*, 51.
31 Wilson, *Honor's Voice*, 72-73.
32 Dodge, "Abraham Lincoln: The Evolution of His Literary Style," 18.
33 Burlingame, *Abraham Lincoln: A Life*, 1:316.
34 Hiram W. Beckwith, a student in a law office that Lincoln shared on the circuit, in Ida M. Tarbell, "Lincoln as a Lawyer," *McClure's Magazine* 7, July 1896, 179.

35 Hiram W. Beckwith, "Lincoln: Personal Recollections of Him, His Contemporaries and Law Practice in Eastern Illinois," *Chicago Tribune*, December 29, 1895.
36 Herndon and Weik, *Herndon's Lincoln*, 2:397.
37 Joshua F. Speed, *Reminiscences of Abraham Lincoln and Notes of a Visit to California: Two Lectures* (Louisville, KY: John P. Morton and Co., 1884), 25.
38 Leonard Swett to William H. Herndon, January 17, 1866, *HI*, 162.
39 Leonard Swett in Rice, ed., *Reminiscences of Abraham Lincoln*, 467.
40 Abraham Lincoln. Buoying vessels over shoals. US Patent 6,469, filed March 10, 1849 and issued May 22, 1849.
41 Burlingame, *Abraham Lincoln: A Life*, 1:33.
42 Wills, *Lincoln at Gettysburg*, 162.
43 Lincoln, "Autobiography Written for John L. Scripps," [c. June 1860], *CW*, 4:62.
44 William H. Herndon, quoted in Weik, *The Real Lincoln*, 240.
45 William H. Herndon, quoted in Weik, *The Real Lincoln*, 240.
46 John P. Frank, *Lincoln as a Lawyer* (Urbana: University of Illinois Press, 1961), 144.
47 Arnold, *The Life of Abraham Lincoln*, 84.
48 Arnold, "Reminiscences of the Illinois-Bar," 22.
49 E. M. Prince, quoted in Hill, *Lincoln the Lawyer*, 211-212.
50 Lincoln, "Speech at Peoria, Illinois," October 16, 1854, *CW*, 2:265-266 (italics in original).
51 Lincoln, "Address at Cooper Institute, New York City," February 27, 1860, *CW*, 3:549-550.
52 Correspondence, June 27, 1857, *Chicago Tribune*, n.d., reprinted in *New-York Daily Tribune*, July 6, 1857 (italics added).
53 Frank, *Lincoln as a Lawyer*, 172.
54 "The Right Man in the Right Place," *New York Times*, September 7, 1863.
55 "The Right Man in the Right Place," *New York Times*, September 7, 1863.
56 Edward Everett to Abraham Lincoln, November 20, 1863, *ALPLC*.

Chapter 6: Knowledge of People

1 Robert L. Wilson to William H. Herndon, February 10, 1866, *HI*, 204.
2 Arnold, "Reminiscences of the Illinois-Bar," 22.
3 Harriet A. Weed, ed., *Autobiography of Thurlow Weed*, Vol. 1 of Thurlow Weed, *Life of Thurlow Weed* (Boston: Houghton, Mifflin and Co., 1884), 603.
4 Mentor Graham to William H. Herndon, [1865-1866], *HI*, 450.
5 White, *A. Lincoln*, 178.
6 Greeley, "Greeley's Estimate of Lincoln," 381.
7 James Russell Lowell, *The Writings of James Russell Lowell* (Boston: Houghton Mifflin, 1892), 5:208.

8   Benjamin P. Thomas, *Abraham Lincoln: A Biography* (New York: Barnes & Noble, 1952), 94.
9   Oates, *With Malice Toward None*, 105.
10 Hill, *Lincoln the Lawyer*, 208.
11 Ogilvie, ed., *Life and Speeches of William McKinley*, 208.
12 Greeley, "Greeley's Estimate of Lincoln," 373.
13 Greeley, "Greeley's Estimate of Lincoln," 373 (italics in original).
14 Jesse J. Dunn, "Lincoln, the Lawyer" (continued), *Oklahoma Law Journal* 4 (February 1906): 253.
15 Abraham Lincoln to Erastus Corning and Others, [June 12,] 1863, *CW*, 6:263.
16 Mark E. Steiner, *An Honest Calling: The Law Practice of Abraham Lincoln* (Dekalb, Illinois: Northern Illinois University Press, 2006), 20.
17 Steiner, *An Honest Calling,* 20-22. Among others, Steiner cites: Edward J. Fox, "The Influence of the Law in the Life of Abraham Lincoln," Report of the Thirty-First Annual Meeting of the Pennsylvania Bar Association (1925), 350; Julius E. Haycraft, "Lincoln as a Lawyer Statesman," 12 *Minn. L.Rev. (Supp.)* (1927): 100; Jesse J. Dunn, "Lincoln the Lawyer," 4 *Okla. L.J.* (1906): 249, 260.
18 Albert A. Woldman, *Lawyer Lincoln* (New York: Caroll & Graf Publishers, 1936), preface.
19 Abraham Lincoln, "Temperance Address," February 22, 1842, *CW*, 1:273 (italics in original).
20 Lincoln, "Temperance Address," February 22, 1842, *CW*, 1:273.
21 Lincoln, "Temperance Address," February 22, 1842, *CW*, 1:273 (italics in original).
22 Lincoln, "Temperance Address," February 22, 1842, *CW*, 1:273.
23 Lincoln, "Temperance Address," February 22, 1842, *CW*, 1:273.
24 Lincoln, "Temperance Address," February 22, 1842, *CW*, 1:273 (italics in original).
25 Lincoln, "Temperance Address," February 22, 1842, *CW*, 1:273 (italics in original).
26 Herndon and Weik, *Herndon's Lincoln*, 2:325.
27 Abraham Lincoln, quoted in Chauncey M. Depew, *My Memories of Eighty Years* (New York: Charles Scribner's Sons, 1922), 166-167.
28 Abraham Lincoln to Usher F. Linder, February 20, 1848, *CW*, 1:453 (italics in original).
29 White, *A. Lincoln*, 146-147.
30 Herndon and Weik, *Herndon's Lincoln*, 3:478.
31 Abraham Lincoln to William H. Herndon, February 2, 1848, *CW*, 1:448.
32 Abraham Lincoln, quoted in William M. Dickson, "Abraham Lincoln at Cincinnati," *Harper's New Monthly Magazine* 69, June 1884, 64.

33 Abraham Lincoln, "Speech at Chicago, Illinois," October 27, 1854, *CW*, 2:283 (italics in original).
34 Abraham Lincoln, quoted in Edward Dicey, *Six Months in the Federal States* (London: Macmillan and Co., 1863), 1:227.
35 Comments of Garry Wills in praise of Holzer, *Lincoln at Cooper Union*, book jacket.
36 Comments of Garry Wills in praise of Holzer, *Lincoln at Cooper Union*, book jacket.

Chapter 7: Preparation and Timing

1 Abraham Lincoln to John M. Brockman, September 25, 1860, *CW*, 4:121.
2 Brian Dirck, *Lincoln the Lawyer* (Urbana, IL: University of Illinois Press, 2008), 28, citing "Stephen Logan Talks about Abraham Lincoln," *Bulletin of the Abraham Lincoln Centennial Association* 12 (September 1928): 3.
3 Herndon and Weik, *Herndon's Lincoln*, 3:594.
4 Abraham Lincoln to Peter H. Watson, July 23, 1855, *CW*, 2:314-315.
5 White, *A. Lincoln*, 242.
6 Donald, *Lincoln*, 100, citing William Henry Herndon, "Lincoln as Lawyer Politician and Statesman," Herndon-Weik Collection, Library of Congress.
7 *Chicago Press and Tribune*, February 16, 1860.
8 Dunn, "Lincoln, the Lawyer," 220.
9 Dunn, "Lincoln, the Lawyer," 220.
10 Lincoln, "Speech at Peoria, Illinois," October 16, 1854, *CW*, 2:256.
11 Lincoln, "Address at Cooper Institute, New York City," February 27, 1860, *CW*, 3:536.
12 Lincoln, "First Inaugural Address—Final Text," March 4, 1861, *CW*, 4:262-271.
13 *New-York Daily Tribune*, September 3, 1863.
14 Wills, *Lincoln at Gettysburg*, 162.
15 Goodwin, *Team of Rivals*, 323-324, quoting "Some Incidents in Lincoln's Journey from Springfield to Washington" in Burlingame, ed., *Oral History*, 130.
16 Abraham Lincoln, "Meditation on the Divine Will," [September 2, 1862?], *CW*, 5:403-404 (italics in original).
17 Abraham Lincoln to Albert G. Hodges, April 4, 1864, *CW*, 7:282.
18 Lincoln, "Second Inaugural Address," March 4, 1865, *CW*, 8:333.
19 John G. Nicolay, "Lincoln's Literary Experiments," *Century Magazine* 47, April 1894, 825 (italics added).
20 Joshua F. Speed to William H. Herndon, December 6, 1866, *HI*, 499.
21 Herndon and Weik, *Herndon's Lincoln*, 2:397.
22 Entry for May 7, 1861, Burlingame and Ettlinger, eds., *Inside Lincoln's White House*, 20.
23 Sandburg, *Abraham Lincoln: The Prairie Years and the War Years*, 186.

24 Abraham Lincoln, "Fragment: Notes for a Law Lecture," [July 1, 1850?], *CW*, 2:81.
25 Harold Holzer, "Avoid Saying 'Foolish Things,'" in McPherson, ed., "*We Cannot Escape History*," 109-112.
26 See, for example, Goodwin, *Team of Rivals*, 309; Holzer, "Avoid Saying 'Foolish Things,'" in McPherson, ed., "*We Cannot Escape History*," 106; Oates, *With Malice Toward None*, 125; White, *The Eloquent President*, 42-61.
27 Abraham Lincoln, "Response to a Serenade," July 7, 1863, *CW*, 6:320.
28 Abraham Lincoln, "Remarks to Citizens of Gettysburg, Pennsylvania," November 18, 1863, *CW*, 7:16-17.
29 R.C. McCormick, "Abraham Lincoln: Interesting Reminiscences," *New York Evening Post*, May 3, 1865.
30 Lincoln, "Address Delivered at the Dedication of the Cemetery at Gettysburg, Final Text," November 19, 1863, *CW*, 7:23 n.19.
31 White, *A. Lincoln*, 255.
32 White, *A. Lincoln*, 255.
33 Abraham Lincoln to Charles C. Nott, May 31, 1860, *CW*, 4:58.
34 Abraham Lincoln to Charles C. Nott, May 31, 1860, *CW*, 4:58 (italics in original).
35 Henry C. Whitney, *Life on the Circuit with Lincoln* (Boston: Estes and Lauriat Publishers, 1892), 177.
36 Mort Reis Lewis, "Abraham Lincoln: Storyteller," in Ralph G. Newman, ed., *Lincoln For the Ages* (New York: Pyramid Books, 1960), 106-107.
37 Lewis, "Abraham Lincoln: Storyteller, 107.
38 *Alleghanian* (Ebensburg, Pennsylvania), September 25, 1862.
39 Browne, *The Every-Day Life of Abraham Lincoln*, 531.
40 Abraham Lincoln, quoted in Francis B. Carpenter, *Six Months at the White House with Abraham Lincoln: The Story of a Picture* (New York: Hurd and Houghton, 1866), 77.
41 Lincoln, "Second Inaugural Address," March 4, 1865, *CW*, 8:333.

Chapter 8: Credibility

1 Goodwin, *Team of Rivals*, 231.
2 Mayson Brayman to William H. Bailhache, February 28, 1860, in Illinois State Historical Society, "Lincolniana Notes: Lincoln Before a New York Audience," *Journal of the Illinois State Historical Society* 49 (Summer 1956): 214.
3 Mayson Brayman to William H. Bailhache, February 28, 1860, in "Lincolniana Notes: Lincoln Before a New York Audience," 214 (italics in original).
4 White, *A. Lincoln*, 238.
5 David Davis, quoted in Herndon and Weik, *Herndon's Lincoln*, 2:335.
6 David Davis, quoted in Herndon and Weik, *Herndon's Lincoln*, 2:335.

7   David Davis, quoted in Herndon and Weik, *Herndon's Lincoln*, 2:335-336.
8   Samuel C. Parks to William H. Herndon, March 25, 1866, *HI*, 238.
9   Ratcliffe Hicks, letter to *Century Magazine*, November 10, 1893, *Century Magazine* 47, February 1894, 638.
10   Samuel C. Parks to William H. Herndon, March 25, 1866, *HI*, 239.
11   Samuel C. Parks to William H. Herndon, March 25, 1866, *HI*, 239 (italics in original).
12   Leonard Swett, quoted in Herndon and Weik, *Herndon's Lincoln*, 2:334.
13   Tarbell, "Lincoln as a Lawyer," 181.
14   Stephen Douglas, quoted in Bouton, introduction to *The Lincoln and Douglas Debates*, xxxviii (italics added).
15   *National Republican* (Washington, D.C.), December 2, 1862 (italics added).
16   "The Next Presidency," *New York Times*, January 15, 1864 (italics added).
17   William Lloyd Garrison to Francis W. Newman in Walter M. Merrill, ed., *The Letters of William Lloyd Garrison: Let the Oppressed Go Free, 1861-1867* (Cambridge, MA: Belknap Press of Harvard University Press, 1979), 5:180 (italics added).
18   Horace White, "Abraham Lincoln in 1854," an address delivered before the Illinois State Historical Society, January 30, 1908, *Transactions of the Illinois State Historical Society for the Year 1908* (1909): 33.
19   McCormick, "Abraham Lincoln: Interesting Reminiscences," *New York Evening Post*, May 3, 1865 (italics added).
20   *Ashtabula Weekly Telegraph* (Ashtabula, Ohio), December 5, 1863 (italics added).
21   Robert L. Wilson, quoted in Whitney, *Lincoln the Citizen*, 140.
22   *New-York Daily Tribune*, February 25, 1860 (italics added).
23   *New York Sun*, March 5, 1861 (italics added).
24   Lincoln, "Speech at Peoria, Illinois," October 16, 1854, *CW*, 2:255 (italics in original).
25   Abraham Lincoln to James C. Conkling, August 26, 1863, *CW*, 6:407.
26   *New-York Daily Tribune*, September 3, 1863.
27   Abraham Lincoln to Albert G. Hodges, April 4, 1864, *CW*, 7:281.
28   Abraham Lincoln to Albert G. Hodges, April 4, 1864, *CW*, 7:281.
29   Abraham Lincoln to Horace Greeley, August 22, 1862, *CW*, 5:389.
30   *Burlington Free Press* (Burlington, Vermont), December 12, 1862.
31   *Chicago Tribune*, December 10, 1863 (italics added).
32   *Alleghanian* (Ebensburg, Pennsylvania), December 17, 1863 (italics added).
33   Scott, "Lincoln on the Stump," 10.
34   Scott, "Lincoln on the Stump," 12-13 (underlining in original).
35   John Strong, quoted in Moores, "Abraham Lincoln, Lawyer," 509.
36   Lincoln, "Address at Cooper Institute, New York City," February 27, 1860, *CW*, 3:522.

37 Abraham Lincoln to Albert G. Hodges, April 4, 1864, *CW*, 7:282.
38 John B. Clarke, quoted in Pride, "The First N.H. Primary?," *Boston Globe*, July 11, 2010 (italics added).
39 Lincoln, "Address Delivered at the Dedication of the Cemetery at Gettysburg, Final Text," November 19, 1863, *CW*, 7:23.
40 Lincoln, "Second Inaugural Address," March 4, 1865, *CW*, 8:332-333.
41 The sentence was: "But when he went on to say that five millions of the expenditure of 1838, were payments of the French indemnities, *which I knew to be untrue*; that five millions had been for the Post Office, *which I knew to be untrue*; that ten millions had been for the Maine boundary war, *which I not only knew to be untrue, but supremely ridiculous also*; and when I saw that he was stupid enough to hope, that I would permit such groundless and audacious assertions to go unexposed, I readily consented, that on the score both of veracity and sagacity, the audience should judge whether he or I were the more deserving of the world's contempt." Abraham Lincoln, "Speech on the Sub-Treasury," December [26], 1839, *CW*, 1:177 (italics in original).
42 *New York Herald*, March 5, 1865.
43 *New York Times*, March 6, 1865 (italics added).
44 Lincoln, "Temperance Address," February 22, 1842, *CW*, 1:273 (italics in original).
45 Charles Maltby, *The Life and Public Services of Abraham Lincoln* (Stockton, CA: Daily Independent Steam Power Print, 1844), 44.
46 Scott, "Lincoln on the Stump," 10.
47 James S. Ewing, speech given at the Banquet of Illinois Schoolmasters' Club, Bloomington, Illinois, February 12, 1909, in Owen T. Reeves, James S. Ewing, Richard P. Morgan, Franklin Blades, and John W. Bunn, *Abraham Lincoln by Some Men Who Knew Him* (Bloomington, IL: Pantagraph Printing & Stationary Co., 1910), 48.
48 Felix Ryan, quoted in Moores, "Abraham Lincoln, Lawyer," 509.
49 J. Henry Shaw to William H. Herndon, September 5, 1866, *HI*, 333.
50 J. Henry Shaw to William H. Herndon, September 5, 1866, *HI*, 333 (italics added).
51 Scott, "Lincoln on the Stump," 2.
52 Scott, "Lincoln on the Stump," 2.
53 Herndon and Weik, *Herndon's Lincoln*, 1:197.
54 Herndon and Weik, *Herndon's Lincoln*, 1:197-198.
55 Herndon and Weik, *Herndon's Lincoln*, 1:198.
56 Thomas J. McCormack, ed., *Memoirs of Gustave Koerner 1809-1896* (Cedar Rapids, IA: The Torch Press, 1909), 1:444. Koerner, who emigrated from Germany, was a lawyer, politician, associate justice on the Illinois Supreme Court, and close confidant of Lincoln.

57 James A. Garfield to his wife, Lucretia Garfield, February 17, 1861, in John Shaw, ed., *Crete and James: Personal Letters of Lucretia and James Garfield* (East Lansing: Michigan State University Press, 1994), 107 (italics added).
58 Lincoln, "Speech at Peoria, Illinois," October 16, 1854, *CW*, 2:248.
59 Lincoln, "Speech at Peoria, Illinois," October 16, 1854, *CW*, 2:255.
60 White, *A. Lincoln*, 229, citing *Amboy Times* (Illinois), July 24, 1856.
61 *New-York Daily Tribune*, February 25, 1860 (italics added).
62 *New-York Daily Tribune*, February 28, 1860 (italics added).
63 John B. Clarke, quoted in Pride, "The First N.H. Primary?" (italics added).
64 Henry C. Bowen, "Recollections of Abraham Lincoln," in Ward, ed., *Abraham Lincoln: Tributes from His Associates*, 29.
65 Ogilvie, ed., *Life and Speeches of William McKinley*, 210 (italics added).
66 Brooks, *Abraham Lincoln: The Nation's Leader*, 242.
67 George W. Julian in Rice, ed., *Reminiscences of Abraham Lincoln*, 50.
68 Schurz, *Abraham Lincoln: An Essay*, 65-66.
69 "The Right Man in the Right Place," *New York Times*, September 7, 1863 (italics added).
70 Abraham Lincoln, "Response to a Serenade," November 10, 1864, *CW*, 8:101.
71 Lydia Marie Child to Eliza Scudder, 1864, Lydia Marie Child, *Letters of Lydia Marie Child* (Cambridge, MA: H. O. Houghton & Co., 1882), 184.
72 Lincoln, "Second Inaugural Address," March 4, 1865, *CW*, 8:333.
73 Arnold, "Reminiscences of the Illinois-Bar," 22.
74 Burlingame, *Abraham Lincoln: A Life*, 1:319.

Chapter 9: Clarity

1 John P. Gulliver, quoted in Carpenter, *Six Months at the White House*, 311 (italics added).
2 John P. Gulliver, quoted in Carpenter, *Six Months at the White House*, 312-313.
3 Sarah Bush Lincoln to William H. Herndon, September 8, 1865, *HI*, 107.
4 Dunn, "Lincoln, the Lawyer," 220.
5 *New-York Daily Tribune*, February 25, 1860 (italics added).
6 *Chicago Tribune*, September 3, 1863.
7 Lincoln, "Speech at Peoria, Illinois," October 16, 1854, *CW*, 2:248.
8 Lincoln, "'A House Divided:' Speech at Springfield, Illinois," June 16, 1858, *CW*, 2:461 (italics in original).
9 "'Our fathers,'" Lincoln quoted Douglas as saying, "'when they framed the Government under which we live, understood this question just as well, and even better, than we do now.' I fully endorse this, and I adopt it as a text for this discourse." Lincoln, "Address at Cooper Institute, New York City," February 27, 1860, *CW*, 3:522 (italics in original).

10 White, *The Eloquent President*, xxii. White says that he "estimated the figure at 105 to 110 words per minute by dividing the number of words in . . . the Gettysburg Address (272 words) and the Second Inaugural (701 words), by the time it took to deliver them (2 ½ to 3 minutes and 6 to 7 minutes)." White, *The Eloquent President*, 403-404 n.4.

11 Abraham Lincoln to James C. Conkling, August 27, 1863, *CW*, 6:414.

12 Wilson, *Lincoln's Sword*, 90.

13 Lincoln, "Speech at Peoria, Illinois," October 16, 1854, *CW*, 2:248 (capitalization in original).

14 Lincoln, "Address at Cooper Institute, New York City," February 27, 1860, *CW*, 3:535 (italics in original).

15 Lincoln, "Address at Cooper Institute, New York City," February 27, 1860, *CW*, 3:550 (capitalization in original).

16 Hugh McCulloch in Rice, ed., *Reminiscences of Abraham Lincoln*, 415.

17 Putnam, *Abraham Lincoln: The People's Leader*, 134-135.

18 *Daily Intelligencer* (Wheeling, Virginia [West Virginia]), March 6, 1865.

19 Lincoln, "Address at Cooper Institute, New York City," February 27, 1860, *CW*, 3:522 (italics in original).

20 Abraham Lincoln to Horace Greeley, August 22, 1862, *CW*, 5:388-389. Lincoln replaces "Union" with "it" three times.

21 Wills, *Lincoln at Gettysburg*, 172-173.

22 Wilson, *Lincoln's Sword*, 15.

23 Lincoln, "Speech at Peoria, Illinois," October 16, 1854, *CW*, 2:255.

24 Lincoln, "'A House Divided:' Speech at Springfield, Illinois," June 16, 1858, *CW*, 2:467 (italics in original).

25 Lincoln, "Address at Cooper Institute, New York City," February 27, 1860, *CW*, 3:537.

26 Lincoln, "First Inaugural Address—Final Text," March 4, 1861, *CW*, 4:271 (italics in original).

27 Abraham Lincoln to Horace Greeley, August 22, 1862, *CW*, 5:388-389. This refers to the twelve sentences after the introduction (beginning with "As to the policy . . .").

28 Abraham Lincoln to Erastus Corning and Others, [June 12,] 1863, *CW*, 6:266.

29 Abraham Lincoln to James C. Conkling, August 26, 1863, *CW*, 6:409.

30 Lincoln, "Address Delivered at the Dedication of the Cemetery at Gettysburg, Final Text," November 19, 1863, *CW*, 7:23.

31 Lincoln, "Second Inaugural Address," March 4, 1865, *CW*, 8:332-333 (italics in original).

32 Chauncey M. Depew quoting Abraham Lincoln in Rice, ed., *Reminiscences of Abraham Lincoln*, 427-428.

33 Silas W. Burt, "Lincoln on His Own Story-Telling," *Century Magazine* 73, February 1907, 502.
34 Pinsker, *Lincoln's Sanctuary*, 102. The intoxicated major slapped Lincoln's knee on making the request, and did so when the exhausted Lincoln was falling asleep, which may well have contributed to Lincoln's rebuff. Burt, "Lincoln on His Own Story-Telling," 502.
35 Burt, "Lincoln On His Own Story-Telling," 502.
36 Robert L. Wilson to William H. Herndon, February 10, 1866, *HI*, 205.
37 Arnold, "Reminiscences of the Illinois-Bar," 22.
38 Scott, "Lincoln on the Stump," 13.
39 Scott, "Lincoln on the Stump," 14.
40 Villard, *Memoirs of Henry Villard*, 1:143.
41 Chauncey M. Depew quoting Abraham Lincoln in Rice, ed., *Reminiscences of Abraham Lincoln*, 428.
42 Goodwin, *Team of Rivals*, 675.
43 Edward Bates, quoted in Carpenter, *Six Months at the White House*, 68.
44 Lincoln, "Speech at Peoria, Illinois," October 16, 1854, *CW*, 2:258.
45 Abraham Lincoln, "Speech at New Haven, Connecticut," March 6, 1860, *CW*, 4:18.
46 Lincoln, "Speech at Springfield, Illinois," June 26, 1857, *CW*, 2:404.
47 Lincoln, "'A House Divided:' Speech at Springfield, Illinois," June 16, 1858, *CW*, 2:465-466 (italics in original).
48 Lincoln, "Address at Cooper Institute, New York City," February 27, 1860, *CW*, 3:547.
49 Abraham Lincoln to Erastus Corning and Others, [June 12,] 1863, *CW*, 6:267.
50 Holzer, *Lincoln at Cooper Union*, 112.
51 Holzer, *Lincoln at Cooper Union*, 112, quoting Carl Schurz, *The Reminiscences of Carl Schurz* (New York: McClure Co., 1907), 2:95.
52 Herndon and Weik, *Herndon's Lincoln*, 2:407.
53 Scott, "Lincoln on the Stump," 12.
54 Albert D. Richardson, *The Secret Service, the Field, the Dungeon, and the Escape* (Hartford, CT: American Publishing Co., 1865), 314.
55 Moncure Daniel Conway, *Autobiography, Memories and Experiences of Moncure Daniel Conway* (Boston: Houghton, Mifflin and Co., 1904), 1:317.
56 John Hill to Ida M. Tarbell, February 17, 1896, Ida M. Tarbell Collection of Lincolniana, Allegheny College Pelletier Library, 5.
57 John Hill to Ida M. Tarbell, February 17, 1896, Ida M. Tarbell Collection of Lincolniana, Allegheny College Pelletier Library, 5-6.
58 *Alleghanian* (Ebensburg, Pennsylvania), December 17, 1863.

59 Burlingame, *Abraham Lincoln: A Life*, 1:228, citing George H. Honig, "Abe Lincoln and the Cosmic Ray," 12, typescript dated August 11, 1947, Honig Papers, Willard Library, Evansville, Indiana.
60 Albert T. Bledsoe, "Lamon's Life of Lincoln," *Southern Review* 7 (April 1873): 334.
61 Edward Everett to Abraham Lincoln, November 20, 1863, *ALPLC* (italics added).
62 *New York Evening Post*, January 7, 1863.
63 Harriet Beecher Stowe, "Abraham Lincoln," *Littell's Living Age* no. 1027, February 6, 1864, 283, reprinted from *Watchman and Reflector*.
64 Tarbell, "Lincoln as a Lawyer," 181.
65 Richardson, *The Secret Service*, 314.
66 *Burlington Free Press* (Burlington, Vermont), December 7, 1861.
67 *Green Mountain Freeman* (Montpelier, Vermont), September 30, 1862.
68 *New-York Daily Tribune*, April 29, 1864.
69 "The Right Man in the Right Place," *New York Times*, September 7, 1863.
70 Lowell, *The Writings of James Russell Lowell*, 5:208 (italics added).
71 John D. Defrees, quoted in Carpenter, *Six Months at the White House*, 126-127.
72 John D. Defrees, quoting Abraham Lincoln, in Carpenter, *Six Months at the White House*, 126-127 (italics in original).
73 Wilson, *Lincoln's Sword*, 27.
74 Bledsoe, "Lamon's Life of Lincoln," 334 (italics in original).
75 Burlingame, *Abraham Lincoln: A Life*, 1:141.
76 Whitney, *Life on the Circuit*, 5.
77 Lincoln, "Speech on the Sub-Treasury," December [26], 1839, *CW*, 1:178.
78 Herndon and Weik, *Herndon's Lincoln*, 1:191.
79 Abraham Lincoln, "Address Before the Young Men's Lyceum of Springfield, Illinois," January 27, 1838, *CW*, 1:108.
80 Lincoln, "Address Delivered at the Dedication of the Cemetery at Gettysburg, Final Text," November 19, 1863, *CW*, 7:23.
81 Robert G. Ingersoll in Rice, ed., *Reminiscences of Abraham Lincoln by Distinguished Men of His Time*, 311.

Chapter 10: Facts

1 Steven R. Weisman, ed., *Daniel Patrick Moynihan: A Portrait in Letters of an American Visionary* (New York: Public Affairs, 2010), 2.
2 Scott, "Lincoln on the Stump," 12.
3 Scott, "Lincoln on the Stump," 12.
4 White, *A. Lincoln*, 243.
5 White, *A. Lincoln*, 243.
6 White, *A. Lincoln*, 243.

7   White, *A. Lincoln*, 243.
8   White, *A. Lincoln*, 243.
9   Abraham Lincoln, "Speech in United States House of Representatives: The War with Mexico," January 12, 1848, *CW*, 1:439 (italics in original).
10 Lincoln, "Speech at Peoria, Illinois," October 16, 1854, *CW*, 2:277.
11 Lincoln, "Speech at Peoria, Illinois," October 16, 1854, *CW*, 2:277.
12 Lincoln, "Speech at Peoria, Illinois," October 16, 1854, *CW*, 2:278.
13 Lincoln, "Speech at Peoria, Illinois," October 16, 1854, *CW*, 2:277.
14 Lincoln, "Speech at Peoria, Illinois," October 16, 1854, *CW*, 2:279.
15 Lincoln, "Speech at Springfield, Illinois," June 26, 1857, *CW*, 2:398-410.
16 Correspondence, June 27, 1857, *Chicago Tribune*, n.d., reprinted in *New-York Daily Tribune*, July 6, 1857.
17 Lincoln, "'A House Divided:' Speech at Springfield, Illinois," June 16, 1858, *CW*, 2:461-469.
18 Abraham Lincoln, "First Debate with Stephen A. Douglas at Ottawa, Illinois," August 21, 1858, *CW*, 3:1-37; Abraham Lincoln, "Second Debate with Stephen A. Douglas at Freeport, Illinois," August 27, 1858, *CW*, 3:38-76; Abraham Lincoln, "Third Debate with Stephen A. Douglas at Jonesboro, Illinois," September 15, 1858, *CW*, 3:102-144; Abraham Lincoln, "Fourth Debate with Stephen A. Douglas at Charleston, Illinois," September 18, 1858, *CW*, 3:145-201; Abraham Lincoln, "Fifth Debate with Stephen A. Douglas, at Galesburg, Illinois," October 7, 1858, *CW*, 3:207-244; Abraham Lincoln, "Sixth Debate with Stephen A. Douglas, at Quincy, Illinois," October 13, 1858, *CW*, 3:245-283; Abraham Lincoln, "Seventh and Last Debate with Stephen A. Douglas at Alton, Illinois," October 15, 1858, *CW*, 3:283-325.
19 Lincoln, "Address at Cooper Institute, New York City," February 27, 1860, *CW*, 3:522-550.
20 Abraham Lincoln to Erastus Corning and Others, [June 12,] 1863, *CW*, 6:260-269.
21 Abraham Lincoln to James C. Conkling, August 26, 1863, *CW*, 6:406-410.
22 Abraham Lincoln to Albert G. Hodges, April 4, 1864, *CW*, 7:282.
23 Lincoln, "Second Inaugural Address," March 4, 1865, *CW*, 8:332.
24 Lincoln, "Second Inaugural Address," March 4, 1865, *CW*, 8:332.
25 Lincoln, "Second Inaugural Address," March 4, 1865, *CW*, 8:332 (italics in original).
26 Lincoln, "Second Inaugural Address," March 4, 1865, *CW*, 8:332.
27 Lincoln, "Second Inaugural Address," March 4, 1865, *CW*, 8:332.
28 Lincoln, "Second Inaugural Address," March 4, 1865, *CW*, 8:332.
29 Lincoln, "Second Inaugural Address," March 4, 1865, *CW*, 8:332.
30 Lincoln, "Second Inaugural Address," March 4, 1865, *CW*, 8:332.
31 Lincoln, "Second Inaugural Address," March 4, 1865, *CW*, 8:333.

32 Lincoln, "Second Inaugural Address," March 4, 1865, *CW*, 8:333 (italics in original).
33 Lincoln, "Second Inaugural Address," March 4, 1865, *CW*, 8:333.
34 Lincoln, "Second Inaugural Address," March 4, 1865, *CW*, 8:333.
35 Lincoln, "Second Inaugural Address," March 4, 1865, *CW*, 8:333.
36 Lincoln, "Second Inaugural Address," March 4, 1865, *CW*, 8:333.

Chapter 11: Logic

1   Dispatch of November 4, 1860 in Burlingame, ed., *Lincoln Observed*, 6.
2   Goodwin, *Team of Rivals*, 234, citing Gideon Welles' editorial in *Hartford Evening Press*, quoted in Richard S. West, Jr., *Gideon Welles: Lincoln's Navy Department* (Indianapolis and New York: Bobbs-Merrill, 1943), 81.
3   Greeley, "Greeley's Estimate of Lincoln," 376, 378-379.
4   John Hay to John G. Nicolay, September 11, 1863, in Michael Burlingame, ed., *At Lincoln's Side: John Hay's Civil War Correspondence and Selected Writings* (Carbondale, IL: Southern Illinois University Press, 2000), 54.
5   Abraham Lincoln to Williamson Durley, October 3, 1845, *CW*, 1:347 (italics in original).
6   Abraham Lincoln to Williamson Durley, October 3, 1845, *CW*, 1:347 (italics in original).
7   Abraham Lincoln, "Fragment on Slavery," [April 1, 1854?], *CW*, 2:222-223 (italics in original).
8   Lincoln, "Fragment on Slavery," [April 1, 1854?], *CW*, 2:222 (italics in original).
9   Lincoln, "Speech at Peoria, Illinois," October 16, 1854, *CW*, 2:264.
10 Lincoln, "Speech at Springfield, Illinois," June 26, 1857, *CW*, 2:406.
11 Lincoln, "Speech at Springfield, Illinois," June 26, 1857, *CW*, 2:405.
12 Lincoln, "Speech at Springfield, Illinois," June 26, 1857, *CW*, 2:405.
13 Schurz, *The Reminiscences of Carl Schurz*, 2:86.
14 Brooks, *Abraham Lincoln: The Nation's Leader*, 172.
15 Lincoln, "Fifth Debate with Stephen A. Douglas, at Galesburg, Illinois," October 7, 1858, *CW*, 3:231.
16 Lincoln, "Fifth Debate with Stephen A. Douglas, at Galesburg, Illinois," October 7, 1858, *CW*, 3:231 (italics in original).
17 Richardson, *The Secret Service*, 315.
18 Lincoln, "Address at Cooper Institute, New York City," February 27, 1860, *CW*, 3:549-550.
19 *New York Evening Post*, February 28, 1860 (italics added).
20 Lincoln, "Meditation on the Divine Will" [September 2, 1862?], *CW*, 5:403-404 (italics in original).
21 Lincoln, "Speech at Peoria, Illinois," October 16, 1854, *CW*, 2:2654-265 (capitalization in original).

22 Lincoln, "Speech at Peoria, Illinois," October 16, 1854, *CW*, 2:265 (italics in original).
23 Lincoln, "Address at Cooper Institute, New York City," February 27, 1860, *CW*, 3:550.

Chapter 12: Emotion

1 Lincoln, "Temperance Address," February 22, 1842, *CW*, 1:273.
2 William Walker to William H. Herndon, June 3, 1865, *HI*, 22 (italics in original).
3 J. Henry Shaw to William H. Herndon, August 22, 1866, *HI*, 316.
4 Stowell, ed., *The Papers of Abraham Lincoln*, 4:36.
5 J. Henry Shaw to William H. Herndon, September 5, 1866, *HI*, 333 (italics in original).
6 Scott, "Lincoln on the Stump," 12.
7 Scott, "Lincoln on the Stump," 12.
8 Scott, "Lincoln on the Stump," 12.
9 Scott, "Lincoln on the Stump," 12.
10 Dodge, "Abraham Lincoln: The Evolution of His Literary Style," 53.
11 Sandburg, *Abraham Lincoln: The Prairie Years and the War Years*,186 (italics added).
12 William T. Sherman, *Memoirs of General William T. Sherman* (New York: D. Appleton and Co., 1875) 1:190 (italics added).
13 Stowe, "Abraham Lincoln," 283.
14 *Daily Ohio State Journal*, November 23, 1863.
15 Browne, *The Every-Day Life of Abraham Lincoln*, 604.
16 *Harper's Weekly* 7, December 5, 1863, 770.
17 Schurz, *Abraham Lincoln: An Essay*, 104.
18 Goodwin, *Team of Rivals*, 165 (italics added).
19 Lincoln, "First Inaugural Address—Final Text," March 4, 1861, *CW*, 4:271.
20 Lincoln, "Address Delivered at the Dedication of the Cemetery at Gettysburg, Final Text," November 19, 1863, *CW*, 7:23.
21 Lincoln, "Speech at Peoria, Illinois," October 16, 1854, *CW*, 2:276.
22 Abraham Lincoln, "Speech in Independence Hall, Philadelphia, Pennsylvania," February 22, 1861, *CW*, 4:240 (italics in original).
23 Lincoln, "Address Delivered at the Dedication of the Cemetery at Gettysburg, Final Text," November 19, 1863, *CW*, 7:23.
24 Lincoln, "Speech at Peoria, Illinois," October 16, 1854, *CW*, 2:271.
25 Lincoln, "Speech at Peoria, Illinois," October 16, 1854, *CW*, 2:278.
26 Lincoln, "First Debate with Stephen A. Douglas at Ottawa, Illinois," August 21, 1858, *CW*, 3:16 (italics in original).
27 Villard, *Memoirs of Henry Villard*, 1:93.

28 Lincoln, "'A House Divided:' Speech at Springfield, Illinois," June 16, 1858, *CW*, 2:468-469 (italics in original).
29 Lincoln, "Address at Cooper Institute, New York City," February 27, 1860, *CW*, 3:550.
30 Sherman, *Memoirs of General William T. Sherman*, 190 (italics added).
31 Lincoln, "Address Delivered at the Dedication of the Cemetery at Gettysburg, Final Text," November 19, 1863, *CW*, 7:23.
32 891 Lincoln, "Speech at Peoria, Illinois," October 16, 1854, *CW*, 2:282.
33 Lincoln, "'A House Divided:' Speech at Springfield, Illinois," June 16, 1858, *CW*, 2:468 (italics in original).
34 Abraham Lincoln to James C. Conkling, August 26, 1863, *CW*, 6:409-410.
35 Lincoln, "Speech at Peoria, Illinois," October 16, 1854, *CW*, 2:282.
36 Lincoln, "Speech at Peoria, Illinois," October 16, 1854, *CW*, 2:276.
37 Lincoln, "'A House Divided:' Speech at Springfield, Illinois," June 16, 1858, *CW*, 2:461.
38 Lincoln, "'A House Divided:' Speech at Springfield, Illinois," June 16, 1858, *CW*, 2:467 (italics in original).
39 Lincoln, "First Inaugural Address—Final Text," March 4, 1861, *CW*, 4:271 (italics in original).
40 Burlingame, *Abraham Lincoln: A Life*, 2:61.
41 Lincoln, "Address Delivered at the Dedication of the Cemetery at Gettysburg, Final Text," November 19, 1863, *CW*, 7:23.
42 Abraham Lincoln to Albert G. Hodges, April 4, 1864, *CW*, 7:282, quoted above at page 152.
43 Ronald C. White, Jr., "Saying What Matters in 701 Words," *New York Times Sunday Review*, January 20, 2013.
44 Lincoln, "Second Inaugural Address," March 4, 1865, *CW*, 8:333.
45 Lincoln, "Second Inaugural Address," March 4, 1865, *CW*, 8:333.
46 Lincoln, "Second Inaugural Address," March 4, 1865, *CW*, 8:333.
47 Lincoln, "Second Inaugural Address," March 4, 1865, *CW*, 8:333.
48 Lincoln, "Second Inaugural Address," March 4, 1865, *CW*, 8:333.
49 Lincoln, "Second Inaugural Address," March 4, 1865, *CW*, 8:333.
50 Lincoln, "Second Inaugural Address," March 4, 1865, *CW*, 8:333.
51 Herndon and Weik, *Herndon's Lincoln*, 3:590.
52 William H. Herndon to Ward Hill Lamon, March 6, 1870, in Douglas L. Wilson and Rodney O. Davis, eds., *Herndon on Lincoln: Letters* (Urbana: Knox College Lincoln Studies Center and University of Illinois Press, 2016), 102.
53 Lincoln, "Address Before the Young Men's Lyceum of Springfield, Illinois," January 27, 1838, *CW*, 1:108.
54 Holzer, *Lincoln at Cooper Union*, 19.

55 "Gus" to Mary P. Christian ("Mollie"), January 28, 1860, in Harry E. Pratt, ed., *Concerning Mr. Lincoln* (Springfield, IL: The Abraham Lincoln Association, 1944), 21.
56 "Gus" to Mary P. Christian ("Mollie"), January 28, 1860, in Pratt, ed., *Concerning Mr. Lincoln*, 21.
57 Abraham Lincoln to John M. Carson, April 7, 1860, *CW*, 4:39; Abraham Lincoln to F. C. Herbruger, April 7, 1860, *CW*, 4:40.
58 Abraham Lincoln to John M. Carson, April 7, 1860, *CW*, 4:39; Abraham Lincoln to F. C. Herbruger, April 7, 1860, *CW*, 4:40.
59 William Walker to William H. Herndon, June 3, 1865, *HI*, 22.
60 William Walker to William H. Herndon, June 3, 1865, *HI*, 22-23.
61 William Walker to William H. Herndon, September 15, 1866, *HI*, 341.
62 J. Henry Shaw to William H. Herndon, September 5, 1866, *HI*, 333.
63 Anthony Thornton, "Abraham Lincoln as Lawyer on Circuit: Repairing His Buggy with Hickory Strips – Apples Instead of Whiskey – Small Fees for Services," *Chicago Tribune*, supplement, February 12, 1900 (italics added).
64 Abraham Lincoln, "Eulogy on Henry Clay," July 6, 1852, *CW*, 2:126.
65 Herndon and Weik, *Herndon's Lincoln*, 2:384.
66 Scott, "Lincoln on the Stump," 19.
67 Correspondence, June 27, 1857, *Chicago Tribune*, n.d., reprinted in *New-York Daily Tribune*, July 6, 1857 (italics added).
68 Villard, *Memoirs of Henry Villard*, 1:93.
69 Special Correspondence, August 23, 1858, in *New York Evening Post*, August 27, 1858.
70 Joseph Hodges Choate, "Abraham Lincoln at Cooper Institute," in MacChesney, ed., *Abraham Lincoln: The Tribute of a Century*, 278.
71 George S. Boutwell in Rice, ed., *Reminiscences of Abraham Lincoln*, 131 (italics added).
72 *Green Mountain Freeman* (Montpelier, Vermont), December 2, 1862 (italics added).
73 Stoddard, *Inside the White House in War Times*, 228.
74 White, "Abraham Lincoln in 1854," 32-33.
75 Horace White to William H. Herndon, May 17, 1865, *HI*, 4.
76 The words "rhythm" and "cadence" are closely related. Rhythm is defined as the "patterned, recurring alternations of contrasting elements of sound or speech," while "cadence" is defined as "balanced, rhythmic flow, as of poetry or oratory." *American Heritage Dictionary of the English Language*, 4th ed., s.vv. "rhythm," "cadence."
77 Lincoln, "'A House Divided:' Speech at Springfield, Illinois," June 16, 1858, *CW*, 2:468.

78 Abraham Lincoln, "Remarks at Dunkirk, New York," February 16, 1861, *CW*, 4:220 (capitalization in original).
79 John Hay, "Buffalo Correspondence," February 16, 1861, in Michael Burlingame, ed., *Lincoln's Journalist: John Hay's Anonymous Writings for the Press, 1860-1864* (Carbondale, IL: Southern Illinois University Press, 1998), 33.
80 Lincoln, "Address at Cooper Institute, New York City," February 27, 1860, *CW*, 3:550 (capitalization in original).

Chapter 13: Conclusion

1 John Hay and John George Nicolay, "Abraham Lincoln: A History," *Century Magazine* 39, January 1890, 436.

Index

Adams, Charles Francis, Jr.   67-68
Albany, New York   52, 61
Annual Message(s) to Congress   39, 45, 49-50, 60-62, 64-65, 111, 113, 158
Appeal(s) (legal)   9, 13-14, 89
Armstrong, William "Duff"   10-11, 87, 115, 124, 140, 147-148, 156
Arnold, Isaac N.   12, 91
Astronomy   90
Atchison, Kansas   29
Bank of the United States   6
Bartlett, D. W.   7
Bates, Edward   36, 128
Beecher, Henry Ward   29, 106
Bible   90, 139, 153-155
Black Hawk War   115
Blair, Francis P., Jr.   28-29
Bledsoe, Albert Taylor   132-133
Bloomington, Illinois   15-16, 20, 149, 157
Border states   37, 40, 46, 62-63
Boutwell, George S.   158
Brady, John T.   148
Brady, Matthew   34
Brayman, Mayson   110
Brinkley, Douglas   9
Brooklyn, New York   29
Brooks, Noah   60-61, 67, 118, 140, 142
Brown, David P.   54
Brown, John   32
Browne, Francis Fisher   107-108, 149-150
Bryant, William Cullen   33, 143
Buchanan, James   25, 39, 129-130
Bull Run (Manassas), Virginia   149, 152
Burlingame, Michael   7, 59, 61, 65, 119
Burns, Robert   88
Burnside, Ambrose   52
Burt, Silas   127
Butler, William   3
Byron, George Gordon   88
Calhoun, John   99
Cameron, Simon   62
Cartwright, Peter   3
Chase, Salmon   36
Chicago, Illinois   9, 13, 35-36, 101
Child, Lydia Marie   119
Choate, Joseph   158
Cincinnati, Ohio   29
Clarke, John   114, 117
Clay, Henry   7, 30, 99, 140-141, 157
Columbus, Ohio   29-30, 150
Concord, New Hampshire   35
Conkling, James (Lincoln's letter to)   55-59, 61, 92-93, 102, 108, 112-113, 122-123, 126, 132, 137, 144, 153
Conway, Moncure D.   131

Cooper Union Speech / Cooper Institute   29-35, 68, 92, 96, 102, 106, 110, 112, 114, 117-118, 122-125, 130, 136-137, 143, 145-146, 149-150, 152, 158, 160
Corning, Erastus (Lincoln's letter to)   52-55, 59, 97, 108, 118, 126, 130, 137, 143-144
Corwin, Thomas   130
Cowper, William   88
Curtis, Benjamin Robbins   22
Curtis, George William   60
Cuyler, Theodore   68
Davis, David   7, 11, 111
Davis, Jefferson   64
Debate(s) (with Stephen Douglas)   6, 10, 15-16, 26-27, 120, 137, 142-143, 152, 156-158
Dennison, William   62
Dodge, Daniel Kilham   68-69, 149
Douglas, Stephen   6, 10, 15-16, 19, 21-32, 35, 44, 92, 99, 106, 111, 120, 122, 124, 129-131, 136-137, 142, 152-154, 156-158
Douglass, Frederick   87
Dred Scott v. Sanford   21-24, 41, 92, 102, 110, 129, 137, 142, 157
Dubois, Jesse   21
Duff, John   14
Dunkirk, New York   159-160
Dunn, Jesse   97, 102
Effie Afton (steamer / railroad bridge collision)   13, 101, 135-136
Eighth Judicial Circuit of Illinois   9-12, 14, 95, 113, 115
Emancipation Proclamation (final)   38-39, 46-47, 50-51, 55-59, 62-63, 65, 99, 107-108, 124, 132, 137-138, 144
Euclid   90
Everett, Edward   93, 132,150

Ewing, James S.   115
Exeter, New Hampshire   34
Fifth Amendment   21
"Fighting Parson"   5
First Inaugural Address   38-44, 54, 59, 66, 102, 112, 118, 125, 146, 150, 154, 158
Forbes, John M.   58
Forney, John W.   54
Forquer, George   5-6
Founding fathers   16, 19, 23, 27-28, 30-31, 102, 123-125, 134, 137, 150
Frank, John P.   91-92
Fremont, John   21, 62, 117
Galloway, Samuel   61
Gardner, Henry J.   8, 90
Garfield, James   117
Garrison, William Lloyd   112, 118
General store   9, 89, 94-95
Gettysburg Address / Gettysburg, Pennsylvania 38, 44, 55, 59-60, 66, 68, 93, 105-106, 108, 112, 114, 124, 126, 132, 134, 138, 149-154, 161
Gienapp, William   39
Gladstone, William   68
Goodwin, Doris Kearns   16, 35, 87, 102, 128, 150
Graham, Mentor   89, 94
Grant, Ulysses S.   69, 158
Gray, Thomas   88
Greeley, Horace (including Lincoln's letter to)   25-26, 33, 46-50, 52. 64, 85, 95-97, 107, 113, 118, 124, 126, 140, 143
Gulliver, John P.   121
Habeas corpus   38, 52-53, 137, 143-144
Hackett, James   88
Hahn, Michael   62, 70

Hanks, Dennis 3
Hanks, John 4
Harper's Ferry, Virginia 32
Harrison, William Henry 7
Hay, John 54, 61, 88, 105, 140, 159-160
Hayne, Robert 99
Herndon, J. Rowan 89
Herndon, William H. 9, 20, 91, 99, 101, 104, 116, 131, 133-134, 155-157
Hill, Frederick Trevor 10, 12-13, 19, 95
Hill, John 131
Hodges, Albert (Lincoln's letter to) 62-64, 103-104, 113-114, 124, 132, 138, 144, 154
Holzer, Harold 39, 130-131
House Divided Speech 24-26, 96, 104-106, 122, 125, 129-130, 132, 137, 146, 152-154, 159
Hunter, David 62
Illinois House 4, 6-7, 9, 19, 156
Illinois Supreme Court 7, 9, 11, 13-14
Indianapolis, Indiana 29
Ingersoll, Robert G. 134
Janney, John J. 61-62
Jones, William 131-132
Judd, Norman 13
Julian, George W. 118
Kalamazoo, Michigan 21
Kansas-Nebraska Act (and Lincoln's opposition) 15-19, 22, 24-25, 27, 96, 102, 107, 112, 136, 146, 151, 153
Lambert, William H. 49
Leach, De Witt C. 44
Lee, Robert E. 69
Lewis, Joseph J. 7
Lincoln, Abraham
Analytical ability 90-93

Antithesis (use of) 124-126
Clarity 121-134
Conciseness 124
Credibility 110-120
Emotion (use of) 88, 147-160
Emphasis (use of in writing) 123-124, 160
Facts (use of) 135-139
Images / illustrations (use of) 99, 126-130, 150, 153-154
Influence of courtroom practice 91, 95-97, 134, 136
Intellect 89-93
Language (study and appreciation of) 87-88
Logic 140-146
Memory 89-90
Pace 122-123
Personality 87-88
Preparation 101-107
Public speaking (enjoyment of) 87
Repetition 124
Rhythm 88, 159-160
Simplicity (in style, theme, words) 99, 130-134
Storytelling talent 126-128
Study of persuasion 95-100
Timing 107-109
Understanding of people / human nature 94-100
Lincoln, Levi 90
Lincoln, Robert 34
Lincoln, Sarah Bush Johnston 3, 89
Logan, Stephen T. 9-10, 101
"Lost Speech" 20-21
Louisiana Purchase 15-16
Lowell, James Russell 95, 132-133
Lowell, Massachusetts 8
Luther, Martin 112
MacDowell, William F. 67
Maltby, Charles 115

Manchester, New Hampshire   114
Mathematics   90-91
McClellan, George   38
McCormick, Cyrus   13, 101
McCormick, Richard   33, 112
McCulloch, Hugh   11, 124
McDonough, John   88
McKinley, William   51, 95, 118
Meditation on the Divine Will   103, 144
Mexican-American War   7, 99, 136
Miller, Joe   107
Missouri Compromise   15-17, 32, 96, 102, 122, 128, 151
Moores, Charles W.   67
Morgan, Edwin D.   44
Moynihan, Daniel Patrick   135
Neely, Mark E., Jr.   54-55
New Salem, Illinois   4, 9, 11, 89
New York, New York   29, 58, 117
Newcomb, Charles King   60
Nicolay, John G.   50, 54, 102-104
Northwest Territory   16, 28
Nott, Charles   106
Oates, Stephen B.   14
Ordinance of 1784   28
Ordinance of 1787   28
Parks, Samuel C.   111
Patent(s)   10, 13, 90, 101
People v. Armstrong   10-11, 87, 115, 124, 140, 147-148, 156-157
Peoria, Illinois   16, 19-20, 50, 91-92, 96, 102, 112, 117, 122-123, 125, 128, 141, 144-145, 150-153
Philadelphia, Pennsylvania   21, 151
Phillips, Wendell   118
Pierce, Franklin   15, 25, 129-130
Pinsker, Matthew   46, 55, 88
Poetry   88
Polk, James K.   7, 99, 136
Pope, Alexander   88

Popular sovereignty   15, 22, 25, 28, 142
Preliminary Emancipation Proclamation   39, 46-47, 49, 51, 107
Pride, Mike   35
Proclamation of Amnesty and Reconstruction   60-62
Providence, Rhode Island   35
Putnam, George Haven   67
Railroad(s)   10, 13-14, 135
Rollins, Edward H.   35
Rutledge, James   4
Safire, William   34
Sandburg, Carl   43, 45, 48, 55, 58, 105, 149
Schurz, Carl   40, 43, 68, 118, 142, 150
Scott, John M.   7, 11-12, 20-21, 113-116, 127-128, 131, 135, 148-149, 157
Second Inaugural Address   38, 65-69, 87, 104, 108-109, 114-115, 119, 124, 126, 132, 138-139, 149-150, 154-155, 161
Seward, William   35-36, 60, 69
Shakespeare, William   88, 90
Shaw, J. Henry   115, 147-148, 156-157
Sherman, William Tecumseh   149, 152
Smith, Albert   61
Snow, Marshall Solomon   34
Speed, Joshua   5-6, 90, 104
Springfield, Illinois   4, 6, 8-10, 12, 14, 16, 19-22, 55, 58, 94, 96, 110, 112, 123, 128, 133, 137, 156
Steiner, Mark E.   97
Stephens, Alexander H.   99
Stevens, Thaddeus   65
Stoddard, William O.   88, 158-159
Stowe, Harriet Beecher   29, 132, 149
Strong, John   114
Stuart, John Todd   4, 9-10

Sumner, Charles 58
Swett, Leonard 11-12, 90
Taney, Roger B. 21-23, 129-130
Tarbell, Ida 49, 111, 132
Taunton, Massachusetts 8
Taylor, Zachary 7
Temperance Address 98
Thirteenth Amendment 50, 64, 70
Thomas, Jesse 116
Treat, Samuel 107
Troy, Kansas 143
U.S. Constitution (constitutional) 17, 21-22, 25, 28, 31-32, 35, 39-42, 44, 47-49, 51-54, 56, 64, 97, 129-130, 137 , 142-144, 150
U.S. Declaration of Independence 19, 22-23, 51, 129, 141-142, 150-151
U.S. House of Representatives (Lincoln) 7-8, 12, 15, 99, 136
U.S. Revolutionary War / Revolution 18, 22, 28, 53, 59, 69, 150
U.S. Senate (Lincoln's efforts) 19, 21, 24, 27, 111
U.S. Supreme Court 9, 21-22, 25, 41, 110, 125, 143
Vallandigham, Clement 52-53
Vandalia, Illinois 6
Veatch, James C. 7
Villard, Henry 128, 157-158
Walker, William 147, 156
Washington, George 33, 61, 69, 111, 151
Webster, Daniel 30, 60, 99, 124, 133
Webster, Edwin H. 44
Weed, Thurlow 69, 94
Weik, Jesse 133-134
Weldon, Lawrence 11, 29
Welles, Gideon 140
White, Horace 16, 106, 112, 159
White, Ronald, Jr. 6, 135-136
Whitney, Henry C. 68

Wills, Garry 87-88, 90, 100, 102, 124
Wilson, Douglas 38-39
Wilson, Robert L. 5, 94, 112, 127
Winchester, Illinois 15
Woldman, Albert A. 97
Worcester, Massachusetts 8
Young Men's Lyceum 133-134, 156

CPSIA information can be obtained
at www.ICGtesting.com
Printed in the USA
BVHW032310240719
554298BV00002B/11/P